ANGELS
of the
NORTH
Volume Two

MORE NOTABLE WOMEN *of the*
NORTH EAST

Joyce Quin & Moira Kilkenny

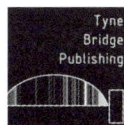

Tyne
Bridge
Publishing

To the two men in our lives, Michael Kilkenny and Guy MacMullen, for their love, support and belief in the importance of highlighting the lives and work of our "Angels of the North".

Contents

Preface

I was delighted to know about this second volume of *Angels of the North* which is a fascinating insight into the women of the region who have made a difference to other people's lives.

I grew up in a household of strong women. My grandmother had been born without the right to vote (she was born in 1900) and always spoke to us about how we should take our place in society. I also remember her being the one who told me that the word "History" was about men, and she encouraged us to think about the women who had made a difference in people's lives.

Growing up in South Wales I started to learn about the women who had changed the lives of coal miners by campaigning for pit head baths and therefore saved women the horrendously hard work of boiling the water. My interest in these experiences encouraged me to investigate further into the history of their lives, but the stories of many of these women are still not known.

The women who have been included in this edition are incredible and come from a wider range of backgrounds including sport, medicine, literature and more. With each name there is much to learn and to admire and we can understand about how hard women have had to fight for change. But it is the known (and unknown) impact that they have had that we should celebrate. Without these women we wouldn't be where we are now. In learning more about these women, we can also learn more about ourselves and the impact that we can make.

Tanni, Baroness Grey-Thompson DBE, DL

Introduction

Welcome to the second volume of *Angels of the North* in which we continue to celebrate the remarkable achievements of notable women of the North East. Women whose actions have led to improvements in different aspects of our national or local life, or women whose personal creativity, bravery and persistence is inspirational and which can encourage and motivate us all. Some of the women profiled are well-known, but some seem to be in danger of being forgotten and some indeed we are seeking to rescue from near obscurity! All of them, we believe strongly, deserve to be widely recognised, remembered and appreciated.

As in volume one, our subjects' lives span a period of over 500 years. From the earliest period - the 15th century - we have Margaret Usher and Matilda Burgh who have a strong claim to be the very first English feminists and who were brought to court in County Durham for their "trickery and defiance" way back in 1417. Our most recent entry is just from last year - 2023 - and is a tribute to that remarkable Durham University Professor, Dame Rosemary Cramp.

The women cover as diverse a range of activities and fields of interest as can be imagined, including aviation, archaeology, architecture, philosophy, medicine, various branches of science and the arts, football, politics, education and social and political engagement.

As in the first volume, the women we have profiled are no longer alive. We decided to do this, partly to avoid setting ourselves a limitless task but also because it is easier on the whole to assess a life's achievements across its entire span and in its historical context. We also wanted to avoid possibly invidious choices! However, we fully recognise and pay tribute to the ever-increasing numbers of women playing key and positive roles in our region today. May this trend continue and become entrenched as the norm.

As in the first volume, too, we had to decide what is a North-Eastern woman and we concluded that it was right to feature those whose life's work and major achievements took place in the region alongside those who were born and brought up here. The geographical definition of the region is the counties of Northumberland, Tyne and Wear, and Durham but with some leeway and flexibility on the southern and western borders!

We have found in writing these profiles that a number of themes have emerged. The key role of education in transforming women's lives has been very much in evidence and education enabled many of the women featured to challenge the limits imposed on them and allowed them to gain new freedoms. Unsurprisingly this meant that many of the women concerned were from the middle or upper classes who were more likely to be given educational opportunities than women from working class and/or impoverished backgrounds. But even middle and upper-class women often had to overcome obstacles to be educated or to be able to pursue careers and take up non-traditional interests. Women in the past were frequently only referred to through their relationship to men - husbands, fathers, brothers - and worked often in their shadows. A well-known saying - and cliché - used to be that "behind every successful man there is a good woman" – well, in this volume we have sought to bring the achievements of good women who have been so overshadowed into the limelight. Particular examples of this would be Teresa Merz and Mary Jane Hancock.

A belief in the importance of education for women as well as men was a vital strand in the thinking of the Quaker religion which helps to explain why a number of the women we have written about grew up in that faith. Although Quakerism was not large in numbers of adherents compared to, say, Catholicism, Anglicanism or Methodism, it was the religion of a significant number of influential women including Elizabeth Pease, Ellen Richardson and Elizabeth Spence Watson. These are women with remarkable achievements to their credit in their chosen fields. It is heartening and satisfying that a number of studies about North East Quaker women have been published in recent years to highlight just how influential and important to our history they have been.

The last women to benefit from educational reform and increased opportunities were those from working-class and poor backgrounds which is why there are frustratingly few of them in this volume. These were the women who because of financial, social and family reasons needed to concentrate on simply surviving from one day to the next. No one painted their portraits, few corresponded with them or wrote about them or discovered their individual talents or potential. Thankfully there are some notable exceptions to this rule.

Indeed, we have felt that the lives of some of the women we have written about are symbolic of countless others whose names are unknown. Elizabeth Shepherd, for example, the supremely talented quilter whose skills only became evident after her husband was so badly injured in a mining accident that he could never work again, and Elizabeth then had to find ways of supporting the family with only a pittance to live on. Given the history of coalmining casualties in our region over the centuries, she is remembered here not only for her own resilience and creativity but as a representative of so many unknown, strong women in our pit communities who had to cope with bereavement or life-changing injuries and the challenge of bringing up children in the most difficult and painful of circumstances - and yet found ways of succeeding and of doing so.

While we have endeavoured to delve into our subjects' lives through reading and research we are aware that a book of this type, featuring many different women, cannot be as detailed as a full-length biography of each. We are conscious too that much still remains to be discovered and written about many of our subjects and if any of our work helps to stimulate new biographies and PhD theses then so much the better!

As a result of both volumes we have been brought into contact with a number of groups and organisations to whom we would like to pay tribute. In particular we have been struck by the region's numerous local history societies, in our cities, towns and rural communities, and how they keep the history of their areas alive, through their meetings, websites, articles and in-depth research. We have also been delighted to have had contact with many individual Women's Institutes and Soroptimist Clubs in our region whose keenness to celebrate exceptional North Eastern women of the past has been clearly evident.

Finally, we have been hugely helped by many libraries, organisations and individuals in compiling this book. As well as recording our heartfelt thanks to them in the Acknowledgements section we have also recognised their help in relation to the individual profiles in the list of sources in the Bibliography section at the end.

Joyce Quin and Moira Kilkenny

Dame Allan's statue on the former school in College Street. In the City of Newcastle upon Tyne there are 113 statues, 97 depicting men, 2 of Queen Victoria and only one of a non-royal woman. Hopefully one day that gender imbalance will be corrected.

Dame Eleanor Allan (1629 - 1709)

A philanthropist who founded a school for poor children in Newcastle which bears her name and still thrives today

This short piece pays tribute to a woman of whose life we know very little, but whose business success and generous personality led her to try to ameliorate some of the consequences of social and economic inequality by establishing a school for 60 poor children in Newcastle in 1704. She also has the distinction of being the only woman, apart from Queen Victoria, commemorated by a statue in Newcastle.

The statue was placed in a niche on the side of College House, in College Street, in 1882, once the site of the school she founded. No one knows who designed the statue of Mrs Allan and, as there is no portrait in existence it is unlikely to be a likeness, it simply depicts an idealised ancient gentlewoman wearing medieval dress with a bible in her hand - a woman whose actions played a part in Newcastle's history, a part as yet not fully known.

What is known is that Eleanor was the daughter of a Newcastle goldsmith, William Link, and that she married John Allan in 1649. By 1657 John had joined the Merchant Adventurers of Newcastle and was a corn merchant, selling such grains as rye, barley oats and maize. By 1665, he was only modestly successful, his tax band being a mere "four hearth house." He had a shop in the Pink Tower ward, near the Side.

It is claimed, in *A History of the Parish of Wallsend* (1923) by William Richardson, that Eleanor and her family were "tobacco merchants," but there are no contemporary documents to confirm this. Certainly the Allan's shop was within reach of both the parishes of All Saints and St Nicholas where the tobacco trade in Newcastle was strongly established and it is probable that with a shop at the heart of the tobacco trade in Newcastle, the Allans may at some stage have drifted into selling relatively small amounts of tobacco bought from wholesalers in England or Scotland, but it is unlikely that they had any direct involvement with the tobacco slave plantations in the Americas.

Richardson tells us that when John Allan died in 1679, Eleanor and her son Francis worked hard in the business and laid up considerable wealth. In 1700 they bought a 130-acre farm in Wallsend and rented it out for income.

Eleanor was a committed Christian and when her only son Francis died unmarried, she decided to found a school to educate some of the poor children of the city. The Charity School Movement supporting such endowments had begun in the 1690s, encouraged by the (Anglican) Society for the Promotion of Christian Knowledge, and Mrs Allen's school was one of these. Ultimately there were six charity schools established in the town. The first was St John's in 1705.

The earliest report of Mrs Allan's generous philanthropy was in 1704 when a clergyman, Rev. Bates, wrote to the Society for the Promotion of Christian Knowledge "Mrs Allen has settled in the hands of Trustees a Dean and Chapter Lease ... for 2 schools one for boys, the other for girls. This Charity to commence at her death, who is now 80 years of age."

So the Charity School of St Nicholas was founded by deed of gift in 1705, which endowed the income from her 130 acre farm at Wallsend for its support.

One year after her death the school was formally opened, for 40 boys and 20 girls. The aim was that the school would instil Christian values in the children while teaching literacy and numeracy.

Following its establishment, the school received donations from other local figures and ordinary parishioners and prominent business people alike. John Fenwick (part of the illustrious Northumberland family which included the founder of Fenwick department store) was one. Aubone Surtees, Bessie Surtees' father and part owner of the Exchange Bank known as Surtees and Burdon, was another. (It was not until 1870 that the State took any responsibility for the education of the poor with the introduction of Board Schools.)

The site of the original school is not known, but in 1786 Newcastle Corporation provided a new site at Manor Chare, where the school remained until 1821 when it moved to Carliol Square. In 1877, St Nicholas Charity School moved again to Rosemary Lane. At this point it was given a new name and completely reorganised as Dame Allan's Endowed schools, with a board of governors, a grammar school curriculum and permission to admit fee-paying pupils. A new building was erected in 1882 in College Street, where the school remained until it moved in 1935 to its present location in Fenham.

Nothing more substantial is known of Dame Eleanor Allan, though her reputation grew as her school flourished and increased in size and importance. In 1801, John Baillie's *An Impartial History of Newcastle* described how the "honourable and laudable" charity school came into existence because of the "pious benevolence of a worthy lady, Mrs Eleanor Allan." On the 200th anniversary of the school's foundation, Rev. Crawford Amour spoke of Mrs Allan as a "saintly person".

Dame Allan's schools continue to flourish today, still within the Anglican fold and true to the philanthropic values of its founder in supporting children from less well-off families with scholarships and free places. There is now a junior school, an 11 to 16 girls' school, an 11 to 16 boys' school, and a coeducational sixth form, about 1,100 pupils in all.

The alumni of the school has some very notable men and women. They include: Dame Myra Curtis DBE 1886-1971 (Principal of Newnham College Cambridge from 1924 to 1954); Margaret Dale 1922-2010 (who became Director of Dance for BBC television) and Peter, Baron Pilkington of Oxenford (Headmaster of the King's School Canterbury and High Master of St Paul's School).

Dame Eleanor's statue is a reminder that this very considerable legacy from the 18th century is only possible because of the far-seeing benevolence of one notable woman, Dame Eleanor Allan. I doubt if she would ever have imagined that her generosity and her kindness would have had such a lasting effect and that her schools would survive so long, thriving as they are today, well into the 21st century.

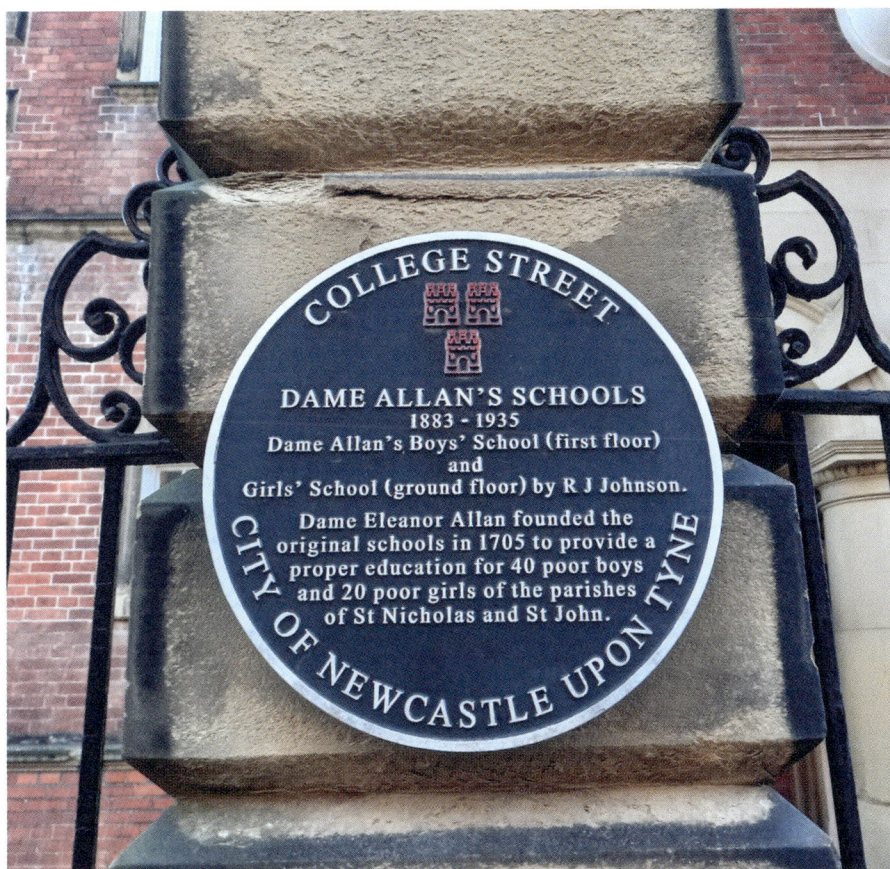

The plaque on College Street honours Dame Allan's achievements.

Susan Auld at the launch of M.S. Polyxene C in May 1957 and, inset, Susan in 1934.

Susan Mary Auld (1915 - 2002)

First woman to receive a degree in naval architecture and successful ship designer

When Susan Auld - then Susan Christie - graduated from Newcastle's Armstrong College (part of Durham University) in 1936 with a BSc in Naval Architecture, so unusual was her success that it aroused great interest and made headlines across the UK. Newspapers in London, Edinburgh, Cardiff and Belfast all reported the event as did the press in Yorkshire, Liverpool, Norfolk and Portsmouth. The *Hampshire Telegraph* asked: "Can we picture her submitting new designs for cruisers and destroyers or creating a record for something entirely new in naval construction?" The same newspaper concluded by saying "The Navy will watch her progress with interest and wish her luck."

While being the first to graduate specifically with a Naval Architecture degree, Susan Auld was not the first woman to study that subject although she was certainly one of the first. Dorothy Rowntree had previously graduated from Glasgow with an engineering degree specialising in naval architecture and had subsequently worked for the Fairfield Shipbuilding yard on the Clyde. Both she and Susan belonged to families with an involvement in the shipping and shipbuilding industries, which helps to explain their interest in these subjects. Nonetheless it was ground-breaking for women to pursue that interest through university and into a successful industrial career. Indeed, they even had to contend with the old superstition that women on board ships meant bad luck!

Susan Christie was born in Tynemouth in 1915, the only daughter of John Denham Christie and his wife Mary. Her father, himself a naval architect and shipbuilder, became the Chairman of the famous Wallsend shipbuilding company, Swan, Hunter and Wigham Richardson Ltd. in 1930. The links with that company were and remained close and involved a number of members of the wider Christie family. Indeed Susan is often referred to as Susan Denham Christie because she, her parents and brother were known as "the Denham Christies" to differentiate them from other family branches. Susan's naval architect grandfather, Charles John Denham Christie, who had originally worked with Brunel, had been a partner based at the company's Neptune Yard back in the 1850s and her brother would become Director at the same yard in 1938. Her own familiarity with the yard began at an early age. At eight years old she, alongside another Director's daughter, launched her first ship, SS Cuba, a passenger ship that began service in 1923. This would be the first of many ships she would name over subsequent years.

The entry for Susan in the Oxford Dictionary of National Biography describes her as a "delicate child" who began her education at home under the care of a governess. At age 10 she was able however to attend a local school in Tynemouth and showed quickly her intelligence and ability to learn. Her son Charles tells an amusing story of the results of a geography test that she took at that time and where she answered every question correctly bar one - the capital of Norway - which she gave wrongly as Kristiania, - denying her a 100% score. In fact this was the old name and Susan had been ill at home and unaware when the name had been changed to Oslo! At age 14 she was admitted to Cheltenham Ladies' College, the school where her mother had been a pupil. It was from there, in 1932, that she won a place to study naval architecture at Armstrong College under the direction of the Department's nationally renowned Professor, Sir Westcott Abell. Also in 1932, she was the first woman to be admitted as a student member of the North East Coast Institute of Engineers and Shipbuilders. After a successful period of study, she graduated with her B.Sc in 1936.

In response to questions from journalists about her graduation, Susan confirmed that she had been aware of the importance of shipbuilding from an early age and had dreamed of the day when she would be able to design big ships. She said, modestly, of her achievement, "I've always been interested in ships and you have to know a lot about their designs to pass the examination". She also later in an interview on BBC Radio's Home Service, she asserted that the shipbuilding industry would benefit from the participation of women.

Following the award of her degree, Susan began work in 1936 in the design office of the Neptune Yard of Swan Hunter and Wigham Richardson. She joined the Neptune Yard at what would turn out to be a key moment. The slump of the late 1920s and early 1930s had had a devastating effect on the shipbuilding industry and many former Tyneside shipyard workers had become unemployed and had suffered great hardship. From 1936 onwards however things started to change with the realisation that the international situation, and in particular the rise of Nazism, meant that the navy needed to be ready in case of attack, and that new warships were necessary. Within a couple of years, Tyneside's shipyards including the Neptune would be working at full capacity and be busier than ever seeking to fulfil the orders for new vessels. The outbreak of war in 1939, unsurprisingly, fuelled this demand even more.

In the pre-war period Susan, in addition to her principal responsibilities, contributed regularly to the company's magazine *The Shipyard* which appeared on a quarterly basis. Susan mostly wrote humorous pieces, providing some light relief in a publication otherwise restricted to factual reports on the vessels being built and launched at the company's yards. One of her articles describes the strange layout of the drawing office which had been extended above the yard's railway line and which involved, to get from one part to another, going up 2 steps and then down 2 steps to accommodate the trains below, and which also entailed coping with the all too frequent emission of smuts!

Susan was part of the design team for the battleship *HMS Anson,* which was completed and launched in 1940. It undertook many wartime tasks, notably assisting in the re-occupation of Hong Kong in 1945 after the victory over Japanese forces. Susan's work in the war was highlighted in the publication *The Woman Engineer* in an article in 1942 referring to her as "the only woman ship designer in the country". Part of her wartime work was as a key member of the team designing the landing craft used by allied troops in the Normandy Landings of 1944, pioneering work that demanded new technical skills and repeated tests to ensure the vessels would operate as intended. Another of her tasks was as one of the designers of the aircraft carrier *HMS Albion.*

The pressing need for ships and qualified people - including women - to build them just before and during the war seems, happily, to have helped eradicate the old superstition of not allowing women on board during construction and Susan no doubt benefitted from this new freedom. Previously, it is said, she had to board and inspect vessels she was designing on a Saturday afternoon when no shipyard workers were present to avoid causing alarm or offence!

During the war, and because of being recognised nationally as Britain's only woman naval architect, Susan's help was enlisted by the wartime coalition government in two different, but related, ways. Firstly, the Ministry of Labour contacted her in 1941 to get her advice on how women could be better and more extensively used in the shipbuilding industry. The correspondence between Susan and the Ministry shows that the government had concerns that the shipbuilding sector, as opposed to other engineering and scientific sectors, was making very little use of women employees and failing to recognise the economic potential of doing so. Susan's experience in the industry was seen as highly relevant and as helpful in compiling the information needed to tackle this problem. Secondly the Ministry of Information recruited Susan, in 1943, to broadcast to the UK's war allies, the United States and Russia, to encourage them to harness the skills and abilities of women in their war efforts.

Like all in wartime Susan had to take shelter during warnings of air raids and, according to her obituary in the *Times,* her air raid position was underneath the battleship. Susan would laugh at the irony of this, recognising that the strength of the ship did offer protection but was at the same time a prime target for enemy bombing.

Locally, besides her wartime work as a naval architect, she was also involved in the Civil Defence Committee in Newcastle in charge of a section of ambulances. She assisted Mrs Wynn Reed, the full-time worker, by working part-time at evenings and weekends. After the war (in 1953) she received a Coronation medal in recognition of her work. Susan's sons remember playing with her white steel war-time helmet with its black "A" on the front.

Once the war was over Susan worked primarily on commercial and cargo vessels. Notably she was a member of the team that designed the *Leda*, the Passenger Ferry which sailed twice-weekly between Tyneside and the Norwegian ports of Bergen and Stavanger.

In 1952 she married John Gwynne Auld, an engineer and graduate in electrical and mechanical engineering, at which moment she gave up her position as a naval architect. This was at a time when women routinely ceased working upon marriage. Two sons resulted from the marriage and the family settled in Jesmond Park East, near to the Armstrong Bridge and Jesmond Dene. Their elder son Martin recalls that his parents would often discuss technical and scientific subjects together such as "strengths of materials" and which for him and his brother made "dinner table discussions quite complex"!

Susan's official involvement with the company in succeeding years was limited to the occasional appearance at the yard for ceremonial events. For example shortly after leaving in September 1952 she was asked to present the annual awards to apprentices which she did "in an able and charming manner". Speaking at the presentation, she said how pleased she was to be invited back to the yard and congratulated those receiving the awards. However, she added "The only thing that worries me is why is it always the boys who get the prizes? Where are all the apprentice tracers? I do hope that next year there will be a long row of pretty women!" Throughout her career Susan fully recognised the contribution and the potential contribution of women to the industry - not only in wartime - and in particular she wanted to salute the tracers (usually women) whose precise and careful work was essential in ensuring the accuracy of the final original design of a vessel, and who had to serve an apprenticeship to gain the necessary qualifications.

Five years later in May 1957 she was again invited to the yard to launch the cargo ship, *MS Polyxene - C*. She gave another lively and well-chosen speech with literary allusions and amusing touches. She declined the present of a diamond brooch - the customary gift to a woman launching a ship - choosing to have a sideboard instead. She declared "a brooch would have been lovely for state occasions but it would have spent most of its life under lock and key because I do not go to many state occasions. This sideboard I shall see every day and no doubt dust it every day and every time I see it I shall remember the *Polyxene - C* and this lovely day."

Both Susan's writings and her speeches convey someone with a keen sense of humour and this is confirmed by her sons in their affectionate memories of her. She comes across as an entirely unstuffy person in an occasionally stuffy working environment. Her sons also remember her no-nonsense attitude and of getting on with what you had to do and doing it to the best of your ability.

While Susan's official appearances at the shipyard after her marriage were few and far between she no doubt, through her brother's continuing role as a Director who specialised in training, innovation and research, was kept up to date on the company's strategy. Given, too, how close she was to her brother she perhaps also acted as a sounding board for him and was able to give her own views about his and the company's plans and prospects.

However, along with the rest of her family's involvement in the company her activity ceased after shipbuilding nationalisation and the formation of British Shipbuilders in 1977.

She lived on Tyneside for almost all of her life and was obviously deeply attached to her home area. Showing an early musical ability, she was a talented pianist. She also, at some point during her childhood, took up playing the Northumbrian pipes and was tutored by Tom Clough, one of the foremost exponents of the instrument.

Susan died on 9th March 2002 in Newcastle's Freeman Hospital after suffering a cerebral haemorrhage. Her husband and two sons survived her.

What Susan felt about the decline in shipbuilding in the 1980s, its complete demise on Tyneside and the loss of shipbuilding skills and jobs throughout the North East is a matter for speculation since she did not write publicly about it. But it is hard to imagine anything other than her regretting that such an important industry, which had played such a vital part in our region's economy and identity, had ceased to exist. Nevertheless her own contribution as a woman in a sector almost entirely male dominated was a part of the history of that great industry in our region - and its national significance - and should be properly remembered. North Tyneside Council has recognised this and, along with heritage charity The Common Room, installed a plaque to Susan on the house where she was born, 12 Northumberland Terrace in Tynemouth. Appropriately the plaque was unveiled on Trafalgar Day, 21st October, in 2022. Speaking about Susan at the unveiling North Tyneside Mayor Dame Norma Redfearn said, "It is very fitting that we can bring people together on Trafalgar Day to celebrate Susan's life and achievements. Her ideas and designs brought about important advances in shipbuilding technology that helped turn the tide of the Second World War."

Florence Nightingale Harrison Bell in 1929.

Florence Nightingale Harrison Bell (1865 - 1948)

Social reformer and pioneer of the labour movement

Florence Nightingale Harrison Bell is a striking example of someone who was well known throughout the length and breadth of Britain during her lifetime but who, until very recently, had been almost entirely forgotten even in her native North-East. She has begun to be rescued from this neglect by the work and research of the Heaton History Group and through her life being celebrated in the production *Heaton!* at Newcastle's Peoples Theatre in 2018. Happily, Florence is now commemorated by a blue plaque on the house in Hotspur Street, Heaton, where she lived from 1901 to 1920.

An indication of Florence's past renown lies in the fact that there are two portraits of her in the National Portrait Gallery in London, the gallery whose stated purpose is "to promote through the medium of portraits the appreciation and understanding of the men and women who have made and are making British history and culture." So what was her record and what significance does her contribution to our national story have for us today? The blue plaque in Hotspur Street describes her as "Socialist, Suffragist, tireless campaigner for healthcare, women's and children's rights. First Federal Secretary of the Independent Labour Party." That is a good summary which hopefully can whet appetites for a fuller knowledge of her life and achievements.

Florence's place of birth was 1 Alexandra Place, Newcastle. The house no longer exists, having been demolished in the 1970s during the construction of the city's central motorway. The circumstances surrounding her birth are intriguing and, following early confusion and mystery, have recently been revealed in research done by Professor John Heckels and published in an article in the *Family History Society Journal* in 2019. She was born, illegitimate, to Isabella Tait on 8th October, 1865, with no father's name appearing on the birth certificate. However, she was baptised in St Andrew's Church, Newcastle, on 17th December the same year and the names of the parents were given as Thomas Latham Harrison (gentleman) and Isabella Harrison of Alexandra Place. Thomas was a well-known and successful bookmaker, nicknamed "Doc", thereby causing confusion by some assuming subsequently that he was a medical practitioner. He died two years after Florence's birth and left his estate to Florence's mother, described as his "widow" despite the absence of any wedding certificate. She and Florence then lived in Scotland for some time before returning to the North-East by 1878 when Isabella married Thomas

Hedley Thompson, an engine fitter of Gateshead. Thereafter, Florence was Tyneside-based, living with her mother, stepfather and three half-siblings.

Fortunately, the stigma of illegitimacy, which so often in Victorian times meant children facing prejudice and ostracism, did not seem to attach itself to Florence or make her life difficult during childhood. Neither did it impede her education when - following a brief spell as a cook - she became a teacher after successfully studying at Armstrong College (now Newcastle University). At some point during her childhood or early adulthood she became Florence Nightingale Harrison. While it can well be understood that either Florence or her mother - or both - shared in the general public adulation of Florence Nightingale (and in fact the name Florence was a popular girl's name because of this) it would be interesting to know more about when and how this name was added.

Florence became politically and social active from her early adult years. She was a keen and committed suffragist as well as supporting the campaigns of the expanding trade union and labour movements in favour of better living and working conditions. Doubtless her work as a teacher in impoverished Newcastle neighbourhoods reinforced her commitment to such causes. Florence was one of the founding members of the Independent Labour Party, joining in 1893 when it was first established, and in that same year stood as the first socialist candidate of the Newcastle Board of Guardians who were responsible for administering the Poor Law in the city.

In 1896 Florence married Joseph Nicholas Bell in Newcastle. In that year he became General Secretary of the National Amalgamated Union of Labour, an organisation that he had helped to found in order to advance the interests of railway workers. The marriage, which produced a son, Percy, born in 1902, was a very successful personal and political partnership, lasting some 26 years until Joseph's death in 1922, aged 58. Sadly, he died less than two months after he had been elected as MP for Newcastle East in that year's general election.

While Joseph was a well-known and a well-respected figure in trade union and labour circles, his public profile was not so evident as Florence's who, through her various activities and speaking engagements, was increasingly in the public eye both regionally and nationally. Nationally, she was the Independent Labour Party's first Federal Secretary, and was also the first woman member of the party's National Administrative Council. Locally she was also prominent in various ways becoming, for example in 1902, a Director of the Newcastle Cooperative Society.

Along with many ILP members, Florence became involved with the Labour Representation Committee which led to the formation of the Labour Party in the early years of the 20th century. Up to and after the First World War she fulfilled a number of roles in the Party, being one of the first women to serve on its National Executive Committee when women were admitted to membership of that body in 1918. She had earlier helped to establish the Party's Labour Women's League and had been a member of a number of committees dealing with specific social and educational issues. Reading some of the proceedings of these bodies it is clear that Florence was an assiduous and active member but it is also clear that she did not see these organisations and bodies as ends in themselves, but as a means of promoting causes she believed in, such as improved living and working conditions for the least well-off through the creation of high-quality public services.

Much of her early campaigning up to the First World War focused on votes for women. While she was a suffragist rather than a militant suffragette, she nonetheless always spoke passionately against any attempts by the organisations to which she belonged to dilute or delay the all-important commitment to deliver the vote for women. She shared platforms with many prominent suffragists and suffragettes including Mrs Pankhurst.

Not surprisingly, education was another key issue for her and this included both improved educational provision for all children and better working conditions for teachers, particularly for women teachers. At the time women teachers invariably got paid less than their male counterparts and they had to resign their posts upon marriage.

Equal pay and equal terms and conditions were always Florence's goals. In an article for *Labour Woman* in 1913 she proposed "An Education Programme" calling for a number of measures to support children from disadvantaged backgrounds, measures that were badly needed at the time but that still resonate today, such as good quality school meals, airy school buildings, access to health care, measures to provide for children with mental and physical challenges, a wide expansion of kindergarten provision and baby clinics. This last proposal in particular bore great similarity to the Sure Start scheme introduced by the Labour Government some 80 years later. She also advocated changes to the curriculum to improve the teaching of both academic and practical subjects as well as financial support to enable children to stay on at school beyond 15 and a much-needed expansion of evening classes and further education facilities.

The many social causes she took up included penal reform, housing policy (including detailed proposals about housing design) and ways of tackling unemployment and of improving working conditions, including a shorter working week without a reduction in pay. As was pointed out in the affectionate obituary written by the former Labour Party General Secretary, J. S. Middleton, so many of the things she campaigned for had been realised by the time she died in 1948, with one exception being her unsuccessful campaign - but one many would agree with - of supporting a change in polling day from a Thursday to a Saturday!

Delving into the British Newspaper Archive it is striking just how many reports of Florence's activities there are from newspapers across the whole of the UK. Michael Proctor, who researched Florence's life for the Heaton History Group, said that he was "astonished by the volume of newspaper coverage of her speeches" and that it was "remarkable that none of the articles found it necessary to explain who she was".

At the end of the First World War in 1918, when (some) women were at last given the right to vote and were able to stand for Parliament, Florence was touted in the press as a likely candidate. In the event it was her husband Joseph who was chosen to stand for Labour in their home constituency of Newcastle East and, in the expectation of being elected, he and Florence moved to London in early 1922. He indeed won the seat later that year but he sadly died shortly after, following two operations to remove cancerous growths.

Newspaper reports at the time predicted confidently that if Florence were to stand as a candidate to replace her husband, being so well known and respected, she would be certain of selection but in the circumstances it is understandable that she declined the opportunity, a decision that also had the effect of allowing the senior Labour figure Arthur Henderson - who had lost his previous seat a few months earlier - to be re-elected in the city where he had lived most of his early life.

Although bereaved, Florence was determined to continue to work for the causes she and Joseph had championed and in the year following his death she served on a national committee to look at the conditions of women domestic servants - as well as speaking at conferences and events around the country and abroad. With the election of the First Labour Government in 1924, Florence was asked to participate in a number of official activities and inquiries including assisting Margaret Bondfield MP (who would become Britain's first woman Cabinet Minister) on a visit to Canada to investigate the problems faced by some British immigrants, especially the plight of children - often orphans - who had been sent there unaccompanied under barbaric forced resettlement schemes.

She was also appointed by the Government to a Royal Commission to inquire into the National Health Insurance Scheme. This Commission's work continued until 1926, after Labour had lost power, and led to a split between those favouring the existing scheme and those - like Florence - in the minority who disagreed. The minority report published by Florence and her colleagues called for sweeping reforms and its detailed recommendations presaged in large part the measures that would, after 1945, be part of the establishment of the Welfare State.

Florence also had a keen interest in international policy. She was a strong supporter of the move to establish the League of Nations after the First World War. In 1923 she was a delegate at the International Federation of Working Women congress in Vienna and she worked on a number of Labour's Overseas Committees on aspects of foreign policy during some momentous years, marked by the Russian revolution, the Spanish Civil War and the rise of the Nazis.

In the 1929 election, Florence, aged 64, was selected to stand as Labour's candidate in Luton. The publication *Labour Woman*, talking of the Party's candidates, proclaimed: "Some of them need no introduction to any of our readers. Mrs Harrison Bell is an old stalwart who has worked in the Movement for more years than some of us can remember." Florence, interestingly, also received endorsements from prominent people outside the Labour Party with Canon Donaldson of the Church of England particularly warmly recommending her to the voters. Florence's son, Percy, was also a candidate in the election - the only mother-son duo amongst the candidates of any party - but neither was successful, although years later, after Florence's death, Percy was elected for Labour to the Greater London Council, representing the Newham area of East London from 1964 until 1981.

During the 1930s, Florence maintained her involvement in the Labour movement. She served on the Standing Orders Committee - responsible for the conduct of Labour's Annual Conferences and gave her last speech as a delegate at the Conference in 1936 in Edinburgh as "she had reached the age of 71 and it was time to let somebody else come". Nevertheless, 10 years later we find her once again at a Labour Women's event, speaking eloquently in support of their work and efforts!

Two years after that, in October 1948 aged 83, Florence died in north London. Her obituary, quite rightly, described her as a "Pioneer of the Labour movement" who had "given a lifetime of service to socialism." Frustratingly for would-be biographers, not much has been written about her personality, although intriguingly her interests were once listed as reading, walking ... and motorcycling. Motorcycling would have been unusual for a woman of her generation, although it would have provided a useful, and stylish, way for her to turn up at her meetings and conferences.

Perhaps there are some people even today who remember meeting Florence and have personal recollections of her. They may be prompted by the renewed interest in her life and work to share those memories. Given her record and achievements, she surely deserves to be recognised long into the future.

Norah Balls, c1910, in her suffragette summer "uniform".

Norah Balls (1886 - 1980)

Dedicated her life to public service and the women's movement

Norah Balls is celebrated for her life dedicated to public service and uniquely for her contribution to no less than three nationwide feminist organisations, the Suffragettes, the Girl Guides and the Women's Engineering Association.

Norah spent most of her life in Tynemouth until she was 65 when she retired to live in a flat in Bamburgh Castle, lent to her by Lady Armstrong. The Balls were a fairly affluent family. Norah was the older of the two children of William Balls, a sea captain who was away at sea for much of the time. Norah attributed her life-long love of geography and travel to her father, who sometimes allowed her to accompany him on his voyages.

Norah's mother, Elizabeth, was a great supporter of good works and, in particular, the RNLI and the NSPCC. Educated locally at dame schools, Norah completed her formal education at a local college where she developed her interest in elocution. When she was in her 20s she placed advertisements for pupils in local papers, offering "weekly lessons in Recitation, Gesture and all branches of Elocution." It is not known what response there was to her advertisements but there was no financial pressure on Norah to earn her own living. Norah's voice production stood her in very good stead when addressing public meetings, a skill which never left her.

From the outset, Norah Balls displayed an interest in helping all those less well off than herself. When only 12 she was reported in the local press as having raised £5 /10 shillings from a bazaar organised to support the local lifeboat. Whatever else she was involved in, over the next years Norah served the community in diverse ways, through membership or Chairmanship of committees, as an Air Raid Warden during the Second World War. She served as a JP from 1944 and was a local Councillor for the Dockwray Ward from 1946 to 1951. For a time she was Aunty Norah on BBC's *Children's Hour North*.

But it was the struggle for equality with men that was always her prime concern, and in the years before the outbreak of the First World War, Norah's activities were centred around the movement for women's suffrage, the campaign that had a huge impact on Edwardian Society, ultimately forcing it to reappraise the role of women. Newcastle was a major stronghold of both the moderate and militant campaigns, though the wealth and organisational strength of the Women's Social and Political Union, the WSPU, the more militant group, gave it dominance from 1910 onwards. From 1908 until the outbreak of war the WSPU, had a permanent organiser and premises in Blackett Street. Regular weekly meetings were held, new members initiated, activities planned and members exploits were reported on and published in the W.S.P.U's national periodical, *Votes for Women*. It was this group which Norah joined and reports in *Votes for Women* indicate that she very quickly became thoroughly immersed and a high-profile activist. She herself said: "I never joined anything to become a sleeping partner."

Norah was primarily active in the North East though she travelled widely to give lectures and speeches. A great deal of time had to be spent explaining and recruiting support from men as well as women, and Norah gained her experience of public speaking from the back of a lorry or a crude platform of beer crates outside public houses and factories as far afield as Edinburgh, Galashiels and Yorkshire, as well as Newcastle. On one occasion, at a meeting of quarry workers in Yorkshire, the men threw stones at them. She said afterwards that she was not afraid and put some of the stones in her bag for her rockery at home! North East area reports indicate that Norah organised meetings in towns and villages across the region, as well as musical and theatrical evenings. Mrs Emmeline Pankhurst stayed briefly at her family home, Deneside, in Tynemouth.

A popular tactic of the WSPU was to heckle cabinet ministers at public meetings. When, in 1909, Winston Churchill, then Home Secretary, came to Newcastle's Station Hotel to speak to the liberal Society, it was Norah Balls who stood in his way at the door of the hotel and told him that women's votes must be included in the King's speech.

When Asquith failed to introduce the Conciliation Bill in 1910, Norah was one of six militants from the North East who travelled to London (along with over 100 women from all over the country) to "storm Parliament."

In a taped interview, Norah described events: "They would not let us get near the buildings. We just stood outside the railings and eventually we were taken to Canon Row police station and charged with obstruction. We were allowed to go to our lodgings but had to attend police court next morning." They were charged and then released. Over the next few days there was some stone throwing and window breaking and Norah was rearrested twice and then released, but not before the magistrate referred to her as "a most dangerous woman". The Government were keen to avoid imprisonments, so as not to create martyrs for the cause, and only two of their number were imprisoned - Cissie Wilcox and Norah Armstrong. Norah Balls had a narrow escape.

Norah was missing from the 1911 census - this was also part of the Suffragette campaign. Mrs Pankhurst called upon women to boycott it saying "If we are not intelligent enough to place a cross on a ballot paper, we cannot fill in census forms." The Headquarters in Blackett Street remained open all night to help shelter the census dodgers.

1912 and 1913 saw increasingly violent protests against the Government's failure to grant women the vote. These began in Newcastle in February, 1913. Corrosive liquid was poured into letter boxes; telephone wires were cut; windows in the Globe theatre, Gosforth, were smashed; the Pavillion and bowls house at Heaton Park were burnt out. That same year Kenton Railway Station was razed to the ground. Although Norah is on record as "hating destruction and violence", she did admit some part in the arson attack on Brandling House in Gosforth Park, though what that was is not known.

When war was declared, a truce was agreed, all WSPU prisoners were released and women decided that their prime duty was to fight on the home front. In the event, after the War in 1918 all women householders over the age of 30 were given the vote, and in 1928, women were given the vote on the same terms as men.

The second National feminist movement Norah was involved with was the Girl Guides Association. In 2012, the chief executive of the Girl Guides Association described it as "the ultimate feminist organisation", established, as it was, in 1910 when a group of girls gate-crashed the first ever Boy Scouts' rally, demanding something for the girls. At a time when girls were "discouraged" from swimming, cycling and running, it is amazing that soon they were completing badges in sailing, aviation, home electrics, cooking and good citizenship, as well as tracking and signalling. The movement now has a long history of empowering girls and young women to be their best and is a worldwide organisation.

It was Norah Balls who established the Girl Guides in Northumberland in 1916, when she became the first secretary of Northumberland County Girl Guides and was heavily involved with the movement for the next 20 years. She was encouraged in this by some of the great ladies of the day - such as Lady Katherine Parsons, Earl Grey's daughters, Lady Howick and Phyllis Craster. She threw herself into the work with great gusto, organising a training camp at Dilston and, in 1917, the first regional Girl Guide rally in Jesmond Dene. Suffice to say that in 1929 she was awarded a Medal of Merit, and in 1932 the Association's governing body gave her the Oak Leaf in recognition of her outstanding contribution to Girl Guiding. In 1936 she became County Commissioner and later President of Northumberland Girl Guides. Her legacy is that today, over 100 years after the Northumberland Girl Guides Association was established, it continues to flourish and has approximately 2000 members.

One of the greatest scientific developments of the 20th century was the application of electricity for use in the home. After the setting up of the

National Grid in 1926, domestic electrification developed apace, so that by the outbreak of the Second World War, 66 per cent of homes were using electricity, at least to light their homes.

The Electrical Association for Women, the EAW, was established by women, mostly scientists and engineers, who recognised that electricity could lighten the burden of housework and bring enormous benefits in terms of health, hygiene and comfort. Caroline Haslett, its director and driving force from 1924 -1956, dreamed of transforming society and liberating women from drudgery through the use of electricity in the home. The spread of the EAW was rapid and immediate, with branches springing up all over the country, and in 1927, Norah Balls became the director of the North East branch of the Electrical Association for Women.

The aim was to educate women about science and about the great benefits that electricity could bring, in heating, lighting, cleaning, refrigeration, laundry and other new labour-saving devices. They organised speakers and conferences and produced a flagship publication, *The Electrical Handbook for Women* (1930). They also produced a quarterly magazine written for the ordinary housewife and entitled *The Electrical Age*.

Norah embraced the work with her usual energy and flair. She herself travelled widely, certainly far afield as Aberdeen, to promote the ideas of the Association. One of her major and very successful initiatives was to invite the Association to hold its fourth annual conference in Newcastle in 1929. The conference was a huge success with delegates from the United States, the Netherlands and Austria, among those in attendance. Visitors to Newcastle could also see the spectacular King George V Bridge (the Tyne Bridge) which had just been opened in October 1928, and enjoy the North East Coast Exhibition, which was also taking place in Newcastle that year.

Norah Balls was an exceptional lady, a tireless, brave and dedicated worker for good causes, with the conviction that suffrage was vitally important but just the beginning of the move towards equality, fairness and fulfilment for girls and women. Her work locally, especially with the Girl Guides Association and the Electrical Association for Women, helped move society in the right direction.

On 2nd March, 2022, North Tyneside Council and the Old Low Light Heritage Centre unveiled a blue plaque outside Norah Ball's family home at 36 King Edward Road, Tynemouth, to honour her life and achievements. It reads: "Norah Balls Suffragette. 3 August 1886 - 26 May 1980. Lived here 1902 - 1936. A leading North East Activist in The Women's Social and Political Union, campaigning for women's suffrage in the United Kingdom. Writer historian, lecturer, guide leader, magistrate and councillor, her life was committed to public service."

Matilda Burgh and Margaret Usher (c1417)

First feminist activists ever recorded

Although little is known about Matilda and Margaret, what we do know is too interesting to be left untold. They were two serving maids who set themselves up against the absolute power of the Prince Bishops of Durham. They attempted to break the law that prohibited all women from entering the shrine of St Cuthbert in Durham Cathedral. Their actions were brave and quite exceptional in that most women at the time simply accepted their ancillary role in Church and State, but not Margaret and Matilda. They protested the equal right of women to enter the shrine. They were fully aware that if they were caught the punishment could be severe.

The simplicity of St Cuthbert's shrine today, behind the high altar of Durham Cathedral, belies its original importance and grandeur. In the Middle Ages St Cuthbert (634-687) was the most important northern saint, the patron saint of Northumbria with many miracles and stories attributed to him. Durham Cathedral itself was built to honour him. The cult of Cuthbert extended throughout the Kingdom and included kings and peasants. King Alfred of Wessex had a great devotion to Cuthbert, King Cnut walked barefoot to his shrine and nearly every Mediaeval English King visited his shrine, a major pilgrimage site.

The beauty of the shrine was legendary. Wealthy pilgrims donated valuable gifts, which were placed in gilded cupboards on either side of the shrine. These cupboards were opened to display their priceless contents only when the shrine was uncovered. The shrine itself, which supported St Cuthbert's coffin, was made of green marble, gilded and carved with dragons and mythical beasts and studded with jewels and semi-precious stones. It was said that just one of the jewels decorating the shrine would have been worth a king's ransom. Four seats were carved into each corner of the shrine where pilgrims, male pilgrims that is, could kneel and pray for the Saint's blessing. The shrine or feretory itself was usually covered by a richly embroidered cloth, with two sumptuous depictions of Christ, as child and judge. At the edge of the cloth were six silver bells that rang when the cloth was lifted. The full grandeur of the shrine was displayed on limited occasions such as St Cuthbert's birthday and at weekly High Mass.

Women however were denied sight of this spectacle, this lavish wonder, and were excluded from the possibility of closeness to the relics of the Great

Saint. They were allowed into the cathedral but were not allowed to enter the shrine itself. There was a cross marked on the cathedral floor, beyond which point women were not allowed to go.

Matilda and Margaret staged their protest. Dressed in men's clothing they attempted to enter the forbidden area. But they were caught and detained. At their trial they confessed to their "crime" and on September 18th, 1417, the consistory court passed sentence upon them.

The order freely translated reads: "Whereas Matilda Burgh and Margaret Usher, servants as they declare of Peter Baxter of the said town (Newcastle) led by devilish incitement and their own desperate audacity and boldness, came clad in men's clothing to the Cathedral at Durham, with this purpose and intent that they might enter the feretory of the most holy confessor Cuthbert, knowing that it is forbidden to all women whatsoever under pain of excommunication... And whereas they have confessed this great crime before us sitting in judgement; and whereas from such crimes an intention to proceed to others afterwards is inferred... We have enjoined upon the said women, in form of law... that each of them shall go before the procession on three festival days round the church of St Nicholas; and on three other festival days round the church of All Saints dressed in the same men's clothes in which they so rashly came to the cathedral church of Durham."

The order went on to say that before each of these occasions the women had to stand before the congregation and explain why they were being punished. This was to further shame them and "so that no other women ever after shall dare break forth into such boldness of crime".

It will have occurred to the reader that the punishment imposed on the two women must have suited them. What better publicity for their cause than to be made to explain their grievance on six separate occasions and before what would have been huge audiences.

I have been unable to establish any more information about these two ladies and, although protests like that of Matilda and Margaret were rare and not part of any movement for women's rights, it was a protest for the right of women to be treated equally with men. And so these two Newcastle women, Matilda Burgh and Margaret Usher, can be seen as the first "feminist" activists, recorded as they are, in the proceedings of the consistory court of Durham in 1417.

Photo: A D Teasdale

Top: Durham
Cathedral and
left, the
simplicity of St
Cuthbert's shrine
today in the
Cathedral.

Photo: J B A Hamilton

A portrait of Dame Maud Burnett
by Frank Eastman.

Dame (Annie) Maud Burnett (1863-1950)

Feminist, politician and the first female Mayor of Tynemouth

In order to fully understand what a pioneering spirit Maud Burnett was, it is important to remember the context of her life. The prevailing ethos was the Victorian, patriarchal view of women. Women were thought weaker and with smaller brains than men, so there was no place for them in the professions, in politics, in the military, even in the church, except as nuns. Their roles, it was thought, were best confined to the home and family, and so until 1918 women had absolutely no parliamentary voting rights. However, in the 50 years before 1928 they gradually gained access to some aspects of local government. They were allowed to serve as elected members of school boards and poor law boards, and from 1907, on rural and borough councils. It was in local government that Maud Burnett was to make her mark.

This period from 1870 to 1934, the span of Maud Burnett's political life, was also one of unprecedented economic and population growth and of major social upheaval in the country and in the region. Issues arose that couldn't be dealt with by employers or philanthropists, but which required Government intervention. Driven by social and industrial necessity, a system of local government evolved to deal with matters such as sanitation, housing, water supply, health and education.

The women's movement welcomed the opportunity to participate in local government but, even so, given the social mores of the day, it required considerable courage and bravery for women to dare to put themselves forward for election, to speak at public meetings or to chair committees because, initially at least, many saw such actions as inappropriate for women - an affront to social propriety. Maud Burnett had the courage and the conviction to swim against the tide, she sought votes and won seats often in the face of considerable male hostility. She dedicated her life to good works at the same time demonstrating that women could and should be equal participants in political life, national as well as local.

Maud was born at 10 Prior's Terrace, Tynemouth, and was the second daughter of Jacob Burnett (1825-96), and his first wife Annie Dalgleish (1830 -1866). Her mother died when she was three years old and there were two boys from a second marriage. Her father was a wealthy man, the last of the Tyneside alkali manufacturers and a shipowner, he was a patron of arts and a collector of pre-Raphaelite paintings. Her two younger brothers founded the very successful Burnett Steam Shipping Company in 1889. It was run by the family until 1980.

Educated in local schools in Tynemouth, Miss Baker's and then Miss Hoald's, she completed her education at Vevey, in Switzerland. Upon her return she learned her public social skills by throwing herself into voluntary work, and over the next 30 years ran Bible classes, an invalid children's aid society, play schemes, children's holidays, a school for the blind, penny banks and girl guides. She was also a committee member of the YWCA and became Honorary Secretary of Tynemouth Women's Liberal Federation, serving from 1895 to 1910. In this role she assisted at three parliamentary elections (The Liberals were unsuccessful until the Liberal landslide in 1906 when they took the Tynemouth seat from the Conservatives).

Maud Burnett's first opportunity to be formally engaged in politics came with Balfour's controversial Education Act in 1902. The Act abolished thousands of School Boards and replaced them with 328 Local Education Authorities (LEAs). These bodies were to set local taxes, establish new secondary schools and develop existing schools, as well as ensuring that all teachers were properly qualified. The old School Boards had provided women with their first opportunity to serve as members, and it was to compensate women for this lost opportunity that the new Act specified there must be two women on each municipal education committee. It was Maud Burnett's good fortune to be co-opted on to Tynemouth's Local Education Committee.

Her experiences on the education committee strengthened Maud's resolution to increase the opportunities for women to engage in and win a voice in politics and, in 1907, she founded a Tynemouth Branch of the Women's Local Government Society (WLGS). The WLGS ran a nation-wide campaign, initially to get women into local government, but it soon widened its remit to include parliamentary franchise and seats in Parliament. The passage of the *Qualification of Women Act* in 1907 was a considerable victory for the WLGS, and for the first time women were allowed to stand for election and become members of local and city councils.

In 1909, as soon as she was able, Maud, then aged 46, stood as an independent candidate for election to Tynemouth Council. She said she stood "as a representative woman" to avoid party political prejudices closing doors to canvassers. Although unsuccessful in her first attempt, a year later with Liberal support she was elected for the Dockwray ward, becoming the first woman municipal councillor in Northern England. She was the first and only woman councillor in Tynemouth for the next twenty years, until 1929 when three other women were elected. It was not until 1919 that there were any woman councillors in Newcastle and 1920 in Gateshead.

Maud claimed a mixture of motives for standing for the Council, quoting women's rights, women's duties and women's needs. She saw council work as the most effective way of promoting philanthropic works. Her position was summed up in the *Shields Daily News* of 20 October, 1910: "There were women who saw all the sorrow around them, who heard the cry of the children, who knew there was sorrow and misery in the world and who said, 'You must let us help'. Was it right to answer 'No, stand aside because you are a woman?'"

She did not seek a seat on the Council for her own sake, but because she cared for the weak and the oppressed and because she wished to show that women could help. The whole effort to keep women out of it seemed too small and petty when one considered these things."

Dr. Ethel Williams supported Maud in 1910 and had this to say: "Under the changed conditions of modern life, much of the work that was especially women's work ... was now being taken over by Town Councils. There was work to be done on these public authorities which, unless a woman did it, was left undone. She hoped that Miss Burnett would not go on to the Council in too quiet a spirit. Fighting was good, and the interests of women and children, housing reform and tuberculous, were things that were worth fighting for." (Reported in *Shields Daily News* of 22nd of October, 1910)

Maud, who was by this time well known locally for her energy and effectiveness (it was she who had persuaded the Local Education Society to provide free spectacles for short-sighted children), was duly elected. Far from being "in too quiet a spirit", she immediately took her place on several committees - these included education, health, infant welfare, housing, insurance, public libraries, local pensions and mental deficiency and distress committees. She was assiduous in her work and while the success of committees cannot be attributed to a single member, by 1939 the council could point to many areas where there had been significant improvements in the standard of living for people in Tynemouth and North Shields. For example in housing. Whereas in the 1920s one third of all children born in North Shields were born in one-room homes, by the mid-thirties, following a slum clearance project and the building of 2,000 new houses, the number was reduced to 10 per cent.

While a councillor, Maud established a guild for mothers and a day nursery. Both were so successful that the first was taken over by the health committee, and the second qualified for a Department of Education grant. Maud served on the Council from 1910 until 1921, when she retired for a while to concentrate on her voluntary work. She was re-elected in 1926 and went on to become the first ever woman to serve as Mayor of Tynemouth, in 1928-9 and 1929-30. There were only four other women in the country who had been so honoured (Elizabeth Garrett Anderson was the first, in 1908). While the mayoral role itself was largely ceremonial, the moral victory was enormous.

She had been elected by her male councillor colleagues, it was a huge honour and indicates just how effective she had been as a councillor and how impressed her colleagues were with her work. She continued as a councillor until 1934, when, aged 71, she retired from politics.

Maud Burnett was partly driven by her belief in women's suffrage and was described in the *Tyneside Weekly News* (January 1909) as a "charming suffragette". But it was the non-militant campaign for women's parliamentary suffrage that she supported. Her chosen route to achieving women's suffrage was to show by her own success what women were capable of when they were allowed to operate in public life. She understood that suffrage was not the end but the beginning of the move towards equality and fairness for women.

Maud was awarded a D.B.E. (Dame Commander of the Order of the British Empire) in 1918 for her war work. Throughout the war she was Chair of committees concerned with war aims, food control and food economy. She served on the YMCA committee on comforts for the forces and on the military and naval war pensions committee, but her most outstanding contribution was as President of the War Savings Association in Tynemouth.

In an attempt to raise much needed funds for the war effort from the public, a National War Savings Committee was established, supplemented by volunteer local committees. The aim was to encourage small savers to lend their money to the Government to help pay for the war. The goal was to get people to buy War Savings Certificates. They cost 15/6 each (made up of thirty-one sixpenny stamps.) and could be redeemed after five years for £1.

Under her leadership, the Tynemouth Savings Committee was so successful that local people raised over two million pounds in Savings Certificates, prompting the military to present a tank, newly returned from Flanders, along with two captured field guns, to the town. It was received with great ceremony and stood in Northumberland Park, Tynemouth, until 1923.

In 1920, Dame Maud Burnett was appointed a Justice of the Peace and served the town as a magistrate from the time of her appointment until her retirement.

Indomitable in old age, when she lost her sight in her 70s she learned braille and became involved in blind welfare. She died at her home, 10 Prior's Terrace, Tynemouth, in November 1950, aged 87 and was buried at Preston cemetery, North Shields.

In 1990 North Tyneside Council erected a blue plaque outside her birthplace, 10 Prior's Terrace. It reads: "Dame Annie Maud Burnett b.1863-1950d. lived here. Elected in 1910, she was the first and only woman member of Tynemouth Council until 1929 when 3 others were elected. Created a Dame

Commander of the British Empire in 1918 for services during World War 1, she became the first woman mayor of Tynemouth in 1928. She was appointed a Justice of the Peace in 1920."

Photo: North Tyneside Libraries

Dame Maud Burnett is celebrated with a blue plaque.

NORTH TYNESIDE COUNCIL

Dame
ANNIE MAUD BURNETT
b.1863 – 1950 d.
lived here

Elected in 1910, she was the first and only woman member of Tynemouth Council until 1929 when three others were elected.

Created a Dame Commander of the British Empire in 1918 for services during World War 1, she became the first woman Mayor of Tynemouth in 1928. She was appointed a Justice of the Peace in 1920.

1990

Christine Elizabeth Cooper, consultant paediatrician in the children's departments of Newcastle and Northumberland.

Photo: RCP Museum.

Dr Christine Elizabeth Cooper (1918 - 1986)

Internationally distinguished paediatrician and expert on child abuse

Christine (Tina) Cooper was a remarkable doctor, a consultant paediatrician in the children's departments of Newcastle and Northumberland for over 30 years. Successful in what was then a male dominated profession, her dedication to the care of sick children led her to challenge many of the orthodoxies of children's medicine and to become a pioneer of both psycho-social medicine and the understanding of child abuse.

Tina was the first child of William Francis Cooper, an industrial chemist and later physician in general practice. Her mother died when she was only six months old and her father remarried. Later, two sisters and a brother completed her happy and affectionate family. In 1924 the family moved to Surrey where Tina attended Surbiton High School, St John's Bexhill, and a finishing school in Switzerland. After completing a two-year course in nursing and mother care, Tina decided she wanted to become a doctor.

This was an exceptional path to choose because at the time only six per cent of doctors were women. The prejudice against the recruitment of women as medical students was so ingrained that in 1944 the Government threatened to withdraw public funds from any medical school whose admissions did not include at least 20 per cent of properly qualified female students. Tina's other problem was that she lacked the appropriate entry qualifications. Undaunted, she set to and by the age of 21 gained admission to medical school. She then embarked on a further six years of medical training. She studied throughout the war years at Girton College, Cambridge and the Royal Free Hospital, London. A prize-winning undergraduate, Tina Cooper qualified as a doctor in 1945.

In appearance Tina was a tall, attractive and imposing woman, she was an entertaining companion and a warm and caring person. It is said she had infinite patience and empathy, as well as an extraordinary gift with children.

In the period after the Second World War there were massive and momentous changes in healthcare. The National Health Service was founded in 1948 and thousands of previously independent Voluntary and Municipal hospitals became State funded. The use of new medicines such as penicillin led to new ways of treating patients, as did the impact of developments in the new science of psychology. Changes in attitudes were necessary too, not least among some doctors, of whom the British Medical Journal said at the time:

"The medical man is intensely individual and must become more and more aware of his responsibility to the whole community." The process of modernisation impacted on all fields of medicine, including children's medicine, then something of an under-developed specialism.

Very broadly these were the circumstances in which Tina Cooper began her career in the field of paediatrics, a field for which she was exceptionally well qualified, with her general medical training, her additional two-year training as a mother and baby nurse and her Diploma in Child Health. After spending her early graduate years in London, in 1949 she made her home in Newcastle and took up an appointment as senior registrar to the distinguished paediatrician, Professor Sir James C. Spence, in the Dept of Child Health at Newcastle General Hospital. One year later she was appointed consultant paediatrician to the children's departments of Newcastle and Northumberland, a post which she filled with distinction until her retirement in 1983.

The Department of Child Health in Newcastle was the perfect place for Dr Cooper, for she shared the philosophy of the Department, namely that paediatricians should be concerned with the whole child, their general wellbeing and their emotional state, and not just the symptoms of their condition. Here, in the first ever Department of Social Paediatrics at Newcastle, Tina Cooper's unrelenting and energetic championing of the psycho social approach to children's medicine throughout the next 30 years, earned her the reputation as a pioneering paediatrician of local, national and international standing.

Dr Cooper treated children suffering from the full range of serious diseases and injuries and to each young patient she gave meticulous care. A key to her professional success was that she kept detailed notes of every one of her patients, including their family and social situation. It seems her "notes" filled every available space in the Department and in her home. As a consultant she ran a tight ship, though her detailed note taking, as well as her own propensity for forgetting the time, meant that parents were often kept waiting for their appointments. However they were always beaming with satisfaction when they left.

She had important leadership responsibilities; to train up the registrars and senior registrars in the department and to lecture and contribute to the teaching of medical students in Newcastle. She was soon recognised as a truly inspirational teacher and practitioner.

For a period of 20 years, Dr Cooper was part of a group of younger paediatricians, who, guided by Anna Freud and Dr John Bowlby, studied the impact of developments in psychology and psychoanalysis on paediatric practices. Membership of this London-based group, which met once a month, had a profound effect on every aspect of her work.

Her attention was increasingly taken by the possible adverse impact of institutions such as hospitals and residential nurseries on children's well-being and development, even on their recovery. At the time when most physicians were men, many were ignorant of or disregarded children's emotional welfare and its effect on treatment and recovery. Dr Cooper became part of the campaign to introduce more enlightened arrangements in children's wards, especially regarding visits from parents.

Whereas today children's wards are bright, and appropriately furnished, with opportunities for parents to stay with their children or to visit them at will, this was rarely true 70 years ago. In general, hospitals were miserable places for children in the 1950s, with rigid regimes and arrangements driven by professional convenience rather than the wellbeing of the children. Parental visits were believed to upset the children and cause noise and disruption to hospital routines and so they were severely limited to weekly or at best twice weekly. If a child cried too much when parents left, the solution was often simply to ban the parents from visiting altogether. The "old school" argued that even if the child did not see their parents they soon settled down.

Modern medicine recognises that children should not be treated as little adults, but that childhood is a vulnerable and vital stage of development. One of a child's most basic needs was a close bonding with their mother or a mother substitute. Without this bonding a child's mental and emotional development could be damaged for life. Research by Dr John Bowlby and James and Joyce Robertson into the hospitalisation of children, demonstrated that when the child appeared to "settle down," it had become detached from its parents, an abnormal state denying the child the close relationship essential to its development.

Tina Cooper threw herself into the campaign for more parental visits. This was a long hard-fought campaign, despite having won official support in the 1956 Platt Report. As late as 1980 only 40 per cent of hospitals allowed parents unrestricted visiting.

As her professional life progressed and her reputation grew, Tina Cooper involved herself with many bodies concerned with the welfare of deprived and disadvantaged children. She was medical adviser to the Northern Counties Adoption Society for 30 years. From 1960 she worked with the Association of British Adoption and Fostering Agencies. In 1969 she was invited by the Home Office to sit on the Houghton-Stockdale committee, contributing significantly to the report which formed the foundation for the *1975 Children Act*, which put the welfare of the child at the very centre of the adoption and fostering process. She could have written the opening words of the Act herself, "The Child's welfare shall be of paramount importance".

A second strand in Dr. Cooper's professional journey was her involvement in the Third World. In 1963 she spent six weeks in West Africa, in Sierra Leone, Ghana and Nigeria at the invitation of the Colonial Office. She travelled 25,000 miles, visiting doctors who had trained in Newcastle and who were working in isolated communities to establish whether their training had equipped them properly for their roles. The relevance of medical training was a theme she returned to again and again.

In 1964, at the invitation of the Government of Sierra Leone in West Africa, she was seconded to establish basic child health services throughout the country. In her own words she wrote: "I had the privilege to work for two and a half years in Sierra Leone, and I made two visits there afterwards. The aim as the country's first paediatrician was to assist the Sierra Leoneans, first to organise the hospital services for children and at the same time to develop a comprehensive child health programme in the remote areas and that would of course mean maternal and child health. We developed rural clinics and mobile teams using a Land Rover and the health sisters, who were fully trained state registered nurses, midwives and health visitors, they and I and nursing auxiliaries, we gradually organised ourselves into teams doing health education nutrition work and immunisation across the country as well as the simple curative medicine." For her work in Sierra Leone she was awarded an OBE.

The third important strand in Dr Cooper's professional life was her pioneering work on child abuse. She became one of the first child specialists to recognise the extent and nature of child abuse, physical, psychological and sexual. Child abuse is a very difficult area to work in. It requires an open mind, an ability to use the intellect when emotions are high, a commitment to the child and yet compassion for the parents. Tina had all these characteristics. A former colleague described the following case by way of illustration:

"A small baby had sustained a subdural haematoma, (from having been shaken). Tina spent a long time interviewing the parents. Mother was a rather beautiful lass whereas husband was more on the side of "rough trade" having already been through three liaisons and left five children in his wake. Police involvement at this stage would have targeted the father as the obvious culprit. Tina however while retaining the option of referral to the police, kept probing each parent on their own. After taking a minute-by-minute account of the previous week, she finally got the mother to confess that, after her husband had walked out during a row, leaving her furious and the baby crying, she had shaken the baby, having transferred her anger to the hapless child".

Her wisdom and experience gained through hard work meant that she was consulted widely, and her example inspired many paediatricians in training. Her skill as an expert witness was widely recognised and she became involved in many access and custodial cases.

Tina Cooper was a founder member of both the British Association for the Prevention of Child Abuse and Neglect and the International Society for the Prevention of Child Abuse and Neglect, becoming its second chairman. She advised the N.S.P.C.C., The National Children's Bureau, the Advisory panel of the National Foster Care Association and the Social Committee of the Council of Europe. She was writing a book on Child Abuse at the time of her death.

Though she never married, she was a great advocate of maternity leave for women doctors and used her position on the committee of Medical Women's Federation from 1970-76, to champion this.

Despite all that she accomplished professionally, Tina Cooper did make time for many interests and friendships outside medicine. She had a passion for music, ballet and particularly opera. When after a tiring day her colleagues were going home Tina could be seen setting off for London to go to Covent Garden or the Festival Hall. Just before she died, ill as she was, she insisted on going to Glyndebourne, for one last time. She travelled widely and had an encyclopaedic knowledge of Venice and Florence. She had an extensive library of books on history, philosophy, art and travel. She bequeathed her unique collection of works on the subjects of child abuse and adoption to the Walton Library of the University of Newcastle on Tyne.

Although she retired in 1983, she continued consulting, advising and lecturing until just before she died. In 1984 she concluded a lecture at the Medical school in Newcastle with a quotation from the Chilean poet, Gabriela Mistral ... which summarises her own lifelong dedication to children and the mantra of her own inspirational career: "We are guilty of many errors and many faults, but our worst crime is abandoning children, neglecting the fountain of life; many of the things we need can wait, the child cannot. Right now is the time his bones are being formed, his blood is being made and his senses are being developed. To him we cannot answer tomorrow, his name is today."

Dr Tina Cooper died of cancer at her home, 3 Kenton Road, Gosforth, in September 1986, after a long illness borne with great dignity and fortitude. Her ashes were scattered in the churchyard of Gosforth church, Newcastle.

Professor Dame Rosemary Cramp pictured at archaeological excavations.

Professor Dame Rosemary Cramp (1929 - 2023)

Durham University's first woman professor and archaeologist

Rosemary Jean Cramp was born in Cranoe, Leicestershire, to a farming family and it was on the family farm that she had her first experiences of archaeology. When she was around 12 years old, she and her younger sister discovered some tiles which, after consulting her children's encyclopaedia, she decided were Roman, perhaps part of a Roman Villa. She shared her discovery with the local vicar, who, to her disappointment, merely took the tiles to his own garden. Still intrigued by what she had found she wrote to Kathleen Kenyon, well-known in Leicester for her excavations beside the Jewry Wall, who took the matter seriously, advising Rosemary that "this is evidence and you must not destroy it!"

A few years later, another archaeologist, perhaps alerted by Kenyon, turned up and did some excavations on the site, helped by an eager Rosemary. They found traces of the walls of a building and, aged 19, Rosemary made notes of these excavations that were published in the *Journal of Roman Studies*. The local newspaper, the *Market Harborough Advertiser*, also covered the story and published a photograph of Rosemary leaning on a spade, the first of many such photos of her to be taken, over many subsequent years.

Following her schooldays at Market Harborough Grammar School, Rosemary won a place at St Anne's College, Oxford, to study English. However, archaeology continued to fascinate her. During her undergraduate years she joined the Oxford University Archaeological Society, became involved with the Ashmolean Museum and attended an archaeological field school near to the Roman Wall in Corbridge, possibly her first visit to the North East.

She was awarded her degree in 1950 and was then encouraged to study and do research to obtain a Bachelor of Letters (B Litt). This gave her an opportunity to combine her earlier degree work with her interest in archaeology by researching the link between archaeological finds and Old English, particularly Old English poetry. In Rosemary's words "in those days there weren't many people bringing those two together" but her research proved crucial to setting her on a career path of connecting archaeological evidence with Anglo-Saxon life and culture, at that time a neglected and undervalued approach.

From 1950 to 1955 Rosemary was a tutor at St Anne's College and as a young don became part of the life of the Senior Common Room. One of the people there, with whom she became close friends, was Iris Murdoch and that friendship would prove to be lifelong. Later in 1978, Iris dedicated her novel *The Sea, the Sea* (which won the Booker prize) to Rosemary, apparently - and charmingly - because coming from mid-Leicestershire Rosemary had been a landlocked child at a time when war-time restrictions on public access to the coast were in place.

Rosemary was alerted to a vacancy for a lectureship at Durham University by Professor Christopher Hawkes, her Oxford B Litt supervisor, in 1955. The post would allow her to lecture on her combined interests of English, History and Archaeology, and Rosemary, although initially somewhat uncertain about the move, decided to apply and was appointed. It was to prove ideal for her as she was then in a part of the country particularly suited to her archaeological interests and the timing meant that she could play a key part in setting up Durham's Department of Archaeology, alongside Eric Birley, already a renowned authority on the Roman Wall.

The Department flourished and Rosemary became a senior lecturer in 1966 and Professor of Archaeology (and Head of the Department) in 1971, the first woman Professor of the University. Under her leadership, the Department became internationally known and one of the most prestigious university departments in the country. She was tenacious in defending and promoting its interests, causing, as Dennis Harding, a fellow lecturer recalled, the University Registrar Ian Graham to characterise her as "spreading like an insidious weed" across the university"! However, she was also described as running the department "like a family, knowing just the right moment to open a bottle of wine." While undoubtedly hugely effective and inspiring as Head of Department, she also had traits of the stereotypical absent-minded professor - regularly leaving her handbag in various places and having a filing system which only she understood.

Her successes within the university are only a part of her story however, as over the years Rosemary's reputation and renown spread far and wide. Leicester University, which awarded her an Honorary Degree, recently summed it up by describing her as "one of the towering figures of 20th century archaeology." Her achievements fall into two categories. Firstly her pioneering excavations, particularly in the North East and secondly the vast project she initiated, aiming to compile a record of every piece of Anglo-Saxon sculpture in England (a task now approaching completion). Overarching these achievements was her vision for the development of her subject, in her early recognition of the transforming possibilities of science-based archaeology, and also of the importance of establishing accredited formal training of archaeologists.

The excavations in the North-East centred on the twin monastery of Monkwearmouth-Jarrow, founded in the seventh century, which was a centre of Anglo-Saxon learning and the home of the Venerable Bede. The monastery occupied sites both in Sunderland alongside St Peter's Church and in Jarrow next to St Paul's Church near the Tyne. Until Rosemary and her team began excavating from 1959 onwards, few remains at either site, apart from the churches, were known. Over the years up to the 1990s finds included the remains of several large buildings and some of the earliest stained glass ever found in Britain, the fragments of which were described by Rosemary as "jewels lying on the ground." These discoveries, important physical witnesses to the golden age of Northumbria must have been immensely exciting for all involved and created widespread regional, national and international interest.

Rosemary's work demonstrated the importance of the Anglo-Saxons to English and British culture and showed that, despite the arrival of the Normans, it was the English language which continued to prevail and that had produced some of the earliest vernacular literature in Europe. It also showed how important Northumbria was to British and European history and culture.

Although the major part of Rosemary's excavations were in Durham and Northumberland, she also undertook significant archaeological digs elsewhere including at the Hirsel in the Scottish Borders and at Catterick Garrison in North Yorkshire.

Rosemary's second great achievement in compiling a comprehensive record of Anglo-Saxon stone sculpture in England led to a first volume appearing in 1984, dealing with Durham and Northumberland, followed by 12 others, most recently in 2018. Only three volumes now remain to be completed and it is fitting - and heartening - to realise that Rosemary would have been able to anticipate the completion of this magnum opus before she died in May 2023.

Although Rosemary formally retired from Durham University in 1990, she continued to contribute to archaeology in various ways. In 1992, for example, she was a visiting fellow at All Souls College, Oxford. Over the years she also participated in and contributed to many archaeological and historical bodies, sometimes serving as President or Vice-President. Notable amongst these were her role over 25 years as a Trustee of the British Museum (where she became a friend of her fellow Trustee Sir David Attenborough), her 25-year membership of the Royal Commission on the Ancient and Historical Monuments of Scotland, and serving as President of the Society of Antiquaries of London from 2001-2004. Other bodies included the Historic Buildings and Monuments Commission England (later Historic England), the Advisory Board for Redundant Churches, the Reviewing Committee on Exports of Works of Art, the Validation Panel of Museums Training Institute, the Royal Archaeological Institute, the Council for British Archaeology, and the Cumberland and Westmorland Archaeological Society. This non-exhaustive list shows how much she was esteemed and how keenly her advice was sought.

As recently as 2017 she was in France, discovering French links to the Anglo-Saxons, a visit that confirmed her long-held view that some of the carvings found in Jarrow and Wearmouth came from there.

Rosemary, unsurprisingly, was the recipient of a number of honours. She was made a CBE in 1987, and then a DBE in 2011, "for services to scholarship". Honorary degrees were awarded to her from the universities of Durham, Bradford, Cork, Dublin, Leicester and Cambridge. She was elected a Fellow of the British Academy in 2006 and awarded, in 2008, the Gold Medal from the Society of Antiquaries of London for distinguished services to archaeology. A "Festschrift", a book in honour of her academic achievements was published in 2001, followed by a second volume in 2008.

She also reached out beyond the academic world in a number of ways. She made several media appearances including in a special edition of the BBC TV Programme *Animal, Vegetable, and Mineral* as well as contributing to the BBC 4 Radio Programme *In Our Time*. She also, crucially, engaged with local communities during her excavations, realising how important it was to share her discoveries with residents of the areas concerned, thereby fostering a greater awareness of local history and engendering pride in local achievements and culture. She was particularly keen to involve local youngsters, sometimes organising them into guarding the trenches and giving them opportunities for looking through excavated soil for any missed treasures. In Jarrow she launched what eventually became Bede's World with exhibitions that continue in Jarrow to this day.

Rosemary's death in May 2023 occasioned an outpouring of affectionate tributes from family members, close friends and colleagues, and from many of the huge number of students who benefited from her teaching and her unstinting support.

A close Durham friend told how "friendships and family were of fundamental importance to her" and described her as "kind, perceptive, funny, a rigorous teacher and an excellent communicator, with a vibrant enthusiasm for sharing her knowledge and vision." She and others marvelled at Rosemary's extraordinary energy, how generous she was with her time both within the university and in the public duties outside which she took on, being involved in such a wide range of learned and local societies and groups.

Richard Morris, who worked closely with her, wrote of his admiration of her style "a persuasive mingling of humour, strategic thought and eye for the pith of an issue" adding that "if you backslid she could be fierce, but admonitions were followed by a smile like a sunrise, and you were encouraged to start again." The Archaeology Department, after her death, published *Memories of Rosemary Cramp* - a long list of tributes to her from former students on whom she made a life-changing and deeply positive impression.

Outside the Archaeology Department the other focus of Rosemary's life within Durham University was her involvement in St Mary's College and this brought her regularly into contact with colleagues from other departments and disciplines, and many close friendships ensued as a result. The College has many entertaining memories of her. She apparently used the college basement from time to time as a depository for her archaeological finds, including even some human remains. This gave rise to the joke that "when they talk about skeletons in the cupboard at St Mary's they are talking literally not metaphorically." There are also many accounts of her dragooning St Mary students and others into helping her with her digs and then returning with them, caked in mud, for College formal dinner. The current Principal of St Mary's College, Professor Adrian Simpson, recalls meeting Rosemary through the Durham Town and Gown Society and how he treasured time spent in her company. In his words: "If I was able, I always tried to manoeuvre myself onto the table at which she was sitting - in that way I could guarantee a wonderful evening of conversation, and the chance to see that insightful and incisive mind at work on whatever topic came up was a joy."

For relaxation Rosemary enjoyed gardening, cooking and entertaining friends. She also, remaining a country girl, treasured any opportunity to escape when she could into the remote and beautiful areas of Weardale. She remained close to her family throughout her life and her niece and nephew Helen Milner and Robert Beesley have been left with the fondest memories of a very generous aunt who always came home to Cranoe for Christmas and Easter and who encouraged them to visit her "digs" and, according to Helen, "endeavoured to bring some culture into their rural lives!"

Rosemary has left an important legacy that will last long into the future. Her name will forever be associated with the stirring history of Wearmouth and Jarrow, and her trailblazing scholarship in Anglo-Saxon history and culture will likewise endure. Even back in 1990, Durham University set up a "Rosemary Cramp Fund" to support and provide grants for individuals and groups who make a significant contribution to the archaeology and heritage of Britain and Ireland. Not surprisingly other similar initiatives, in the light of her recent death, are currently being planned.

Dame Rosemary in later life.

Photo: Natural History Society of Northumbria

common violet

viola canina

Viola Canina (Common Violet) by botanical artist Margaret Rebecca Dickinson.

Margaret Rebecca Dickinson (1821 - 1918)

Victorian botanist and botanical illustrator

Margaret Rebecca Dickinson was a talented botanical artist who left a treasure trove of exquisite watercolours of wildflower specimens from all over Britain. A member of the Berwickshire Naturalists' Club, she spent her life collecting, painting and researching plants with meticulous and detailed care. Her paintings are only now, 200 years after her birth, more widely appreciated and available for us all to see.

Margaret was born in Newcastle to William Ogle Dickinson and Elizabeth (nee Davidson) Dickinson, the eldest of five children, a boy and four girls. Father and son, George, ran the long-established (1740) family tobacco and snuff manufacturing business from their premises at 22 and 24 Bigg Market, while the family home, was the "Head of the Side". The Side in Newcastle was then a bustling centre of trade and commerce. Both parents came from tobacco manufacture and retailer families, and three of their children, George, Elizabeth and Ann, all married into merchant families. Margaret and her sister, Rebecca Ann, remained unmarried but were wealthy, independent women. There are no portraits of the children, only of the parents, depicting an affluent well-dressed couple of the early 19th century. There are no records of the education of the Dickinson children, though the girls are likely to have had a governess rather than attend a school.

As her biographer Elizabeth Towner has observed, it is difficult to know how the child of a family without any known interest in the arts or science developed such a real passion for botany and botanical art that she spent almost the whole of her life dedicated to its study, except to say that, at the time, botany was a very popular area of study for women. In the first half of the 19th century botany was not seen as a science but more as a cousin to flower arranging, flower painting and gardening, a sort of high-status occupation for women, and no challenge to any male preserves. But when it did find its place in natural history and was recognised as a science, then the men moved in! I'm thinking of the young Beatrix Potter whose advanced work on lichens in the 1880s and 1890s was not taken seriously, leading, many years later, to an apology from the Royal Society, and of the occasion when the Director of Kew gardens refused even to look at Potter's highly accurate botanical drawings.

In Margaret's day however there were plenty of opportunities in Newcastle for her to pursue her interest. Margaret may have attended a series of botanical evening lectures, given in 1837 by Sir William Hooker and/or a summer day course in botany, advertised in the *Newcastle Journal* in 1838 as "illustrated with fresh and dried plants, drawings and diagrams, as well as, occasional Botanising Excursions with the pupils." In 1844 William Bell Scott was appointed Master of the new Government School of Art and Design in Newcastle and more than half of the courses run there were attended by women. One advert in 1847 read: "The Government school of Design, under the Supervision of Mr. Scott will reopen on Monday 6th September in the room in Market Street. LADIES PRIVATE CLASS. For tuition in Pencil, outline shading in chalk from copies and flower Painting on Monday and Friday mornings from ten to twelve o'clock. Fee 5s per month ..." Margaret's home was near Market Street, and of course she had the means to pay any fees.

Though the actual details are unknown, it is evident that Margaret took full advantage of the opportunities around her. As a single woman of independent means, she had the time and resources to devote to her studies. Her book collection indicates that she studied seriously. Hooker's, *British Flora* 1842, Withering's, *A Systematic Arrangement of British Plants* 1845, and Coleman's *Our Woodlands, Heaths and Hedges* 1859, were among the books she owned and annotated, while her plant paintings illustrate that she became a talented artist with a sound knowledge of botany and different habitats.

Margaret was 25 in 1846 when she began collecting and painting wildflowers within reach of her home in Newcastle. Over the next 40 years she painted 458 delicate and forensically accurate paintings, mostly though not entirely, from the Border Counties areas where she lived. She collected plants from within Newcastle itself, and from wetland habitats just outside Newcastle like Prestwick Carr, then a renowned beauty spot, plants from along the lower reaches of the Tyne Valley and along the coasts of Northumberland and northern County Durham, such as Whitley Bay, Cullercoats, and Tynemouth, as well as Marsden and Whitburn, Boldon and Sunderland. In the 1850s she began travelling further afield to Wetherall and Warwick Bridge, also to Cirencester in Gloucester and Cavan in Ireland. She began making trips to areas of mid Northumberland such as Otterburn and parts of the Cheviots as well as Yetholm in Roxburghshire.

In the late 1850s the family moved to Friar's Hill in Gattonside, a village one mile north of Melrose, a perfect location for a botanist. They moved again, and for the final time in 1869, to a large house in Boathouse Lane, Tweed Villa, in the village of Norham, eight miles from Berwick. Sadly, both parents died soon after they moved, William in 1870 and their mother Elizabeth in 1871. Margaret and Rebecca continued to live in Tweed Villa, with one servant. 20

years later in 1894, Rebecca, Margaret's lifelong companion died too.

But back to happier times. The move to Norham in 1869, brought Margaret many advantages. It seemed to act as a stimulus to her, in that in her first three years in Norham, Margaret painted as many as 42 specimens from in and around the village. The railway station at Norham allowed her to travel more widely. She could catch trains to Berwick with connections to take her to Edinburgh and Newcastle or travel west to Cornhill and Melrose. Another great benefit of this move was that she could easily travel to the Berwickshire Naturalists' Club, which she joined in 1872, and which proved to be the beginning of a long and happy association. (Women were only allowed as honorary members)

The Club, concentrated on field activities, with meetings held in different parts of the district and she attended meetings until she was in her late 80s. Her last recorded attendance was in October 1908. The Secretary, Dr. James Hardy, was very taken with Miss Dickinson's paintings, her enthusiasm and knowledge of botany. He was keen for her to exhibit her work at their meetings, and although only ever shown locally during her lifetime, wherever her work was seen it was greatly admired. A local newspaper described her work as showing "how close a student of nature that lady is, and her excellency as an amateur artist" (Report of a Berwickshire Naturalists' Club meeting, 1877). Another local source, *The Histories of Berwickshire Naturalists' Club*, 1882-84, commented ... "her beautiful delineations of our flora have secured for her a place in the very front rank of floral artists".

Margaret went on at least one field trip with the Berwickshire Naturalists' Club, to Holy Island in 1874 and later painted seven of the plants she collected there, several of which are very rare and endangered. It was more than 100 years later that Dr Linda France, Climate writer in Residence at Newcastle University, was so inspired by these beautiful watercolours that she wrote the poem, *Portrait of the Artist as an Island Flower*, a moving tribute to Miss Dickinson's life's work.

1874 was also the year that Margaret collected three specimens from near the High Force waterfall in Upper Teesdale in County Durham, which had long been an area of special interest to botanists. The area was recognised as one of a small number of remarkable localities distinguished by a collection of rare or purely local species of plants growing there. In the case of Upper Teesdale they included plants that were widespread in the British countryside 12,000 years ago. Margaret illustrated her finds, which were Spring Gentian, Shrubby Cinquefoil and Yellow Mountain Violet, now known as Mountain Pansy. All are rare and precious plants.

Margaret also had a special fascination for orchids and "ballast flora", and went to great lengths to find them. Her wildflower collection includes 13 paintings of orchids, five of which are rare specimens from Kent and one from Cirencester. Ballast flowers are a relic of our industrial past and are plants transported into the area unintentionally as seeds among the ballast of soil, rock and sand, carried by ships sailing into the rivers to collect their cargoes especially of coal, bound for London and elsewhere. The ballast was dumped by the riversides and formed hills on which these "imported", seeds germinated. Some such plants came from the south coast of England and others from Europe. One of these plants, Perennial Wall-rocket, she collected from South Shields and it can still be found in Amble and around Berwick today, but many such plants did not survive in Northumberland into the 20th century.

It is chastening to think how widely Margaret did travel to collect her plants. Victorian dress was cumbersome and although the development of the railways was a huge help, there were then no motor cars. "Shanks pony" or horse-drawn carriages were the only other forms of transport. I wonder how she decided which plants to collect and illustrate, who went with her on these trips and how she organised herself. Perhaps some of her visits further afield arose simply from holidays and visits to friends, while others would have a more deliberate "scientific," purpose. Margaret had other wide-ranging interests in natural history that included seaweed, freshwater algae, mosses, moths and fungi.

About a decade after she had finished the wildflower collection, Margaret embarked on another project, and between 1886 -1893, produced an Album of 30 watercolours of Narcissus cultivars, 27 of which were of flowers she, herself a keen gardener, had grown at Norham. (Three were grown at Paxton House nearby, by a Mr. Muirhead a fellow member of the Berwickshire Naturalists' Club). It is likely that as Margaret grew older, she was less keen to travel or that she too was affected by the craze for daffodils that gripped the nation at that time. However the fact that her Album of 30 Narcissus drawings was bought by the RHS for its prestigious Lindley Library Collection in 1996, is itself a great endorsement of the botanical paintings' artistic merits.

Margaret's many paintings are exquisitely beautiful and of the highest quality. There is a delicacy and freshness about them, as though each plant has just been picked. Her lightness of touch seems to emphasise the vulnerability and fragility of the plants, her use of background colours and her subtle use of shadow, gives the paintings a three-dimensional effect. Each of the watercolours is a carefully arranged portrait of the whole plant, roots, leaves, stems and flowers in different stages of development, painted with great skill.

Little is known of Margaret's personal life. Dr James Hardy described her

Above, Margaret's illustration of Geranium Sanguineum and, left, Blue Anemone.

as, "amiable and good". We know that she and her sister were very sociable. During the bathing season, they decamped to Spittal, just south of Berwick, and stayed at either No.1 or No.184 Spittal Well Terrace for several weeks. Their next-door neighbour and several friends from Norham went too and stayed nearby. Their arrival at Spittal was first reported in the local press in June 1874 and again as late as 1906, when Margaret was 85. In between walks by the sea and sea bathing Margaret made time to search for plants to paint. Unfortunately, there is no portrait or picture of her, she pre dates the widespread use of photography, and although she was fastidious about giving the names, dates and locations of her specimens, she left no other field notes, no notebook, no diary nor any letters to help us know her other than through her work.

Her life though, was a long one, spanning the period from just after the Napoleonic Wars until the end of the First World War, and she must have been concerned, as all naturalists were, about the impact of industrialisation on the countryside and its effect on the different habitats of the flora in particular. The changes in land use were huge, with the development of railways, mines and factories, the drainage of wetlands to increase agricultural productivity, and in coastal areas the development of holiday resorts. All of these things brought change and loss and were of great concern. The President of the Berwickshire Naturalists' Club addressed all lovers of natural history when, in 1859, he wrote of "The wanton destruction of rare birds and beasts, some of which have entirely disappeared; and also of the eradication of plants, many of which once common enough are no longer to be found." He blamed drainage and new farming methods. In 1873 George Clayton Atkinson published his *Catalogue of the More Remarkable Trees of Northumberland and Durham*, in which he detailed the tree damage arising from chemical pollution.

Clearly Margaret loved her subject, loved collecting, observing and painting, loved the study of botany, but she also had a profound understanding of the importance of soil and soil conditions on plants and her underlying motivation was to preserve for posterity the images of hundreds of flowers that she felt were endangered by the rapid changes going on all around her.

Margaret lived until the great age of 98 and is buried in the churchyard at Norham. She bequeathed her specimens of dried flowers, 1000 of them, and her 458 watercolours to the Hancock Museum. She wrote, "my botanical collection of dried plants and my paintings of them, my collection of seaweeds and my paintings of fungi to the Hancock Museum Newcastle upon Tyne, as well as any other articles of mine of scientific interest which the Committee of the Museum may choose to accept." (The Hancock is now known as the Great North Museum).

The Museum was delighted to receive her work and in 1919 the Curator wrote ..." the most remarkable acquisition of the year has come to us, by bequest of the late Miss M. R. Dickinson of Norham, a lady who retained to an advanced age a boundless energy and unusual versatility. The bequest includes a great series of beautifully executed watercolour drawings of wild flowers, in itself a remarkable life-work".

Although Margaret received little attention or recognition during her lifetime, her own personal fulfilment would come from knowing that she had used her talents to the full and left a huge visual legacy to encourage future generations to value our native flora. She was probably considered by her contemporaries as merely a well-informed amateur or a hobbyist, yet the range of her specimens, the extent of her travels and the quality of her artwork, make it hard to think of her as an amateur.

In recent years, two hundred years since her birth, and with the growing interest in biodiversity, the importance of Margaret Rebecca Dickinson's work is being acknowledged. An excellent biography was published in 2021, which has been the major source of information for this short profile. Her Wildflower Collection was digitised in 2002 and in 2021 was transferred to the prestigious JSTOR website, which means that, potentially at least, Margaret Dickinson's work can now be seen by a world-wide audience. For general interest and simply for pleasure, one can easily access her illustrations on the Northumberland Natural History site, "The Watercolour Drawings of British Wild Flowers" by Margaret Rebecca Dickinson.

458 of Margaret's watercolours were bequeathed to what is now the Great North Museum.

Pauline Dower (1905 - 1988)

Environmental activist and important pioneering figure in the development of Britain's national parks

Pauline Dower was an expert on Britain's National Parks

Pauline Dower, 1905-1988 (nee Trevelyan) was an important pioneering figure in the development and implementation of Britain's National Park system. An environmental activist, she also helped to raise awareness of environmental issues nationwide.

The National Parks were established in 1949 to protect England's beautiful landscapes and to give the people of Britain access to the hills and countryside. Today when we all enjoy access to the fells and forests, to lakes and rivers and mountains, it is easy to forget how recently this access was won. In the past the public were denied access to huge swathes of our landscape, either because the rights of landowners to prohibit entry were protected, or the construction of roads and other amenities were considered paramount. It took a determined mass campaign in the 1920s, 30s and 40s to open minds to what was then considered a radical idea, that the rights of private property, the rights of public and private developers alike, should be limited in order to protect the needs and rights of the wider community and the beauty of the countryside itself.

When Britain was recovering from the ravages of the Second World War, a vision emerged of a better world, including protection of the beauty of the landscape and provision for the physical and spiritual refreshment of the nation, enshrined in legislation.

The National Parks were to be part of the "New Jerusalem", alongside the National Health Service, education and social welfare reforms. The *National Parks and Access to the Countryside Act* transformed the idea of National Parks into a real possibility by establishing the National Parks Commission, whose job was to define and create National Parks in Britain and to implement the new law. This was a huge and innovative task, without precedent, very controversial and extremely important. Pauline Dower was to become a most influential lady, the longest serving and highest profile woman on the Commission.

Pauline was the eldest of the six children of Sir Charles Philips Trevelyan and Mary Lady Trevelyan, who was the youngest daughter of Sir Hugh Bell and half-sister of the great Gertrude Bell. Pauline grew up in Cambo House, Cambo, one mile from Wallington Hall.

Because of her father's pacifism the children were sent to a Quaker school in Somerset, Sidcot, one of the earliest coeducational schools in the country. Pauline was her father's favourite and he intended that she should help him run the Wallington estate and so, when her schooling was completed, Pauline went on to study at Reading, where she gained a Diploma in Agriculture. She also studied at the Central School of Art in London where she gained a Diploma and became an accomplished watercolourist and etcher. On the death of her grandfather in 1928 the family inherited Wallington Hall and the 14,000-acre estate. Pauline had just completed her training and had returned home ready to help farm the estate lands.

But then John Dower arrived for a visit and there was a complete change of plans. On the Wednesday, she took delivery of 300 pigs, on Thursday John Dower visited Wallington, and the next day they announced their engagement. He was 28 and she 23.

John was a Yorkshireman who became an architect and town planner. He was heavily involved in environmental matters and was an active speaker about National Parks throughout the 1930s, and wrote the brilliant and seminal report, *The Case for National Parks*, published in 1938.

They were married in September 1929, and over the next years Mrs John

Dower, as she became known, had three children; Susan Michael and Robin. Pauline certainly fulfilled the conventional roles of mother and doting wife of a distinguished public servant, although letters to her parents during the later years of her 15-year long marriage, indicate that she often found confinement to the domestic role frustrating. The war years, in particular, were dark for her. While John was away in Whitehall she was stuck in Kirby Malham, Yorkshire, with the house to run and only children for company. She longed to be more involved in public life.

When war broke out John joined the Royal Engineers but very unfortunately contracted TB and was invalided out of the army in October 1940. He was then recruited by Lord Reith to join a think tank on post-war planning and to write a paper on national parks. Sadly, in October 1942 he was told his TB was incurable. Despite this devastating news, John decided he would rather work on for as long as he could. In preparing his paper on National Parks it was necessary for him to visit potential sites and when he became too weak to do this Pauline acted as his chauffeur and drove him about in their little Vauxhall coupe, helping him with the surveying and report writing.

John Dower bravely finished his report in the winter of 1946 and died in October 1947. His final report, the Hobhouse report as it is known, became the basis of the legislation that led to the creation of the national parks in 1949.

John was only 47 when he died and obituaries acknowledged the importance of his work, and his ambition that the national parks would take their place in Mr Attlee's New Jerusalem.

Pauline and the children were devastated, she was 42 years old and the children still quite young. Their sense of loss can hardly be imagined. In an effort to help during her period of mourning, her father, as Lord Lieutenant of the County, arranged for her to become a Justice of the Peace in the hope that a public role might distract her from her grief. She embraced the opportunity with enthusiasm and was an active magistrate in Northumberland for over 30 years. It was also during this period of mourning that Pauline embraced Anglicanism and throughout the rest of her life remained a practising Anglican.

The Trevelyans were a wealthy and influential family, with a history of involvement in access and land preservation. In 1908, Charles Trevelyan, Pauline's father, a lawyer and Liberal MP, introduced four successive Access to Mountains Bills in Parliament, though they all failed. Then, incredibly and in keeping with his radicalism, in 1941 Sir Charles donated Wallington Hall and his 13,000-acre estate, including the village of Cambo, to the National Trust. The family view was that "nobody had the right to own and enjoy all the beauty there is at Wallington ... without sharing it with people". (*Living at Wallington* by Pauline Dower) Pauline's mother Molly, Mary Katherine Lady Trevelyan, 1881-1966, was awarded the MBE in 1963 in recognition of her work for the community and the countryside.

And so, in 1949 Pauline Dower was invited to become a member of the National Parks Commission. Her close involvement and absolute commitment to her husband's work, meant that by then Pauline herself was recognised as an expert on National Parks. There were 11 Commissioners, whose principal task was to follow the recommendations of the Hobhouse Report and designate the National Parks, and then to act as advocate for the parks at all levels of government. While they did not have executive powers as Hobhouse had suggested and were "advisory" rather than "executive ", they had great authority and influence in Whitehall. This was a mammoth task involving travelling the country, surveying areas, deciding boundaries and negotiating with interested parties, would-be developers, farmers, landowners and government departments. Pauline Dower's involvement in these matters is not surprising, the level of her commitment and the sheer breadth of her achievements indicates her enthusiasm and dedication to the work.

During the first months in post. Pauline found herself on five sub-committees. Her greatest responsibility then was her chairmanship of the sub-committee for the designation of the first ever national park in the UK, The Peak District National Park. To give a flavour of the intensity and complexity of the work, this process took 14 months to complete. A site visit was made in May 1950 and a draft map prepared. Comment was sought from the Local Authorities and the Council for the Protection of Rural England, the Joint Committee of Peak District, the Limestone Federation, the National Trust, the Nature Conservancy, the Forestry Commission and the Ministry of Agriculture and Fisheries, and as a result the map was revised. Then a series of conferences was held with the local authorities, which led to further revision of the original map. The minister, recognising the strength of objections decided there should be a local public enquiry. Pauline's role in all this was to drive the process forward and represent the Commission. The public enquiry lasted for three days, and afterwards the Minister, Hugh Dalton, confirmed the designation in April 1951.

Nearer home, Pauline was very closely involved in the designation of Northumberland National Park whose boundaries were a matter of the most complex and heated debate for over three years. Northumberland County Council rejected the Commission's first proposal for a small national park of some 200 square miles. They wanted a much larger park covering 570 square miles including the Cheviots, Hadrian's Wall, the Ministry of Defence Artillery

Range at Redesdale and Forestry Commission Land at Kielder, Wark and Redesdale. Resolving the issues involved dealing with many powerful bodies, the MOD, the NFU, the Forestry Commission, Northumberland County Council, the Council for the Protection of Rural England, the Minister and of course local interests. After strenuous efforts demanding profound local knowledge and tact, and avoiding a public enquiry, Pauline was able to produce the designation map that was finally agreed in 1956.

Today Northumberland National Park lies to the west of the county and covers one quarter of Northumberland, spanning 410 square miles. It encompasses the Cheviot Hills, the southern tip of Kielder Forest at Wark, and the central section of Hadrian's Wall. Years later, JB Ross, Clerk of Northumberland County Council, commenting on Pauline Dower's retirement wrote: "this will be specially severely felt in Northumberland because we all realise that the creation and development of Northumberland National Park owes far more to you than can ever be learned from printed reports." (Ross to Dower, 22 June 1966, Cambo papers.)

An important function of the Commission was to prevent the disfigurement of beauty spots and beautiful landscapes and so, over the years, there were innumerable issues to deal with, many of them low key, but each requiring careful consideration. Pauline was involved in these on an almost daily basis.

Meetings were endless and might take Pauline to London four days a week. At other times she was away from home for nights on end, travelling to visit sites or chairing local public enquiries. Pauline's home was littered with maps of the national parks, annotated in black and showing proposed boundaries. She sometimes illustrated her explanations with useful watercolour drawings and sketches, as at the public enquiry into the proposed Old Moor extension to Tunstead Quarry. There she used her watercolour sketches to show the potential impact of the proposed extension.

In the first 10 years of its existence, the Commission designated 10 National Parks. First the Peak District, then the Lake District, Snowdonia and Dartmoor in 1951, followed by the Pembrokeshire Coast, North York Moors, Yorkshire Dales, Exmoor, Northumberland and the Brecon Beacons. Together they covered 10 per cent of the land area of England and Wales.

Pauline had been promoted to Deputy Chair in 1958 and served until the Commission was replaced by the Countryside Commission in 1968. She was awarded a CBE in 1966 in recognition of her work. She was the longest serving and highest profile woman on the National Commission, and she served with huge dedication, bringing her local knowledge, her energy, experience and talent to all that she did. She travelled widely, spent many a night at her desk and defended the principles of the National Parks passionately. Indeed, when the Commission was disbanded in 1968 its first secretary wrote to Pauline saying: "no one could have done more for the National Parks than you". Pauline's commitment to the National Parks was total and must have been reinforced by her wish to fulfil her husband's dream. With few financial resources and a small staff, Pauline and her fellow Commissioners in designating 10 national parks established a territorial footprint that remains the basis of the system today.

Her work for the National Parks is, in itself, a considerable legacy, however Pauline's career in public life did not end there. She continued as a magistrate for over 30 years, for six years she served as a member of the British Waterways Board. She was a member of the Northumberland National Park Committee for 10 years, and the first woman President of the YHA in 1981-2.

The gender issue never deterred Pauline but it seems that newspaper reporting locally remained gender obsessed. In October 1958, the *Newcastle Journal* used the headline "Granny Stays Active," to describe her presentation of a prize to Allendale, as Northumberland's best kept large village and described her as one of Northumberland's most active grandmothers. She was 53 at the time and would live for another 30 years!

In 1984 Pauline's booklet *Living at Wallington*, was published. It is a personal account of the cheerful, happy family life she experienced as a child and young woman, enjoying gracious living, with multiple servants and carriages, and a lively and loving family. Throughout the book, which is an excellent family and social history, there are glimpses of her strong and energetic personality, although she only mentions herself on a couple of occasions.

Pauline's two sons followed in the Trevelyan family tradition and worked for the environment. Michael became National Parks Officer in the Peak District 1985-92 and then Director General of the Countryside Commission 1992-96. Robin, an architect, was a member of the Countryside Commission 1992-96.

Pauline used her wealth and position for the public good while gaining a huge amount of personal satisfaction and pleasure from her work. Administrators, by the nature of their work, which is mostly behind the scenes, are generally little known, as Pauline Dower is little known, but as the beneficiaries of her efforts, we should all be grateful that she was so effective and successful.

Pauline Dower died in 1988 and is buried at Cambo.

Mary Baxter Ellis' leadership qualities were vital during wartime.

Mary Baxter Ellis (1892 - 1968)

Commanding Officer of the F.A.N.Y and inspiring leader of women in both war and peacetime

The importance of public service must have been apparent to Mary Baxter Ellis from a very young age. She was born into a prominent Newcastle and Northumbrian family and her father, Joseph Baxter Ellis, described as a grocer and miller, had already served as both Sheriff of Newcastle and Mayor of Newcastle by the time of her birth in 1892. Later her father would become the first Lord Mayor of Newcastle when that title was conferred upon the city by Edward VII in 1907.

Educated at Newcastle's Central High School for girls there were, during her schooldays, various mentions of Mary in local newspapers when helping her father in his civic duties. At age 11, as the Mayor's daughter, she presented a bouquet to Princess Louise on the occasion of her visit to Newcastle in 1904. At age 12 she was reported as delivering "a well-received recitation for Newcastle Tramway staff at a party given for them by her father", her performance being described as "given with admirable emphasis and intelligent expression"! A year later she was helping to organise entertainment for the Fresh Air Fund and for The Poor Children's Holiday Association "and later on was mentioned as supporting local Barnardo homes. Through such activities she must have become aware of some of the economic hardships that many families were having to endure, and how useful such private charitable initiatives were in an age before the welfare state and at a time when publicly-funded social services were only very slowly emerging.

On leaving school she won a place at University College London to study archaeology, a subject that would continue to be of interest to her in later life.

With the outbreak of the First World War in 1914, Mary was determined to play an active role and engage in the war effort, despite the initial reluctance of the British Government and the military to allow women to volunteer their services. Mary, however, was already aware of the work of the First Aid Nursing Yeomanry (FANY), an organisation that she supported strongly. FANY had been founded in 1907 by Edward Baker, an Army Warrant Officer in the 21st Lancers, who, during his service in the Boer War, had the idea that women could have an important role in providing nursing and ambulance services at the front in time of war and should be trained in peacetime to help them be properly prepared for such work. He initially envisaged women reaching the front lines on horseback, although with the advent of the motor car it became obvious that driving skills would be needed in future. Not surprisingly, given the requirement to be able to ride horses or drive vehicles, all the early members of FANY were women volunteers, like Mary, from comfortably off families.

Mary had, at the beginning of the war, signed up for a chauffeur's course, gaining a first-class certificate at the Motor Supply Company School of Motoring. Accepted by FANY, she arrived in France, in 1915, and served with the British Calais convoy and the Corps de Transport Armée Belge. As with other British women volunteers at the beginning of the war, such as women doctors, the members of FANY found that it was Britain's allies, France and Belgium, who initially were much more ready to accept women performing front-line tasks than were their own British authorities.

Even in her native Newcastle, Mary encountered opposition to the idea of women being on active service. In her book *FANY Invicta*, published in 1955, Irene Ward describes how Mary, on her return from her first stint at the front and wearing her military khaki, was stoned on her way down to Newcastle's Quayside to meet her father, a disturbing example of the hostility towards women in military uniform, who were seen as threatening to usurp men in their traditional roles. Mary described the experience to her friend Irene as "Far more frightening than the bombs that rained down in Calais!"

However, Mary also gained local support for her work and her appeal for money to prominent citizens of Newcastle and Northumberland did result in a number of valuable donations for FANY. Men at the Elswick and Scotswood works also raised money for her to purchase an ambulance.

The war work of women, both at the front and at home, doing essential jobs previously the preserve of men did gain increasing respect and, by the end of the war, the record of bravery and service by FANY members was fully recognised in the granting of many medals for gallantry. By the end of her war service, Mary too had been properly commended for her work at the front in dangerous situations and she received a number of awards and medals that recognised this including, from Belgium, the Medaille de la Reine Elisabeth and the award of Chevalier of the Order of Leopold II.

Mary was involved in organising the demobilisation of FANY members at the end of the war in 1918-1919. However, given that FANY was an independent and voluntary organisation, it could not be disbanded as part of the general government-directed demobilisation process, which envisaged women giving up their war roles, and their jobs reverting to the men who were returning home. Mary, at this time - and thereafter - was very convinced that the skills and commitment that FANY members had displayed should be maintained in peacetime, both to be available in national emergencies and to be ready to be used in the unfortunate eventuality of another war. Indeed it is largely due to Mary that FANY, after an understandable reduction in numbers in the immediate aftermath of the war, survived and began to build up again in the late 1920s and 1930s. Her determination, her flair and ability both to lead and to organise proved to be crucial.

While committed to the survival of FANY, there were other prospects offered to Mary at the end of the 1914-1918 war. She had a number of literary and artistic interests. She also, it was reported, was considered as a suitable coalition Parliamentary candidate in the 1922 election, although she must have decided not to stand despite a Newcastle newspaper report at that time declaring that "her abilities as a speaker and organiser are so well known in the city of her birth".

By 1928 Mary had, with others who had served on the Western Front, formed an active Northumberland County Section of FANY, one of only a handful around the country at that time. Four years later she became overall Commandant of the national organisation after the resignation of Lilian Franklin, and from then on her work for FANY absorbed her full-time. By the time she stood down in 1947, her record was described in the *FANY Gazette* in the following words: "For thirty-three years she has been a member of the Corps and during those years she has been for three years Adjutant, for seven years Second-in-Command and for fifteen years Commanding Officer."

Mary's work in building up the organisation after her appointment as its head in 1932 during those key years before the outbreak of the Second World War cannot be overstated. The outstanding contribution of FANY in that conflict - in both the ATS where they were providing transport and vital logistical support - as well as the extraordinarily brave and dangerous work carried out by FANY members behind enemy lines as secret agents - would not have been possible without her success in recruiting new members and in ensuring their high-level training and battle readiness.

Again, to quote the *FANY Gazette*, "Baxter Ellis was, in the true sense of the word, a leader. She had a great capacity for enthusing others, both collectively and individually. She had a creative brain, always full of new schemes, and a gift for public speaking. This she used with increasingly good results, for recruiting campaigns publicly, and within the Corps as a means of making known the Corps's outlook and plans, and for spreading a knowledge of its traditions - traditions which were actually born even before the 1914-18 war and which were strengthened, augmented and finally established on a high ethical and regimental standard by Baxter Ellis and the Officers and NCOs who served with her, particularly during the period 1932-39."

Mary would certainly have wanted to acknowledge those key members who worked with her and supported her in those years. Particular mention needs to be made of her close Northumbrian friend, and her deputy from 1932 onwards, Marjorie Kingston Walker. Marjorie Kingston Walker had, like Mary, seen FANY service in the First World War and with Mary had helped set up the Northumberland Section. Theirs was to be a lifetime friendship and partnership. Kingston Walker was also a recognised and much-praised artist, exhibiting her work successfully in Newcastle, Liverpool and London. A versatile artist she painted landscapes, portraits, flowers and animals.

The Baxter-Walker partnership was referred to in glowing terms by FANY's Commandant-in-Chief, HRH Princess Alice of Athlone, in her introduction to *FANY Invicta* by Irene Ward in the following words: "There are two leaders I must mention because I know all FANYs will agree that it was Mary Baxter Ellis and Marjorie Kingston Walker who held the fort together between the two World Wars. Their zeal and enthusiasm made it possible to keep alive the splendid comradeship of this fine little Voluntary Corps." She also paid tribute to their work "as maintaining FANY's independence and character to the present day."

Irene Ward's description of the Baxter-Walker partnership is less formal as she was friends with both women. She wrote "The close association of Baxter Ellis with Kingston Walker, a fellow Northumbrian, was a great partnership in the FANY world. "Dick" and "Tony" to their numerous friends made a wonderful pair and the close harmony in which they worked was a big factor in the growth and happiness of the Corps."

Mary's character and resilience were to be tested at the outset of the Second World War. In anticipation of that conflict she had changed the name of the organisation to "Women's Transport Service - FANY" to reflect their area of expertise. However the War Office then decided to create its own women's service the Auxiliary Territorial Service (ATS) and originally asked Mary to lead this. She declined feeling that her loyalty was to FANY as a unique, independent organisation, while agreeing enthusiastically that close working between FANY and the ATS was essential, particularly with the imminence of war. Accordingly, she negotiated a deal for FANY with the War Office to provide 1,500 trained drivers and mechanics for the transport wing of ATS, while FANY would, at the same time, retain its administrative independence and particular identity. Helen Gwynne-Vaughan, who subsequently became head of the ATS, reneged on this deal however, refusing to accept FANY's independence and demanding its total absorption into the ATS. Given that by then war had been declared Mary Baxter Ellis - not wanting to distract from the war effort - decided to knuckle down and accept being absorbed into the ATS, although she did manage to ensure that FANY members of the ATS could wear their distinctive FANY flashes on their uniforms. Those members of FANY who decided not to join the ATS became known as the "Free FANYs" and some of them through later work as secret agents, particularly as part of the Special Operations Executive (SOE), became some of the best-known heroines of the war, many being captured behind enemy lines, and tortured, imprisoned and killed in Nazi concentration camps.

Mary Baxter Ellis, while deemed too old for such service abroad, nonetheless kept close links throughout the war with both wings of FANY. Her own war work was UK-based, being, at first, Commandant of the ATS motor companies training centre at Camberley, then attached to the War Office doing training duties and finally becoming deputy director of the ATS in 1943. The previous year, in 1942, she was awarded the CBE (military) in recognition of her outstanding and continuous record of service to the country.

Interestingly it was at the ATS Camberley training centre, and during the time that Mary was ATS Deputy Director in early 1945, that Princess Elizabeth, later Queen Elizabeth II, did her wartime training in driving and in motor mechanics.

Mary was described as tall and slender with her dark hair swept back into a bun. She conveyed an authoritative presence in her khaki uniform but off duty enjoyed relaxing and the company of friends, displaying a keen sense of humour and fun.

Two years after the war ended, in 1947 Mary - and Marjorie Kingston Walker - decided to retire and reside permanently in their moorland cottage near Bellingham, in their beloved Northumberland. Mary felt - and hoped - that a lengthy (if uneasy because of the Cold War) period of peace was likely to ensue and that it was therefore an excellent moment for others to take the work of FANY forward and determine its future priorities. As Popham put it in his book about FANY, Mary and Marjorie "inseparable as ever, went off to the country to breed cocker spaniels and paint in watercolours".

However, her retirement from FANY after 1947 did not mean that Mary retired from all public life or service. In those post-war years she served both as a Councillor on Northumberland County Council and as a member of the Bellingham Rural District Council. She also wrote some fiction and had articles published in various magazines.

Mary died in hospital in Corbridge on 12th April, 1968, aged 75. She and her partner Marjorie passed away within a couple of months of each other that year. We cannot know, of course, how different Mary's life would have been if it hadn't coincided with two world wars. What does seem likely, however, given her skills and talents is that even without those wars she still would have contributed to the public life of her country in a significant way, and in a way in which her undoubted qualities of leadership would have been evident.

Anne Fisher, a woman who refused to accept the limitations of contemporary society.

Anne Fisher (1719 - 1778)

Grammarian, author, educationalist and entrepreneur

In the 18th century there was a widespread belief that women were innately inferior to men both physically and intellectually, that their role in life should be confined to raising families, and men alone should engage in public life. Mercifully there were strong women who refused to accept the status quo and who broke into public life. Anne Fisher was such a woman. Although quite well known during her own lifetime her name fell into obscurity, until, 300 years after her birth, a blue plaque celebrating the life and achievements of Anne Fisher was unveiled on the churchyard wall of St. John the Baptist in Grainger Street, Newcastle in 2019.

It reads: "Anne Fisher, a pioneering educationalist. Published A New Grammar (1745). Ran a girls' school on Denton Chare (1745-1750). Raised nine daughters while working alongside her husband, Thomas Slack (m.1751). They established the *Newcastle Chronicle* in 1764. Buried in this Churchyard."

Very little is known of Anne's personal life before her marriage. She was born in 1719, the daughter of Henry Fisher, yeoman of Oldscale in the parish of Lorton in Cumberland.

We know nothing of her education but by the age of 26 she had published the ground-breaking *A New Grammar* for which she is chiefly remembered. She was the first woman writing on modern English grammar ever to be published. (Elizabeth Elstob's *Grammar of Old English* had been published 30 years earlier in 1715.) As with other grammars, her book sets out the rules governing the sounds, words sentences and other elements of the language, as well as their combination and interpretation. Anne Fisher's, *A New Grammar* was so successful that it ran into over 40 editions and was published in London as well as Newcastle. There were also pirated editions published in Penrith, Gainsborough, Leeds and York. It was one of the most popular English grammars of the 18th century.

Because of the prejudices of the 18th century and the deep suspicion of women writers, the first two editions of her grammar were published under a pseudonym, D.Fisher, the name of an established male writer, with whom she had some sort of agreement. Only when it became clear that the work had been well received in its own right did Anne publish subsequent editions under her own name A.Fisher. Anne went on to publish under her maiden name even after her marriage to Thomas Slack.

The full title of her grammar book was shortened over time but in its early editions it was, *A Practical New Grammar with exercises in bad English, or an Easy Guide to speaking and writing the English Language properly and correctly.* The 1754 edition is a charming Quarto size hardback of only 177 pages, pleasant to handle and written in a simple question and answer format. The key to its success is that it was written to encourage the learner. She wrote, "My principal desire in compiling the Grammar was to render, in as easy a manner as possible a perfect and critical knowledge of our mother tongue, attainable to every person of common capacity and that in a short time".

By 1788 she was justified in writing, "all the best school masters in the kingdom consider mine as the quickest and most effectual mode of inculcating the knowledge of the English Language". It was, at the time, groundbreaking. It dispenses with the need to have any knowledge of Latin, and instead of the conventional division of the grammatical categories into six or eight, they are reduced to four: nouns, adjectives, verbs and particles. The terminology is different to make it more user friendly. So for example "nouns" become "names", "adjectives" become "qualities", an "auxiliary verb" becomes a "helping verb". Anne Fisher's enthusiasm for the beauty of the English language runs through the work and gives it an inspirational tone.

Before her marriage Anne was also running a school. We have to assume that she was teaching in some capacity before 1745 in order to have gained such insights into the existing old school grammar books that enabled her to write her *New Grammar* by 1745. It is most likely that she opened her own school in 1745 because an advertisement in the *Newcastle Journal* in 29th June, 1745, read: "A school will be opened where READING from the best spelling books and grammar extant, WRITING, fine and plain SEWING, will be taught by ANNE FISHER." The school was in Denton Chare, opposite to the Pant in Westgate and was obviously a school for girls, teaching what was then the "home" centred basic curriculum for girls. (It was not too unusual for women to open schools for girls, both Mary Astell and Elizabeth Elstob had done the same to try to earn a living.)

There were no further advertisements until April 1750 when a rather different scheme was launched, evening classes for working girls. "Young Ladies who choose to learn the English Grammar yet cannot conveniently attend on school hours may at Mrs Fishers School in St. Nicholas's Church yard between the hours of Five and Eight be instructed in English Grammar. viz., Vocabulary, Reading, Parts of speech, Adjectives Verbs Pronouns, and Styles of Writing". The advert goes on to say that any young lady, of a tolerable capacity, who can read pretty well and write a legible hand, may in a few months be completed in this way, at a reasonable rate.

These evening classes were directed at young, poor working-class women to enable them to attend after working hours and to complete the course as quickly and therefore as cheaply as possible. At the time, a knowledge of English grammar, reading and writing was required in advertisements for domestic work. As a single lady, Anne may well have run both a day school and evening classes for the period from 1745 to 1751, but what is clear is that by the time of her marriage to Thomas Slack in 1751 the school(s) had closed.

Anne and Thomas were married at Longbenton in Northumberland. Thomas, like his wife, was a Cumbrian. He was from Wreay near Carlisle. He became a successful printer and publisher in Newcastle. They had a fruitful and happy marriage. As well as their joint business ventures they had nine children, all daughters, born between 1752 and 1768. Sadly, four of their girls, Jane, Francis and both Margarets, predeceased their mother. Jane was 21 years old when she died, Frances was only three. There were two babies called Margaret, the first Margaret died in infancy the other died at two years old. It is hard to imagine the heartache and sadness their deaths must have brought to the whole family and especially their mother.

Anne continued to write after her marriage. Her books were mostly on teaching elementary English grammar, to the great benefit of English teaching. *The Pleasing Instructor*, published in 1756, included a preface "New Thoughts on Education," and ran to 29 editions, *The New English Tutor* published in 1774, ran to 13 editions. She also wrote *The New English Exercise Book*, published in 1770, *The Young Scholars Delight*, in 1802, and *An Accurate New Spelling Dictionary*, published in 1773. The number of editions of these books is testament to her popularity and evidence abounds of their use in local schools and further afield. Her "Grammar", was even known on the other side of the Atlantic

For the first ten years of their marriage, Thomas Slack was employed in Newcastle by Isaac Thompson, as manager of Thompson's local newspaper, the *Newcastle Journal*. But in 1763 Thomas fell out with his employer and Anne and Thomas decided to set up their own business. In April 1763 they opened a shop. Known as The Printing Press, this was the first of three prosperous ventures. The shop sold books of every sort as well as maps, paper, mathematical instruments, spectacles, sealing wax, pens, ink and all the stationery items you can imagine. Their shop soon became a place where artists, writers, actors and even politicians met to discuss the issues of the day, and it made a major contribution to the cultural life of Newcastle. "This was due to the public spirit and generosity of the proprietors." (Horsley 1971)

That same year, 1763, they opened a printing press and published their first two books. Over the years they published many books including their own, mainly Mrs Slacks, or rather A.Fisher's. They are said to have produced, "by far the most successful series of school books written in the North in the 18th century". (Robinson 1972)

The printing of books was a large part of their business and they contributed handsomely to the 800 books printed on Tyneside in the century. They served private buyers and the circulating libraries that began to spring up in the town in the 1780s. They also procured the services of a London publisher for their books because, of course, it gave them access to a wider market.

In March 1764, they took the enormous step of publishing a new local paper, the *Newcastle Chronicle*, which would be in direct competition with Isaac Thompson's *Newcastle Journal*. For the next 20 years the papers battled it out, but in 1788 the *Newcastle Journal* was forced to close for lack of readers. The idea of their own newspaper was said to have been Anne's, and it certainly became an excellent channel for advertising Anne's own books, and their own publications, but more importantly it went on to become ... the leading liberal organ of Newcastle for more than 70 years." (*The Hodgson Family*). The *Newcastle Chronicle* remained part of the Slack family business until 1850, when it was sold to M. W. Lambert, who sold it to Joseph Cowen in 1862.

Despite 18th century prejudices against women's participation in public life, Anne took a very active part in the running of their businesses. Her letters indicate that she was virtually running the printing business. For example, she wrote in September 1771 to her friend and client the poet John Cunningham: "We shall dry your title sheets directly to be ready to send a few books to you in a week's time, if you choose it and advise how we are to send them & to what quarter, as you talk of moving to Scarborough."

And in November the same year: "Mrs Montague is not yet come to her house in London but will be in town by the time the books get up. We send Messrs. Robinson & Co., theirs this week & shall send Mr White his at the same time ... and mind to hint to her, Mrs Montague, if any more be wanting for her friends she'll please send her orders either to yourself or me. If she sends to Robertson & Roberts they will expect a booksellers profit upon them, we'll not desire it, we have no other motive than to serve you in the publication."

Biographers of Thomas Slack write that "Thomas Slack found his wife an admiral supporter shrewd and active in prospering their respective ventures." (Horsley1971). Welford wrote in 1907 "Thus working together as authors and publisher, and probably co-operating in in newspaper work, they built up a large and successful business."

Their joint ventures not only served the public well but they made the family wealthy. When Thomas died their estate included five houses, a ship, a freehold estate in Wreay, a shop, a printing office and a thriving newspaper.

Anne counted among her friends many who were prominent in the cultural life of Newcastle in the 18th century. These people included Thomas Bewick, the engraver, who described Anne as, "a woman of uncommon abilities and great goodness of heart" (Myer 1997) and Mrs Montague (1720-1800) the influential bluestocking who was a customer as well as a friend. Anne's daughter Sarah, wrote in her memoir that: "Mrs Montague was a particular friend of my mother's."

After a very full life Anne died from asthma aged 58. (Thomas died six years later in 1784). Her life and death were significant enough to be recorded in the local records of important events of Newcastle: "April 26th, 1778, died in Newgate Street, Newcastle, Mrs Slack, Wife of Mr Slack printer and publisher of the *Newcastle Chronicle*. To her literary abilities the public were indebted for several valuable publications (Fisher's *Grammar and Tutor, the Pleasing Instructor & c*) adapted to the use of schools, as well as *Private Instruction*, which will remain lasting monuments to her memory." (Sykes 1866)

Her obituaries refer to her great energy and enthusiasm, her interest in the world of arts and literature, her literary abilities and accomplishments, her success in running her school, her shrewdness as a businesswoman, her roles as wife and mother. She is referred to as a woman of great fortitude, one of the highest female ornaments.

Anne's name was known to her contemporaries before her marriage because, by the time she was 26, she had published her *New Grammar* and was running a school for girls. After her marriage in 1751 and despite bearing nine children, she continued to engage with the world of work. She wrote and was published. She was recognised as a good businesswoman as well as becoming a leading light in the development of Newcastle's burgeoning cultural life. Above all though, she refused to accept the limitations that contemporary society placed upon women and so provides us all with an inspirational "can do" role model.

Anne Fisher's New Grammar exudes her enthusiasm for the beauty of the English language.

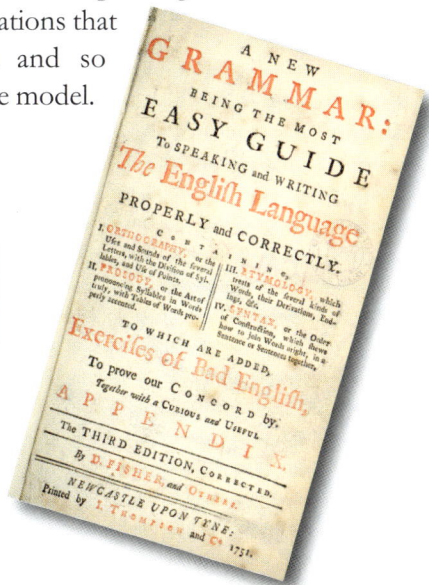

The portrait of Dorothy Forster at Bamburgh Castle.

Photo: Sally Larkin, Bamburgh Castle Viewings

Dorothy Forster (1686 - 1767)

Courageous heroine of an inspirational rescue

The exciting story of Dorothy Forster's courageous rescue of her brother, the Jacobite General Thomas Forster from certain death, has become entrenched in Northumberland folklore. While it is impossible to verify all aspects of the rescue, it is too convincing a story to be ignored, and whatever the details, it involved such ingenuity and personal bravery that it cannot be overlooked or forgotten.

The Forsters were an ancient, well-connected Northumbrian family, cousins to the Earl of Derwentwater, himself cousin of the Old Pretender, James Francis Edward Stuart. Their aunt and devotee was Lady Crewe, the wife of the fabulously wealthy Lord Crewe but the Forster family itself was not wealthy. Thomas Forster had inherited estates in Bambugh and Blanchland in 1701, but these had to be sold off to pay pressing debts, and so by 1715 Thomas Forster had not an acre to bless himself with and certainly no money to bring to the Stuart "cause."

Thomas and Dorothy lived in the family home, Bamburgh Hall, supported financially by Lady Crewe. As children the pair were very close, in part because their mother Frances had died when they were still young and they were drawn together by their vehement dislike of their stepmother.

Thomas Forster was brought up to live the life of a gentleman and politician, while Dorothy would become a lady of leisure. Thomas succeeded his father as a Tory MP in 1708 when elected MP for Northumberland. He remained an MP until 1716 when he was attainted and expelled for high treason. Little is known of Dorothy until she burst onto the scene in 1715.

Shortly after the accession of the Hanoverian King, George I in 1714, those who wanted to restore the Stuarts to the throne began to plot. Those who favoured this cause were called Jacobites, and the Earl of Derwentwater and his cousin Thomas Forster were known sympathisers, largely because of their close family connection to the Stuarts.

In 1715, aware of their Jacobite sympathies, King George issued a writ for their arrest by the House of Commons, but before this could be done Derwentwater and Forster fled North, and on October 6th, 1715, at Green Rigg, near Birtley in the North Country, Derwentwater and Forster went into open rebellion. With only a small band of supporters, they declared the Old Pretender King James III.

Despite having no military experience, (indeed some said he had never even seen an army), and no appetite for the job, Thomas Forster was chosen to become General of the Jacobite rebels. Unsurprisingly he proved to be a very poor leader. After failing to take Newcastle, (which remained loyal to king George, one possible explanation for the present-day nickname, "Geordies") he allowed the rebellion to degenerate into a series of purposeless marches. Although the Jacobite numbers increased when they were joined by rebels from south Scotland led by Lord Kenmure and a detachment of Highlanders led by Brigadier Mackintosh, the expected reinforcements from the Roman Catholic gentry of the North Western counties did not materialise. Without money, supplies, or proper battle plans, they were trapped by the professional loyalist armies led by Generals Wills and Carpenter.

In November 1715 at Preston, there was a decisive battle. The King's troops surrounded the rebels, and heavily outnumbered by about three to one, the rebels were defeated. At this point General Forster decided to surrender and was taken prisoner with the other Jacobite rebels, and the first Jacobite rebellion was ignominiously over.

The rebel prisoners, The Earl of Derwentwater and General Forster, along with upwards of 200 others were escorted to London arriving on the December 9th, 1715. Lords Derwentwater, Kenmure, Nithsdale and Widdrington, as peers, were conducted to the Tower of London. Forster and Radcliff and about 70 others were taken to Newgate and the rest to the Marshalsea and Fleet prisons.

In January 1716 the House of Lords impeached the noblemen, and all were found guilty of High Treason. They offered no defence but pleaded for clemency. In the event, the Earl of Derwentwater and Kenmure were beheaded on February 24th, 1716, on Tower Hill. Lord Nithsdale, due to be executed with them, managed to escape and Lords Widdrington and Carnwath, although not pardoned, were spared their lives but forfeited their lands, wealth and titles.

Meanwhile, Thomas Forster lay for months in Newgate Gaol, helplessly and hopelessly awaiting his fate. It was not until April 10th, four days before his trial was due to begin, that his sister came to his rescue.

The most common account of events around his escape is as follows. On hearing of her brother's incarceration, Dorothy set off from Bamburgh dressed as a servant riding pillion behind a local blacksmith named Purdy. The weather was diabolical and the journey to London took a month. Dorothy then began to visit her brother in gaol regularly, always accompanied by a maid. On her final visit she went alone, but concealed beneath her own dress she wore her maidservants clothing. Thomas then disguised himself in the servant's costume and, because the guards were accustomed to seeing two ladies leaving the General's cell, brother and sister were allowed to pass unchecked. (Another version is that Dorothy managed to make a copy of the key to Thomas's cell which she smuggled in to him.)

The escape was so well organised that horses were waiting to meet Thomas and take him without delay to a vessel lying off the Essex coast. Within 24 hours of his escape he was in Calais. When the escape was discovered the Government issued a reward of £1000 for his recapture. We know exactly what Thomas Forster looked like from the description printed on the reward notices, which were widely circulated: "Of middle stature inclining to be fat; well-shaped, except that he stoops in the shoulders; fair complexioned, his mouth wide, his nose pretty large, his eyes gray, and speaks the Northern Dialect."

Thomas Forster was never recaptured and in June 1716 he was expelled from Parliament by Act of Attainder, found guilty of high treason.

In order to deceive the government and take the heat off her brother, the story was circulated that Thomas had died abroad shortly after his escape. To complete the deception, Dorothy organised a mock funeral and a coffin, filled with sawdust, was placed with due ceremony in the family vault at Bamburgh. In reality Thomas did die in Boulogne but not until 1738, having survived his escape for 22 years. At that point his body was secretly brought back to Bamburgh and buried in the crypt of the church, the genuine coffin deposited beside the false coffin. One hundred years later in 1837, the true coffin and the sham coffin were found together in the family vault.

The sheer ingenuity of Thomas's rescue was an amazing achievement for anyone, let alone a country lady who had probably not travelled far beyond the county before then. Remember, though, that she was driven by her love for her brother and that she was not without friends of great influence and wealth.

Dorothy's close involvement in the escape is not disputed. No punishment was ever meted out to Dorothy - could her guilt be proved? She was too poor to be noticed by the authorities, she had neither wealth nor title to lose and, as a woman, was thought to be without influence or interest. What her heroism gave her brother were riches beyond measure, his freedom and, as it happened, a further twenty years of life.

Little is known of Dorothy apart from these events. It is believed that she married one John Armstrong, who may have been the Blacksmith (aka Purdy) who took her to London. Certainly the grave of Dorothy Armstrong, nee Forster, lies next to Thomas Forster's in Bamburgh Church. Dorothy died childless in 1767.

Visitors to Bamburgh Castle today can see the portrait of Dorothy, as well as one of her dresses and a pair of her shoes. They are as beautiful as she was brave. The novelist and historian, Sir Walter Besant (1836 -1901), was so inspired by the story of Dorothy Forster that 168 years after the event, in 1884, he wrote a three-volume romantic novel entitled simply, *Dorothy Forster*.

Writer Jane Gomeldon was willing to challenge convention.

Jane Gomeldon (c1720 - 1779)

Writer and early feminist

The Wikipedia entry for Jane Gomeldon describes her as "writer, poet and adventurer". Quite an intriguing, and certainly an unusual description of an English woman of the 18th century, and one which, justifiably in this case, hints at an unconventional and interesting life.

She was born Jane Middleton into a Newcastle Quaker family of glassmakers. The exact date of her birth is uncertain although it is thought to be around 1720.

Glassmaking was an important industry in Newcastle at that time and indeed had been so since the Elizabethan age, when a royal edict had forbidden the chopping down of forests to fire glassmaking furnaces, leading to coal being used instead. This helps to explain why wealthy Newcastle merchants on the quayside could afford extensively glazed facades on their smart 17th and 18th century homes, despite any window taxes in force at the time.

Jane, by all accounts, as well as having a comfortable background, was well educated in such subjects as philosophy, science and languages. Described as "a great adept" in natural history, she particularly liked collecting shells. As a young woman, she was also spoken of as a beauty, something that the only known portrait of her seems to confirm.

She was married "at an early age" to Captain Francis Gomeldon who was reported to be a good friend of the well-known local coal magnate, George Bowes. If this is so, it is ironic, as George Bowes was the father of Mary Eleanor Bowes whose second marriage to the unscrupulous and violent fortune-hunter, Andrew Robinson Stoney, was one of the great 18th century scandals.

Jane's marriage proved not much less disastrous as she left Francis within a short time, citing his cruelty, and his determination to have sole use of the fortune, that her mother had left her for her own benefit and use. In 1740, her husband placed an advertisement in the *Newcastle Journal* announcing that she had left him and asking for her return. For her part, she placed a counter-advert in the *Newcastle Courant* declaring that she had left him on account of his cruelty and money-grabbing. She then sought to bring a separation suit to court against him on grounds of cruelty, although to escape him she also fled to France, where she remained until his death. This was remarkable and courageous behaviour for a married woman to display in an age where women were expected to obey their husbands.

What we know of Jane's time in France seems to justify the description of her as an adventurer. It is said that she disguised herself as a man and assumed a number of different roles. She also paid court to a nun whom she was hoping would elope with her! It is not clear whether this was simply to fool people into believing her false, masculine identity, or whether she really was interested in a permanent attachment or romantic relationship.

As is evident from her later writings, she studied French society and culture, and became interested in the different attitudes towards marriage, religion, and other great issues of the day in France and Britain. Her stay in France coincided with the Age of Enlightenment and she was a contemporary of some of the best known "Encyclopédistes", such as Diderot and D'Alembert, leading to speculation, that, as an educated and independent minded woman, she might have had some contact with them, or with their admirers and followers.

Francis Gomeldon died in 1751, having made his nephew the sole beneficiary of his will and it was after that date that Jane felt free to return to her native north-east. We do not know what immediate reception she got from her family or how much of her life in France was known to them, but there is no evidence of hostility towards her. Her subsequent writings and charitable works appear to have been well received, and she renewed her contacts with the Newcastle society of the time.

She was also an early and keen supporter of Newcastle's charitable Lying-in Hospital - a place where poor married women could recuperate after giving birth, but which also operated as an outdoor charity. This was established in 1760 in Rosemary Lane, next to St John's Church - although later, after Jane's day, at the beginning of the 19th century, it moved to a new purpose-built building designed by leading architect, John Dobson, which itself would become well known in more recent times as Newcastle's BBC headquarters. (see illustration).

Jane was a supporter of Newcastle's charitable Lying-in Hospital.

Jane's best known written work, *The Medley,* published in 1766, was in fact produced as a fundraising venture for the Lying-in Hospital and attracted a number of sponsors, comprising many of the "great and good" of Newcastle and Northumberland at the time, as well as enlisting support from a number of prominent citizens from other parts of the country. This work is a collection of 31 essays, ranging over a variety of subjects and containing much amusing and pert commentary on "the polite society" of the time. It is entertainingly written but contained within it are a number of, sometimes thinly disguised, feminist messages and shrewd comments. As was frequently the case in that era, she wrote under a male pseudonym and used that role to praise women, referring to some of the social gains they had made, as well as strongly favouring further change towards greater equality. Indeed, Gomeldon cheekily claims that it is "Gentlemen that now need improvement to render them fit to be women's companions." (See illustration).

The title, *The Medley*, both conveys the variety of topics the work contains as well as, according to Jane's publisher, "something to please the taste of every reader". Subjects dealt with include the transience of fashion; the peculiar attitudes of the "beau monde "; differences between French and English attitudes to marriage; the education of daughters; the fleeting nature of fame; and - of striking relevance to our present-day concerns about "fake news" - a declaration that facts are the only proper basis on which to build opinions! She also touches (understandably given her life experiences) on what might have been thought of as taboo subjects, such as female adultery, and abusive husbands. On this last subject, she advises wives with financial resources to leave their spouses, but recognises that for poor women, such abusive marriages are difficult to escape from and suggests other less easy approaches such as ways of retaining a sense of self-worth and building alliances with others for mutual support.

She also conveys important messages about society through the creation of a number of memorable and highly entertaining fictitious characters. She revels in exposing the differences between appearance and reality, describing Lady Alba, for example, as seeking to appear generous, while in reality being proud, mean, and miserly. Of her pride she says memorably "the appearance of it has got into Lady Alba's features and deformed them more than the smallpox could have done".

The married couples she portrays illustrate a variety of relationships, from stable to tempestuous and evince behaviour, ranging from reasonable to flagrantly and farcically unacceptable. Her witty and satirical descriptions contain sometimes uncomfortable truths but in a way designed to attract and amuse, and thereby appealing to, rather than alienating, her varied readership.

Besides *The Medley,* Jane is also remembered for two other published works. Her poem *Happiness* appeared in print in 1773 and was dedicated to a friend, "Dear Faithful Ann", although, as often happened with women authors, the gender identity of the writer was not made clear. Yet, as the entry on Jane in the *Oxford Dictionary of National Biography* relates, there was at that time "a vogue for celebrating romantic friendships between women". The friendship referred to in the poem is described as "sacred and sublime" as well as one bringing the author much happiness in rural retreat, away from the "vexing scenes of trade". Perhaps this latter phrase refers to her local busy and thriving trading hub on Newcastle's Quayside!

In 1779, and this time under her own name, Jane's book of Maxims appeared. Books of Maxims were fashionable at the time, although Jane, with her knowledge of France, and French, was also familiar no doubt with the famous *Maximes* of Larochefoucauld, which had appeared 100 years earlier. Despite being very much of the time, Jane's maxims, in line with her views, contain feminist and radical elements, showing both her consistency and her unconventionality of thought and opinion.

In addition to her writing, Jane seems to have continued to have a lively interest in the news and events of the time. It is said that she became enamoured of Captain Cook, and his adventures, declaring that she wanted to accompany him on his travels. She was reputedly a cousin of Sydney Parkinson, who accompanied Captain Cook and Joseph Banks on Cook's first voyage in the Pacific Ocean in 1768, and with whom she corresponded.

Jane died in 1779 and was described in a newspaper account at the time as being of "an advanced age". If she was born, as it is thought, around 1720 this would have meant that she was 59 years old. Whether this was her actual age or whether she was older is unknown. Many people at that time did not live long, but the description "advanced age" seems, even for that era, to be somewhat inappropriate.

Her written works live on and are still in print. Indeed, there has been a welcome and considerable renewed interest in her in recent times, not least because of her early and pioneering feminist views. Perhaps more information about her life will still be uncovered. Given her undoubted writing talents, as well as her readiness to challenge convention, and articulate views ahead of her times, it would be fascinating if more details of her life and work were to emerge.

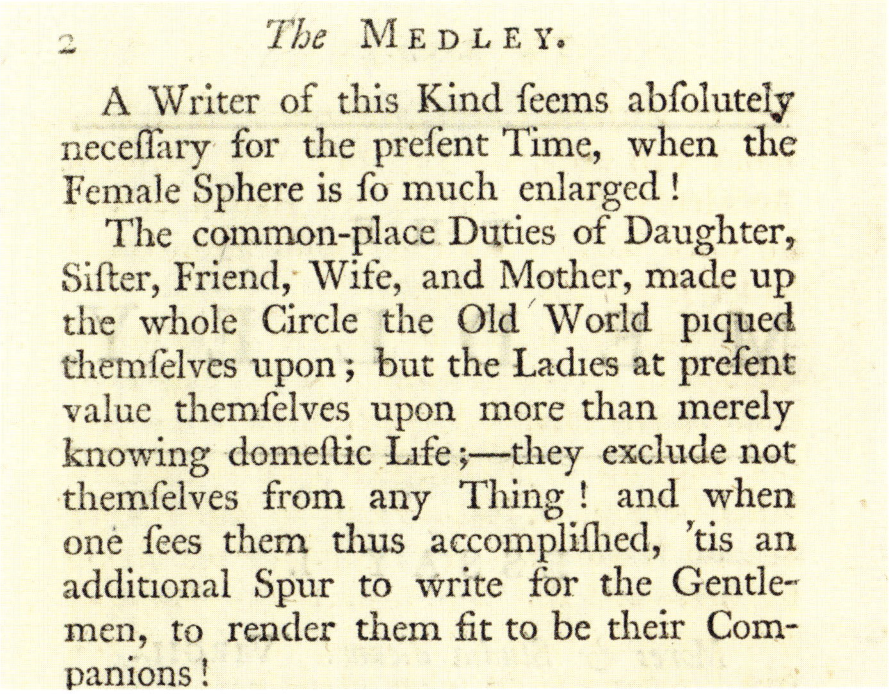

A Writer of this Kind feems abfolutely neceffary for the prefent Time, when the Female Sphere is fo much enlarged!

The common-place Duties of Daughter, Sifter, Friend, Wife, and Mother, made up the whole Circle the Old World piqued themfelves upon; but the Ladies at prefent value themfelves upon more than merely knowing domeftic Life;—they exclude not themfelves from any Thing! and when one fees them thus accomplifhed, 'tis an additional Spur to write for the Gentlemen, to render them fit to be their Companions!

Jane's book 'The Medley' contains many witty, shrewd and feminist observations.

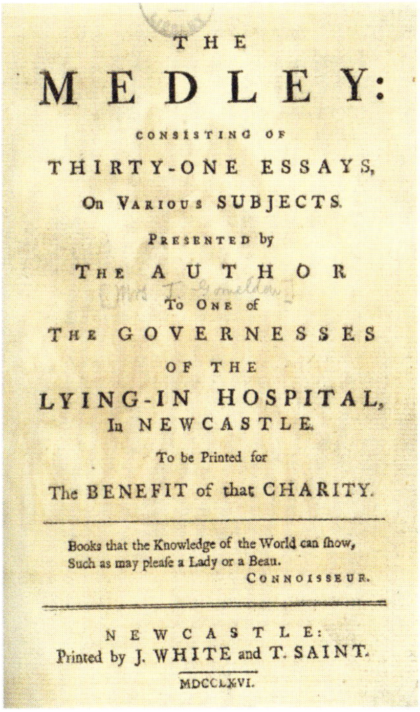

THE

MEDLEY:

CONSISTING OF

THIRTY-ONE ESSAYS,

On VARIOUS SUBJECTS.

PRESENTED by

THE AUTHOR

To ONE of

THE GOVERNESSES

OF THE

LYING-IN HOSPITAL,

In NEWCASTLE.

To be Printed for

The BENEFIT of that CHARITY.

Books that the Knowledge of the World can fhow,
Such as may pleafe a Lady or a Beau.
CONNOISSEUR.

NEWCASTLE:
Printed by J. WHITE and T. SAINT.

MDCCLXVI.

Mary Greaves worked tirelessly to change attitudes towards disability.

Mary Elsworth Greaves MBE, OBE (1907 - 1983)

Pioneer of disability rights

The works and achievements of Mary Greaves have become an accepted and integral part of British life, but largely without her own role being recognised or remembered. Yet there are many reasons why Mary as a person should be celebrated alongside the huge changes in attitudes towards disability that she worked tirelessly and successfully to realise.

Born in Newcastle on April 23rd, 1907, Mary was the daughter of a schoolmaster, Joseph Elsworth Greaves, and his wife, Mary Beatrice Heckels. In a tantalising fragment of her unpublished autobiography (the whereabouts of the complete version is unknown at present) belonging to her relative Bob Frazier, it seems that her forbears were largely of the Dissenting traditions – Unitarians and Quakers – and Liberal in politics. Family fortunes had varied over the years from being comfortably off with a thriving shipowning business in Sunderland to a later downturn after failing to take advantage of some of the technical advances of the Victorian era. On the whole, however, and at time when poverty was widespread, the family was financially more secure than most.

Mary's own young life was to change dramatically for ever when she contracted polio, aged three, on a family holiday in Belgium. A prolonged stay in a London hospital ensued and when she was eventually discharged and the family could be reunited in their native North East, she had to face the future, wearing a steel corset, and with the prospect of never being able to walk more than a few paces from then on. In those days, people affected by disabilities were also often confined to institutions or to home with little chance of finding a role for themselves in the outside world.

In her early childhood, Mary's family moved to a house in Lish Avenue, Whitley Bay, and Mary, a bright and intelligent child, attended local schools. (Another resident of Lish Avenue at the same time, intriguingly, was the young William Fisher, later to achieve notoriety as the Soviet spy Rudolf Abel, who was exchanged in a "spy swap" with US airman Gary Powers in 1962).

Mary did well at school and was supported in her efforts by her family. On leaving she applied to, and was accepted, at the local shorthand and typing school. She doubtless hoped to obtain some kind of employment afterwards while knowing what a challenge this would be, given the fact that workplaces only catered for the able-bodied, and any job other than one in the immediate locality would present difficult if not insurmountable travel obstacles.

She had however obtained a degree of freedom when, aged 17, she came into possession of a hand-propelled invalid tricycle, which allowed her to ride the streets of Whitley Bay. Despite the machine's occasional unreliability, this was something she relished and she became a recognised and distinctive figure in her locality as a result. Mary later recalled that on her first trip out in the tricycle she visited her friend Madge, who lived some two miles away, not realising that her father had followed at a discreet distance to make sure she was safe.

She also, around this time, found some local employment including a three-month stint working as a replacement typist for the local council - Whitley and Monkseaton UDC. She was, however, obliged to work alone in a small, dimly lit room on the ground floor as she was unable to climb the stairs to the main offices above. As her relative, Professor John Heckels, puts it in his article about Mary this experience "must have had a major effect on her attitude to employment and working conditions for the disabled."

Wider economic conditions in Whitley Bay, and on Tyneside more generally, also played their part in severely limiting employment possibilities, as joblessness unrelentingly rose from the late 1920s onwards. Mary, determined and resourceful, decided to set up her own shorthand and typing school, and copying office. She went to London to obtain the required shorthand teacher's diploma, she borrowed money (£50) from her father to buy the equipment she needed and opened her school in her home in Lish Avenue. She only had one pupil in her first year but she persevered and in the end ran the school successfully for a total of 14 years.

By the time she had reached her mid-thirties Mary was ready for new challenges. The Second World War was raging, but undaunted - and keen to be part of the war effort - she applied for various secretarial posts in London, without success. She then decided that extra educational qualifications would help her, saying that "I realised then that for a disabled person to get a job he must have qualifications and, if possible, rather better ones than the man next to him."

Sociology had begun to interest her and so she took a correspondence course in that subject with Ruskin College, Oxford. Her tutor (the head of Extra-Mural studies at Durham University's Armstrong College, based in Newcastle) then encouraged her to go further and read for a London University external degree in Sociology. By this time, she had found a job in Leicester, where her old schoolfriend Madge was living. She lodged with Madge, working through the day and studying in the evening. She subsequently gained an intermediate degree with a distinction in geography and won the prize for economics.

To complete the degree it was necessary for her to study in London but obtaining a job there to enable this to happen proved difficult. It was still wartime, which complicated the situation as employers were nervous about the difficulty of evacuating people with physical disabilities in emergency situations. However, as the war was ending, she was offered a job as a temporary executive officer in the statistics section of the Ministry of Labour where, happily, her boss Stephen Day both admired and was supportive of her efforts and valued her work. He helped with her application to the London School of Economics and with her need for accommodation, by arranging for her to live in the basement of the Ministry, along with people who had been bombed out of their homes. Studying once again in the evening, she gained her degree in Sociology and Statistics. Later she was to attend Birkbeck College and obtain a higher degree in industrial psychology. Given all the circumstances she had had to contend with, her dedication and commitment to gaining qualifications and worthwhile employment, are awe-inspiring.

In a memoir entitled *Defeating the Pied Piper* she describes her early days working, studying and living in the Ministry basement, in the following words: "I have never been in a prison cell, but I imagine this was less luxurious. I was of course free to come and go as I wished, but it consisted only of a camp bed, a wooden chair and a hook behind the door. There was just room to squeeze between the wall and the bed, and there was no window. But to me it was better than Buckingham Palace. I had survived, I had a job, I was living in London, and I could go in the evenings to the London School of Economics. For the first time in my life, I was stretched to my uttermost and it was sheer heaven."

She now became established at the Ministry, being granted permanent employment and valued for the quality of her work. She was to remain there, in her role as a Civil Servant until her retirement. Her last posting, at age 57, was a promotion to the National Economic Development Office. On her retirement she was awarded an MBE in recognition of her work on statistics.

During her time in London, she also became increasingly committed to highlighting the needs of employees with disabilities, including providing proper facilities to allow access to places of work and getting employers to recognise that they were missing out on opportunities to employ gifted people by failing to provide such facilities.

After her retirement, this work became a crusade, as she travelled the country investigating the opportunities and facilities for people with disabilities in the employment market. She had also become involved in the Disability

Income Group (DIG) founded by Megan du Boisson in 1965, the group's main purpose being to campaign for a disability income for all disabled people. While previously there had been some payments - for example to those injured and disabled in wartime, or in some specific industries - it was clear that restricting income support to particular categories caused unfairness, bureaucracy and entailed invidious choices, and the DIG was determined to bring in a fairer and comprehensive system of support that would help all disabled people fulfil their potential.

Megan du Boisson, like Mary, was disabled, having contracted Muscular Dystrophy. Sadly four years after founding the DIG she died, aged only 44, in a car crash in 1969, at which point Mary took over the reins as Director of the organisation. The voices of these two articulate, committed, physically disabled women had begun to provide authoritative direct experience of the problems people with disabilities faced and, importantly, they were beginning to inform public debate at every stage. This was to be vitally important in getting recognition in Parliamentary legislation of the needs of disabled people. As Derek Kinrade put it in his biography of Alf Morris MP (later Lord Morris of Manchester) "Megan du Boisson, Duncan Guthrie, Mary Greaves, Marsh Dickson and Mary Scott among others were leading activists in helping to start the parliamentary impetus for change."

Mary's book entitled Work and *Disability: Some Aspects of the Employment of Disabled Persons in Great Britain* was published in 1969 and became a standard reference work for campaigners and politicians. The wealth of information it contained about the living and working conditions of disabled people was based both on Mary's own life experience and on her extensive research and travels.

Mary was to lead the DIG in a rather different direction to Megan as she had identified the danger of duplicating the many other organisations which had set up - and were still setting up - in the field. As Judy Hunt put it in her 2019 book *No Limits – The Disabled People's Movement*, "Mary knew much more of what was going on in the disabled world and politics than Megan du Boisson and she realised that if you duplicated what the Central Council for the Disabled (CCD) was doing, for example, it was going to lead to bad blood - so she really kept DIG on the economic side."

However, avoiding duplication with other bodies did not stop Mary from co-operating with other organisations, far from it. Furthermore, she accepted invitations to assist and participate in other bodies, chairing, for example the CCD's Legal and Parliamentary Committee set up to shadow the Private Members Bill introduced by disability campaigner Alf Morris MP, in 1969. The Committee, under Mary's chairmanship, helped Alf Morris with drafting sections of the Bill, providing briefing material and drawing up amendments. No doubt the experience Mary had gained of working in Whitehall and of following Parliamentary proceedings proved invaluable in this work.

Lobbying Parliament and working with sympathetic Parliamentarians was a vital part of making progress towards proper rights for disabled citizens. Mary personally lobbied two Prime Ministers, Harold Wilson and Edward Heath, as well as other Ministers and Shadow Ministers. It seems that on the whole she was well, and sympathetically, received. She recognised the importance of cross-party working so that a national consensus on action and legislation to help the disabled could be built and she gained the support of politicians from across the spectrum, from Sir Keith Joseph on the right to Shirley Williams on the left. She also, as a former civil servant, recognised the need, crucially, for support from administrators and officials.

Her contacts with Prime Minister Harold Wilson are particularly interesting. She thought she had first met him at a function for disability campaigners at Admiralty House in London, but he remembered seeing her some years before in the Ministry of Works - perhaps being struck by the unusual sight of a woman in a wheelchair in that working environment. On meeting her at the reception and talking to her, he invited her to 10 Downing Street to brief him further in a one-to-one meeting, which Mary felt gave her a very special opportunity to put her case. She was also struck by his thoughtfulness in realising that the room allocated for their meeting involved steps and at the last minute he changed the arrangement so that they could meet in the easier to access Cabinet Room.

In her discussions with the Prime Minister, she also stressed the importance of the Open University, founded by the Wilson government in 1969, reaching out to disabled people. She can thus take some credit for the fact that the Open University became the largest provider of higher education for people with disabilities.

Subsequently when Wilson decided to call an election in 1970 he honoured the promise that he had given to Mary personally that Parliament would not be dissolved before Alf Morris's landmark Bill on Disability became law. Indeed the Morris Bill - a Private Member's Bill - was given precedence over parts of the Government's own legislation, such as the National Superannuation and Social Insurance Bill, which was abandoned through lack of time. So it was as a result of Mary's successful lobbying of the Prime Minister that the Morris bill, that pioneering legislation enshrining legally enforceable rights for the disabled successfully entered into law as *The Chronically Sick and Disabled Persons Act, 1970*.

Mary paid her own tribute to Alf Morris and his Bill when she contributed a chapter in Duncan Guthrie's 1981 book entitled *Disability Legislation and Practice* and wrote the following: "The awareness that disabled people are people and have the same needs, aspirations and problems as non-disabled has become world-wide. Why did this happen? What brought it about? The single factor which influenced many others was the introduction of the *Chronically Sick and Disabled Persons Bill*."

Once the bill had become law, its provisions could be used to bring in further specific measures. It placed legal obligations on local authorities to make provision for access by disabled people to public buildings and to create welfare services, such as meals on wheels delivered to the home. It also involved measures to facilitate travel to and from home leading, in 1971, to the introduction of the important Blue Badge scheme.

Mary stood down as director of DIG in 1972. She had enjoyed the work and achieved much of what she set out to do, but her own disability meant that she had to do a great deal of work unaided from home and faced practical problems, such as being unable to travel to the Group's headquarters in Godalming.

Happily, however, also in 1972 her efforts were nationally recognised when she was awarded an OBE for her services to the disabled. Her life and views were also referred to in a book about the lives of particular disabled people - published that year - *No Feet to Drag* by Arthur Butler and Alfred Morris. The authors had interviewed her "in her comfortable book-lined flat" and highlighted her life's experience including her past struggles, in the face of considerable challenges, to obtain qualifications for employment.

Furthermore her advice and expertise continued to be sought by those who were concerned with how much progress was being made since her 1969 book in providing facilities for the disabled and in how effective the 1970 legislation was turning out to be in practice.

In 1976 the Trustees of the Eleanor Hamilton Educational and Charitable Trust agreed to fund a report on progress on behalf of the Disabled Living Foundation and asked Mary, along with Bert Massie (another very able wheelchair-bound campaigner) to write the report. Their published report was a thorough investigation and made widespread recommendations for further action to a number of government departments, as well as to other bodies including trade unions, the Post Office, to DIG and to the Association of Disabled Professionals amongst others.

Mary died in London on 16th January, 1983, aged 75. Members of her family still treasure her memory today. Bob Frazier recollects "we grew up hearing stories about her and how cool she was" and Professor John Heckels quotes the *Times* obituary of Mary describing her as "a woman of courage and good sense, who disliked above all things a sentimental approach to disability."

In June 2008, in the House of Lords as part of a debate to celebrate the 30th Anniversary of the coming into force of all the provisions of his *1970 Disability Act*, Alf Morris, by then Lord Morris of Manchester, paid tribute to Mary once again as one of the key people who helped him with that ground-breaking legislation.

Given all that she did, she deserves to be remembered widely, not least in her native North East.

Mary Greaves, front row, fourth from left, at a National Conference on Disability, Ditchley Towers, 1976.

Jane Grigson was a unique and pioneering voice in food writing.

Jane Grigson (1928 - 1990)

Food writer of lasting fame and influence

One of the consequences of the television age, combined with the period of greater prosperity and personal wealth that followed Britain's post-war austerity of the 1940s and 1950s was the emergence of a greater interest in cooking and food, accompanied by the arrival of the TV celebrity chef. Jane Grigson, through her recipes and her extensive writings about food, was a key influence in promoting this greater interest and awareness of how we cook and what we eat.

So many of our present day preoccupations about the importance of good quality vegetables in our diet, about promoting and celebrating locally and regionally produced food, and our concerns about how our food is produced are matters that she wrote about from the late 1950s onwards. She became a well-known national figure and a respected authority on food and cookery, and her many books on these subjects are still in print and widely read today.

When Jane Grigson was asked where she was from on the long-running BBC Radio Programme *Desert Island Discs*, she answered unhesitatingly "I'm from the North East of England, from Sunderland". She was in fact born in Gloucester, where her father, George McIntire, was Deputy Town Clerk, and on her birth certificate her names are recorded as Heather Mabel Jane. When she was four years old the family moved to Sunderland - where her father was appointed Town Clerk - and she spent her formative years there, identifying strongly with it thereafter. Some detected traces of a North-Eastern accent in her speech, although in her radio and television interviews this is not easy to discern since she spoke for the most part in the somewhat stilted BBC "received English," which all programme presenters and many contributors seemed constrained to adopt at that time.

Her Sunderland childhood, it is claimed, also influenced her political outlook, which was left leaning and strongly pro-welfare state, coloured by her knowledge of the poverty and unemployment that had been so marked during the 1930s.

Her early education was at primary school in Sunderland but her secondary education was at a girls' school in rural Westmorland. This was because the Second World War had begun and Sunderland, like many port and industrial areas, was a Nazi bombing target. As a result, many schoolchildren were either evacuated with their schools, or, as in Jane's case, were sent by parents who could afford it to private boarding schools in safer areas. The school she attended, Casterton, had started out life as Cowan Bridge school, the institution where Charlotte Bronte and some of her sisters had been pupils and which was the model for Lowood, the infamous school in her novel *Jane Eyre*. Although Jane Grigson's time at the school took place more than a hundred years after Charlotte Bronte, her description of it is not much less scathing. She disliked it and was not happy. However from there she did win a place to Newnham College, Cambridge, where she studied English Literature.

On graduating from university, she struggled for a while to find a job that would suit her. She spent some time travelling in Italy, learning the language, and showing considerable aptitude in doing so. Her time there included a three-month stay in Florence, where she was able to enjoy its galleries and cultural attractions. Her interest in artistic and creative work had already been awakened during her childhood in Sunderland where she had loved visiting its museum and had become fascinated by its collection of silverware and by the long history of Sunderland's production of quality pottery and glassware. She had also become interested in painting and textiles.

These experiences had made her very keen to work in a museum and following her return to England, she set her heart on finding employment in the Victoria and Albert Museum in London, but despite applying for a number of positions there was unsuccessful. She spent some time working as the assistant to the curator at the Heffer Gallery in Cambridge and then as a junior in a Bond Street art gallery in London. She also, through her Sunderland contacts, began to write art reviews for the *Sunderland Echo* where her subjects included pottery and porcelain, as well as the works of the Sunderland-born artist Clarkson Frederick Stanfield.

Meanwhile, her father, wanting to help her, had approached the Victoria and Albert to try to find out why her applications there had been refused and was told that competition was fierce. It was suggested to him that given her English Literature degree, Jane might try to get some useful experience in publishing where there seemed to be better job prospects.

As it turned out this would be life-changing advice. In 1953 Jane was appointed editorial assistant at the publishing house of Rainbird, McLean, and was assigned to work as a research assistant to the poet and writer Geoffrey Grigson. So began a life-long partnership. Their relationship was not without its initial challenges, however, as Geoffrey was married and, although he and his wife were leading separate lives, she was unwilling to grant him a divorce. Jane, nonetheless, moved to Geoffrey's farmhouse home in Wiltshire, changed her name to Grigson by deed poll and then later, in 1959, gave birth to their daughter Sophie. The early years together were financially difficult but their partnership, both personally and professionally, was and remained solid.

During this period Jane did a lot of work translating Italian books into English. One of the books she translated was *Dei delitti e delle penne* (On Crimes and punishments) by Cesare Beccaria, the 18th century writer of the Italian Enlightenment who was the first to write in opposition to capital punishment. Jane's translation appeared at a time when the debate on whether to abolish the death penalty was high on the political agenda in the UK, and Jane, who opposed capital punishment, was pleased that she played her part in making his writing known to an English-speaking readership. As a result of the quality of her work she was awarded the John Florio Prize for Italian Translation in 1966.

At this time too, Jane and Geoffrey produced together books aimed at bringing art to young people. A successful volume *Shapes and Stories* came out in 1964 followed by *Shapes and Adventures* in 1967.

On a visit to France, Jane and Geoffrey discovered the area of Loir et Cher and, in particular, the village of Troo, sometimes called "the Troglodyte village" because of its cave houses dating from medieval times. They decided to buy one of these, prompted by their friend and neighbour there, Aden Horton, the purchase being made possible by a legacy left to Jane by her father.

They spent as much time as they could in their cave house over subsequent years and Jane began working with Aden on an idea for a book he had about writing on French charcuterie for a British audience. Jane thoroughly enjoyed researching this, and while doing so sampling some of the recipes for local dishes, including recipes provided by her French neighbours. When Aden decided to abandon the work, Jane was persuaded to carry on alone and complete it. The published work was described by Elizabeth David, already one of Britain's best known cookery writers, as a "kitchen classic" written by "a writer who could combine a delightful quote from Chaucer on the subject of pike galantine with a recipe for a modern chicken and pork version of the same ancient dish, without pedantry or a hint of preciousness".

Elizabeth David was enchanted by the lyrical writing, the depth and breadth of the research, and the amount of practical and helpful advice that the book so admirably combined. The book entitled *Charcuterie and French pork cookery* came out in 1967 and was acclaimed in Britain where not much had been written in English on the subject, and not in such an accessible and attractive way. It also came on the market at a time when more Britons than ever were travelling to France and the Mediterranean area and becoming, as a result, more adventurous in cooking and in trying different cuisines.

Shortly after, Elizabeth David was approached by the *Observer* newspaper to write a weekly column. She declined, but suggested, having been so impressed by Jane's book, that Jane would be an excellent choice for this work. So in 1968 Jane began her weekly column for which she would become so well-known and which continued regularly and punctually until 1990.

Over those 20 years Jane also wrote and published a great variety of books on food and cooking. The most successful included *Fish Cookery* (1973); *English Food* (1974) containing some 450 recipes, including some from her native North East; *The Mushroom Feast*, (1975); *Vegetable Book*, (1978); *Fruit Book* (1982); *The Observer Guide to European Cookery* (1983); *The Observer Guide to British Cookery* (1984); and *Exotic Fruits and Vegetables* (1986).

Most of the books she wrote were published in the United States as well as in the UK, the exception being *Fish Cookery*, which was judged by the American publishers as of insufficient interest given that Americans didn't eat much fish!

Many of the books were also shortened by the editors, feeling apparently that Jane's enthusiasm for her subject and wide-ranging references might overwhelm her readers. Jane loved to set the food in its social and historical context and showed much scholarship in the way she did this. In *Food with the Famous* (1979) she talked of John Evelyn's enthusiasm for salad and vegetables. Writing about Jane Austen, she explained some of the dishes referred to in Austen's novels which modern readers would not understand such as the "white soup" mentioned in *Pride and Prejudice*.

Throughout these years of her greatest successes, Jane's life with Geoffrey brought her great personal happiness. They were eventually to marry in 1976 when he was able to get a divorce. Geoffrey said, in appreciation of life with Jane and of her culinary talents, "she ruined my figure and she saved my soul."

Their daughter Sophie eventually followed a similar career path to her mother becoming both a cookery writer and a celebrity chef. Jane, when interviewed on *Desert Island Discs*, said that in contrast to her, Sophie never got recipes wrong! Yet Sophie was equally complimentary about her mother, writing in the preface to her own book *Eat Your Greens* (1993) "I have my mother to thank first and foremost for my love of vegetables. She cooked them perfectly and lovingly and imaginatively", and described her mother's *Vegetable Book* as "by far the best book ever written on the subject."

Geoffrey Grigson died in 1985, bringing to an end over 30 years of their being together and Jane's love for him was again in evidence on *Desert Island Discs* where one of her records was of Geoffrey reading one of his poems. Her chosen book was Geoffrey's *Notes from an Odd Country*, published in 1970.

Jane died, aged 62, in 1990, but her books, writing and influence live on. The year after she died, an educational charity, The Jane Grigson Trust was set up in her honour that includes a library, based on her own collection. The Trust also organises an Annual Lecture and an Award for promising new food and drink writers.

25 years after her death, in 2015, the BBC broadcast a two-part tribute to her on Radio 4. In those programmes many well-known people from the world of food and cookery remembered her with great affection and respect, summing her up as a "unique and pioneering voice in food writing."

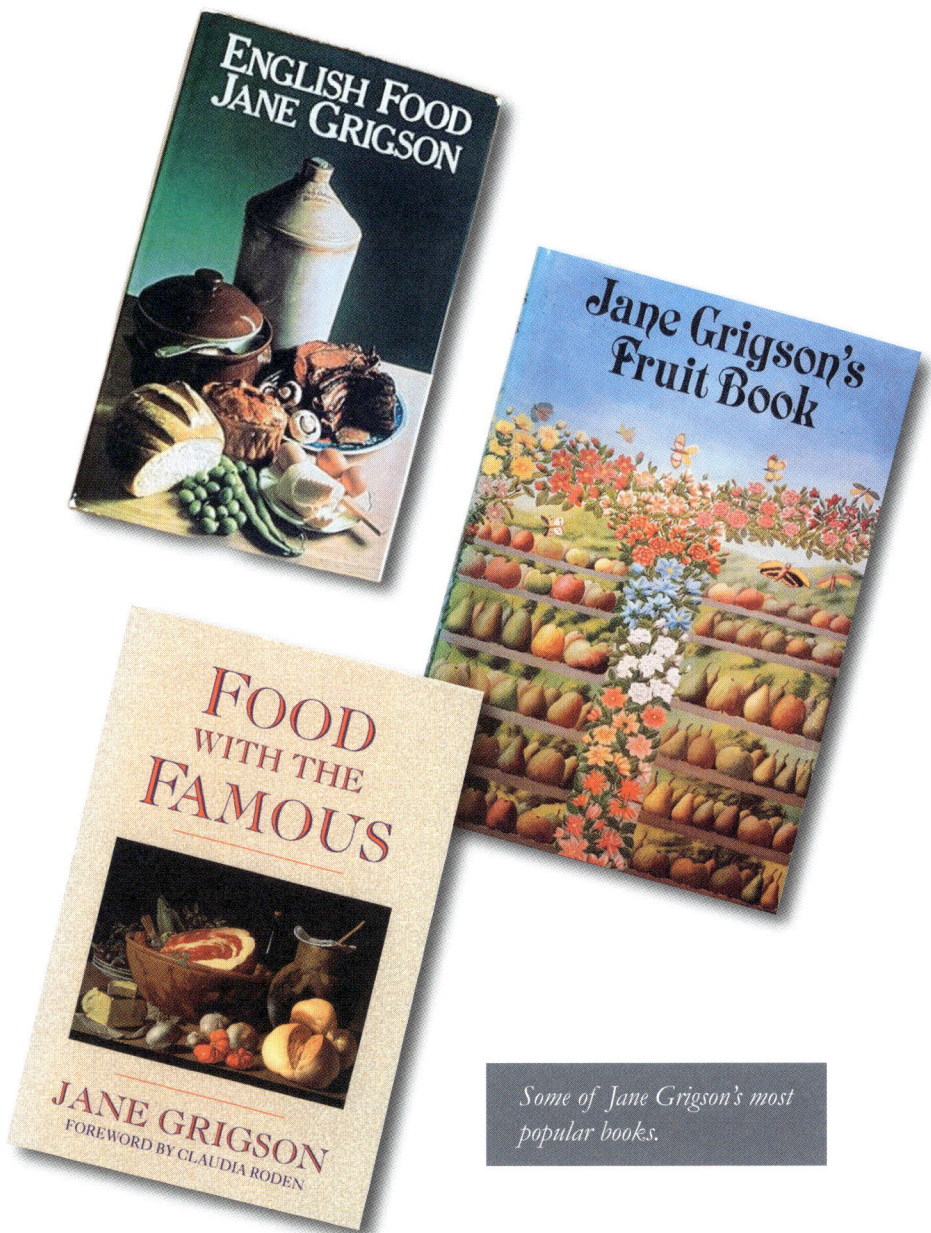

Some of Jane Grigson's most popular books.

Mary Jane Hancock.

Mary Jane Hancock (1810 - 1896)

Botanist and artist

Mary Jane Hancock's life is largely overshadowed by her two famous brothers, Albany and John Hancock, after whom Newcastle's celebrated Hancock Museum (now known as the Great North Museum Hancock) was named. She was devoted to her brothers and acted as housekeeper to them, dying in the family home at 4 St Mary's Place, Newcastle, after they both had predeceased her. For a single woman in the 19th century such circumstances were not uncommon, but there are good reasons for remembering Mary in her own right and acknowledging both the contribution she made during her lifetime as well as the donations and generous bequests she left that considerably augmented the museum's treasures and are still enjoyed by locals and visitors today.

In accounts of her brothers, Mary is frequently mentioned as a supportive figure, but even with the relatively little we know of her it would be more appropriate to think of her as an active partner in the natural history endeavours and achievements of the Hancock family.

Mary was born in 1810, the youngest child of the family. Her father, like his father before him, was a saddler and an ironmonger and had premises close to the stone Tyne Bridge - that had been erected after the medieval bridge had been swept away in a flood in 1771. (Today the Swing Bridge stands on that site).

One side of the family had Huguenot roots and links to the early glassmaking industry on Tyneside. While running his saddlery business, Mary's father John - perhaps as a result of his education or through a natural inclination - had become very interested in natural history, particularly in plants, insects and shells. John also had made friends, possibly through this interest, with Thomas Bewick the engraver, and indeed had helped and advised Bewick about the purchase of his eventual home, Birk Lane near Cherryburn, where he had grown up. Mary was to become a close friend of Bewick's eldest child, his daughter Jane.

Sadly, John Hancock died aged 43 when Mary was only two years old. Mary's mother was left with six children to look after. It is recorded that she treasured her husband's natural history collection and his library. If, as can be supposed, she wanted her children to follow in his footsteps she must have been amazed and hugely proud about their subsequent achievements and scholarship!

Given this background, it is not surprising that Mary and her brothers, from early childhood, began to develop a keen interest in nature and acquired a knowledge of plant and animal wildlife, particularly during their trips to nearby coast and country including Tynemouth, Winlaton Mill, Gibside and Prestwick Carr.

In his book *Men of Mark Twixt Tyne and Tweed,* Richard Welford, in profiling John Hancock, says: "After his father's death, when the family were residing at Bensham he (John) and his sister Mary hunted through the fields and hedgerows for birds, insects and flowers, and during summer trips to Tynemouth wandered together about the banks and sandhills for insects and plants that were new to them".

For John and his brother Albany these childhood interests and experiences would become the basis of their nationally-known works and fame, John concentrating on taxidermy and amassing a huge scientific collection of animals and birds and Albany becoming an expert on molluscs and a prolific writer on many aspects of natural history. However, Mary too had begun a lifelong interest, particularly in botany, and in building up an impressive natural history collection of her own. This was accompanied by an equally strong interest in art and painting. It is said that Mary, as a young girl, studied art under Thomas Miles Richardson, a prominent local artist who has been described as "The Father of Fine Arts in Newcastle". That he taught Mary seems likely, particularly since he was, like the Hancock family, a friend of Thomas Bewick and he was also a teacher of watercolour painting techniques to many pupils Richardson was also a friend of William Bell Scott, the well-known artist and associate of the Pre-Raphaelites, who sketched the portrait of Mary that illustrates this brief chapter about her.

An examination of the collection of Mary's paintings held in the Great North Museum Hancock reveals some of her favourite local haunts from childhood onwards. Denton Burn (then a charming wooded valley); the old bridge at Gosforth over the Ouseburn; Jesmond Dene; Lintzford; Cullercoats; Tynemouth and Whitley Bay. But she also knew, and drew, the wider North East, depicting scenes in the Tyne Valley (Dilston and Corbridge for example); Northumberland (Warkworth, Rothbury, Cartington); and County Durham and Teesdale (Gainford, Rokeby, Staindrop and Croft on Tees).

An attractive collection of her early paintings is constituted by the watercolours she produced, aged 26, during an extended Lake District Holiday with Jane Bewick and her sisters. She also would, over subsequent years, enjoy painting when visiting friends. She and her brothers John and Albany often stayed with Tyneside inventor and industrialist Sir William Armstrong and his wife Lady Margaret and one of Mary's paintings in the Great North Museum is entitled *View from Lady Armstrong's Window.*

Sundays seemed to be Mary's favourite day for drawing. In a later reminiscence about her some of her nephews and nieces claimed that she did not like to go to church but preferred to spend her time on Sunday out with her sketch pad recording the local scenery.

Later in life she also found time to sketch and draw during several holidays with her brother John in Oatlands in Surrey, in a house which had been bequeathed to John by one of his lifelong naturalist friends and admirers, William Chapman Hewitson, who was a well-known entomologist and ornithologist.

While enjoying opportunities for painting and drawing, Mary never neglected her interests in natural history and in plant collecting in particular. She was an active supporter, alongside her brothers, in the work of the Natural History Society of Northumberland, Durham and Newcastle upon Tyne. This had been established in 1829 with the Hancock brothers as founding members. It operated when it first began from a building behind the Literary and Philosophical Society. When her brother Albany died in 1873, Mary ensured that his collections and manuscripts were donated to the Society.

In 1880 she presented to the Society a collection of plants from Switzerland, Norway and Madeira, the result of expeditions undertaken by her brother John and by William Hewitson. In 1884 she was elected a member of the Natural History Society - a highly unusual honour for a woman in what was very much, until then, a masculine organisation. A year later she donated to the Society another large number of ethnographical and social history items including some that had been collected on voyages of Captain Cook. She also donated a collection of her own botanical specimens, numbering some 300 or so, from different parts of the British Isles.

Because of the success of the Natural History Society and because of its growing collections, the members felt in the 1870s that its premises next to the Literary and Philosophical society were increasingly inadequate. The death of Albany Hancock had also motivated John and others to find a suitable way of honouring his life and of housing his publications and extensive collections in an appropriate setting. Funds provided by Lord and Lady Armstrong and by Edward and John Joicey enabled a site to be purchased and for the present fine building to be erected and opened in 1884. At the time it opened it was named the New Museum of Natural History but six years later, after the death of John Hancock, it was decided to rename it the Hancock Museum in tribute to both brothers.

After John's death, Mary lived on for another six years in the home she had shared with her brothers, dying there in 1896. She was buried alongside her brothers in Jesmond Old Cemetery. In addition to all her previous donations she left £100 in her will to the funds of the Natural History Society - quite a considerable amount in the days when most people would earn less than that in a year.

An obituary of Mary in the *Journal of the Natural History Society* in 1896 describes how "botany and landscape painting were favourite subjects with her up to the last year of her life" and in recognition of her devotion to both art and botany how "she left behind a considerable Herbarium of British plants and numerous Portfolios of sketches of rural and marine scenery from every place she visited in England and Scotland."

Currently, the Great North Museum Hancock, named in honour of Mary's brothers, also acknowledges Mary's own contribution by featuring her in a delightful exhibition "Mythquest" - an interactive experience particularly aimed at children and imagining Mary leading visitors to the museum that she had helped create - into a "world filled with magical creatures" where the visitors become adventurers and encounter myths and monsters before completing their quests. In this way the museum, named in honour of Mary's brothers, recognises and proclaims that she too has her place both in establishing the museum and in contributing to its wonderful collections and its continuing successful role in the North East's cultural heritage and identity.

Above: A sketch of Mary by the artist William Bell Scott. Left: A portrait of Mary at her easel. Opposite page: Two of Mary's paintings including Ovingham churchyard with Thomas Bewick's grave.

Hannah Hauxwell at her farm in 1966.

Hannah Hauxwell (1926 - 2018)

Hill farmer and Britain's unlikeliest celebrity

Throughout her life Hannah Hauxwell identified herself as a Yorkshirewoman and it is certainly the case that the farm in Baldersdale, where she lived during her childhood, was situated in Yorkshire's North Riding. However, the area was transferred, under the 1974 local reorganisation to County Durham as was the village of Cotherstone to which Hannah later retired. Teesdale, which she also identified with, has always straddled both Yorkshire and Durham, with Durham's Barnard Castle being the main town serving the area. Given this background, here in the North East we can share in Hannah's legacy and can, along with our Yorkshire neighbours, celebrate her life.

Hannah came dramatically and spectacularly to public attention as a result of a Yorkshire TV programme that revealed her spartan way of life on her isolated hill farm high up in the Pennines. The sight of a woman single-handedly coping with her livestock in the bleakest of winter conditions in a farmhouse without electricity or running water amazed and astonished TV viewers and seemed reminiscent of a bygone age.

In addition, they found Hannah's charming and open personality and her gentle stoicism in the face of adversity quite compelling. In today's language this 1972 programme entitled Too Long a Winter, and Hannah's role in it in particular, went viral. The programme was played and replayed and gained a nationwide audience. What perhaps was just as remarkable was that, once discovered, Hannah, far from being a one-minute wonder, became, from then on a permanent national treasure without ever for a moment losing her simple honesty and authenticity. Even today, five years after her death at the age 91 in 2018 there are millions of hits on the programmes and documentaries that were made about her many years ago but which still continue to inspire and enthral.

Hannah Bayles Tallantyre Hauxwell was born in 1926 in Sleetburn Baldersdale where her parents were farming. When she was three years old the family moved to nearby Low Birk Hatt farm, a family property acquired by her parents on a mortgage. To pay the mortgage and run the farm was a constant challenge and Hannah's father worked tirelessly.

Hannah, an only child, was close to both parents who, despite their economic circumstances and the need to house and support elderly relatives, gave their daughter a happy and secure early childhood. From her mother, who had been the organist at the Mouthlock Methodist chapel, she acquired a love of music that never left her. Sadly, when Hannah was only seven years old, her father died and her uncle Tommy, whose own marriage had broken down, then moved into Low Birk Hatt working alongside Hannah's mother to ensure the farm could continue to operate. He was a supportive and kind uncle to Hannah throughout his life.

By then Hannah attended the local school but, according to her memoirs, her experience there was not particularly enjoyable. As the only child of the family, with very little previous contact with other children, she found school daunting and did not make friends easily. She summed it up by saying that she was glad when she could leave at age 14 and work on the farm which, given the family's need of her, she accepted willingly as her way of life from then on.

Even in Baldersdale, time did not entirely stand still and Hannah recalled how exciting it was when the family acquired their first wireless - in 1939 - and how she enjoyed listening to the programmes, extending her musical knowledge and her awareness of the outside world.

While most of the time farming activities predominated, she also remembered riding on the back of her uncle's scooter into Barnard Castle, going to the cinema there and to the circus in Darlington. The family belonged to the local Methodist Chapel which organised annual bus outings, including to the Lake District and to Scotland, and other social activities. In those days too more people lived in Baldersdale than was the case in later years and there was regular contact with neighbours and friends nearby. During the war, some evacuees were housed in the area, mostly from Tyneside, and there was also an occasional military presence for training purposes. Indeed at one local dance Hannah met a fair-haired soldier to whom she was attracted. She recalled "he was playing with the band and asked me to stay until he finished" but living on a remote farm and, not being allowed to stay out late, this possible romance was sadly and quickly nipped in the bud.

Its remoteness, and the severe winters, meant that Baldersdale was not an area of aristocratic residences but the moors were prized for grouse shooting and tracts of the land were owned by aristocratic families. Hannah recalled that during the grouse season, there was extra employment and more money for local farmers and farmworkers.

In the years following the war, life continued in Baldersdale along traditional lines but Hannah's mother aged 67 died at the end of the 1950s and this was followed by the death of her uncle only three years later. From the beginning of the 1960s, aged 35, Hannah was left to farm Low Birk Hatt on her own and had to cope as best she could. She had a farm sale of most of the livestock, which she felt she could not manage on her own, but this took place at a time when prices were depressed and didn't give her the financial cushion she had hoped for. From then on her lifestyle became increasingly frugal and it was this, combined with the harsh winter conditions, which so astonished the nation at the time of the Yorkshire TV documentary in 1972. Viewers were told that she was living off an annual income of only around £250 a year (roughly equivalent to £4000 a year today) and the bulk of this came from the sale of one cow a year. Her food delivery amounted to £5 a month and was delivered in a box, not to her door, but had to be collected from a couple of fields away. Her food often had to be sealed and suspended in places safe from mice, and even rats, who would come into the farmhouse looking for a billet in the winter months. Hannah even felt she could not afford a dog, a much-needed companion and comfort, because of the price of dog food. Such information which she supplied openly and in a matter-of-fact way in the interview along with the visual impact of seeing her hauling a recalcitrant cow through a blizzard to the shelter of the byre left an indelible impression on those watching and listening.

Yorkshire TV producer Barry Cockcroft had been intrigued by living conditions in the high Pennines and had already filmed a number of times in the area, but even he was taken totally by surprise on meeting Hannah and seeing for himself how she got by. Little did he realise that his meeting with her and the subsequent documentary he made would have such profound and prolonged repercussions - making Hannah a celebrity and leading to some further 15 television documentaries and a dozen or so books. The immediate media frenzy eventually gave way to steadier and calmer ongoing interest in Hannah but her famed endured.

Offers of help for Hannah had poured in from viewers touched by her story. Many of them assumed, from her white hair and from seeing her struggle in winter fields, that she was old and feeble. In fact she was still in her forties and, despite her poor diet, in reasonable health. However help was welcome as it resulted in electricity being supplied to the farm and, as a result of later TV fees, the arrival of a heating system and a much-prized electric kettle! Such improvements allowed Hannah to continue her lifestyle but in somewhat more comfortable circumstances. While she coped with all the attention admirably, she did not want to leave her family home: "the old house and me, we'll stay together", she declared.

Her partnership with Barry Cockcroft was a great success. They became friends and they respected each other hugely. Initially Barry was very concerned that with the media invasion he "had ruined this poor lady's life" but was soon reassured by her realistic and no-nonsense attitude to fame. While she had coped with living alone, having new friends in her life was welcome to her and in one of her early interviews she told of the time, a few years earlier when, perhaps as a result of her impoverished lifestyle and overwork, she had become unwell. The doctor had insisted on a period in hospital, where she was looked after for eight weeks, the longest time she had ever spent away from home. Happily, no serious illness was diagnosed and she recovered, helped by good care and good food. In hospital she made friends whose company she enjoyed and confessed to finding it difficult when she returned home and had no one to talk to. So, although she could cope alone, she was far from deliberately wanting to shun company.

The years following the 1972 documentary found her (with Barry Cockcroft's enduring support) combining her traditional lifestyle with a public role, involving some eye-catching activities. In 1977, for example, she was invited to be guest of honour at the Women of the Year lunch at the Savoy in London, causing her to buy her first new dress since her mother's death some 20 years earlier. At the lunch she met Mary Wilson, the wife of the then Prime Minister Harold Wilson, and the Duchess of Gloucester. Hannah was also thrilled to meet Odette Hallowes, the French Resistance heroine, whom she had long admired and never imagined meeting.

Over the following years she continued to contribute to TV programmes, collaborate with Barry Cockcroft in producing books, and answering courteously a vast amount of correspondence.

Despite more comfortable living conditions, Hannah found winter increasingly difficult to cope with. As she put it: "In summer I live, in winter I exist". Baldersdale, too, continued to suffer depopulation, meaning fewer neighbours for Hannah and fewer local social activities. Towards the end of the 1980s health problems also affected her, with angina being diagnosed. A self-confessed hoarder and having received mountains of mail and gifts from her countless fans over the years, she was also struggling to manage her increasingly messy home. Consequently her friends, new and old, began suggesting to her that she should retire from farming, move to a village and have a more comfortable and easy-to-manage home. Hannah resisted such pressure determinedly for a while but then surprised her friends by finding a house she liked in the Teesdale village of Cotherstone and announcing that she would leave Low Birk Hatt.

Her move to her new village home, Belle View Cottage, featured in another Cockcroft documentary "A Winter Too Many" filmed in 1988, which attracted six million viewers. Not surprisingly, as Hannah faced living somewhere other than the house that had belonged to her family since it was built 200 years previously, she was conflicted and deeply nostalgic about the move, shedding tears at the thought of leaving and no longer having her favourite view over the water from her farmhouse window.

The house and farm were sold in lots, partly because of Hannah's meeting in 1987 with the person she called "The Flower Gentleman". He was Mike Prosser, a botanist, and he was identifying areas where rare plants and flowers flourished, for the Nature Conservancy Council. Hannah's land had a number of such plants and flowers and had never been treated with chemical fertilisers. Mike Prosser quickly realised that her land was "possibly the least improved meadows in upland Durham". Happily, this land was acquired by Durham Wildlife Trust when Hannah's farm was sold, helped by some generous grants from environmental bodies. Now called "Hannah's meadow" it is under permanent protection and attracts visitors from far and wide. Hannah's byre is today a visitor centre and she is remembered, not only for surviving hardship and penury, but also for farming in harmony with nature - a pioneer organic farmer!

Once properly settled in Cotherstone, Hannah took on a new lease of life. While sad at no longer living at Low Birk Hatt, she also felt she had lots of things to look forward to and rejoiced that her health and eyesight were still reasonably good.

Television companies were keen to take advantage of her changed circumstances and suggested a series of travel programmes entitled "Innocent Abroad", again a collaboration with Barry Cockcroft. The series involved an extensive European tour, covering France, Germany, Austria, Italy and Switzerland. A later series also focused on a trip to America. From having travelled only very rarely and not owning a passport, Hannah was suddenly spending considerable time abroad, earning her the affectionate nickname of the "Teesdale Pimpernel" as her friends tried to keep track of her movements.

Some of the publicity attendant on her travels - and indeed the portrayal of Hannah generally - jarred at the time and doubtless does even more so today. Media descriptions of Hannah, invariably including her age, routinely described her as a "maiden lady" and as a "spinster" constantly stressing the absence of men in her life. The simple, frugal life she had led before being discovered encouraged a stereotype of her as innocent, inexperienced and knowing nothing of the world. However this caricature does not describe the reality. Hannah is shrewd about human nature and not naïve. She observed that while a good marriage is wonderful and, she thought, greatly preferable to being on one's own, she also declared that a bad marriage, involving sharing a roof with someone who you were at variance with, was definitely to be avoided. She had known of good and bad marriages within her own family. Similarly, abstaining from alcohol was part of her Methodist upbringing but

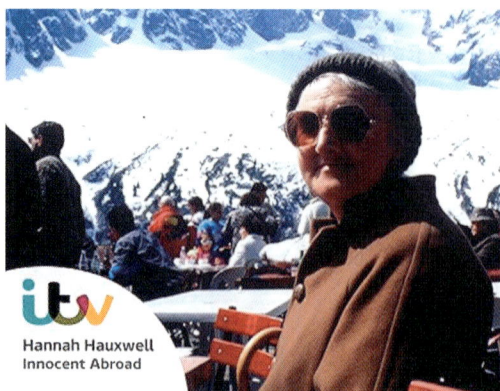

Hannah Hauxwell
Innocent Abroad

was reinforced by her experience of people whose lives had been harmed by drink. One of Hannah's books is entitled *The Commonsense Book of a Countrywoman* and contains many wise comments on a range of issues from politics and religion to the future of agriculture and the role of the media in our society.

Hannah's travels meant that she encountered many celebrities. She enjoyed such meetings for the most part and was always respectful and ready to engage in conversation, but seldom overawed, retaining her gentle composure.

She enjoyed her ventures abroad, falling unsurprisingly in love with Venice, and appreciating Salzburg and Vienna. She was less keen on the Swiss Alps as the snow reminded her of harsh winters and less keen on the treatment of horses in Siena's famous Palio. She also enjoyed cruises where she was an invited speaker and, in her memoirs, mused on the fact that until her sixties the sole sea voyage she had undertaken, many years previously, was the ferry from South Shields to North Shields!

Throughout all her travels and journeys and despite media attempts to overdo the "innocent abroad" image, Hannah, to quote the *Guardian* (9/2/2001) "remained resolutely her excellent self."

In her eighties Hannah naturally spent more time at home in her cottage in Cotherstone but kept in regular contact with her now worldwide circle of friends. She lived there until 2016 and then moved to a care home in Barnard Castle. She died in 2018 in a nursing home in West Auckland, Durham aged 91 and, after a funeral at Barnard Castle Methodist Church, was buried in Romaldkirk churchyard not far from Low Birk Hatt.

While Hannah did move with the times, those first images of her in 1972 continued to remind people of what seemed to be a simpler age, an age when most people passed their whole lives close to where they were born, often carrying on the same tasks as their forbears. Hannah's life at that time was an unforgettable example of how people lived and worked in those remote Pennine upland dales of County Durham and Yorkshire.

As well as the documentaries about her and her own published books, perhaps her most precious legacy is Hannah's Meadow where The Durham Wildlife Trust now has an interpretation centre explaining what is unique about the countryside there. The Trust also organises visits in which the connection between the Meadow and Hannah's life is perpetuated. In addition there is a plaque on Hannah's cottage in Cotherstone and the Fitzhugh Library in Middleton in Teesdale retains documentation about her.

The opening titles of the 1972 programme about Hannah - Too Long a Winter.

Photo: Natural History Society of Northumbria

Grace Hickling tagging a seal on the Farne Islands and, inset, working as an intelligence officer during the war (second from left).

Grace Hickling (1908 - 1986)

Ornithologist and naturalist MBE, MA

Mrs Grace Hickling was rightly hailed by the *Times* newspaper as "Protector of Northumbrian Wildlife." For almost all of her adult life, Grace Hickling worked tirelessly for Northumbria Natural History Society as their Honorary Secretary, while at the same time researching and protecting the Grey Seals and sea birds of the Farne Islands off the coast of Northumberland.

Grace Watt was born in August 1908, the only daughter of Adam and Grace Ann Watt. Her father was an engineer in Newcastle. Grace was educated at Harrogate Ladies' College, and at Armstrong College, Newcastle. From there she went on to study mathematics and geography at Newnham College Cambridge, from 1928 to 31. Although she passed all the exams with flying colours, Cambridge University did not award women degrees until 1948, which was when she too was awarded her MA.

She took up a teaching post but with the growing threat of war was asked in 1938 to do some training in readiness to work in a regional war room if hostilities broke out. On 1 September she was called up to work as one of three Intelligence Officers in the war room at Watson House in Newcastle. Grace records that the salary for this post was £400 a year until the authorities discovered that her "G" stood for Grace and not George and the salary was promptly cut to £300 a year. She was not at all surprised, equal pay was just a dream in 1939.

This posting was to change the course of her life. One of the other Intelligence Officers, recruited at the same time, was Mr T. Russell Goddard, Curator of the Hancock Museum, which was closed for the duration of the war. In quiet times Russell would talk to his colleagues about his museum work and his research visits to the Farne Islands, about the records he had kept since 1925, noting population figures and his observations on the birds and seals. Grace wanted to know more about it and so, in June 1940, the RNVR granted Goddard and Watt a permit to land on the Inner Farne and to visit any of the islands, except Longstone. From that first visit, at the height of the bird breeding season in June 1940, Grace was hooked and became more and more interested in natural history. Further visits to the Farne Islands followed and when the war ended and the Museum re-opened, Mr Goddard resumed his post and his research, but now with support from Grace Watt, who had decided on a career change.

Her deep interest in natural history never waned and she was severely upset by Russell Goddard's death in 1948. In the same year she was elected Joint Honorary Secretary of the Natural History Society of Northumbria.

A few years later she was elected sole honorary secretary, an unpaid role that she fulfilled until her death in 1986. For 38 years she managed the day-to-day administration of the society with devotion and efficiency. One of her first tasks was to arrange for the binding of the most important publications of the thousands of documents in the library. Professor HGA Hickling, a member of the Society helped her in selecting the appropriate documents, they became close and in 1954 they married. Grace became Mrs Hickling, but her happiness was short lived because very sadly her husband died only a few weeks later.

Grace took full control of the library which was in a deplorable condition in 1948, but she transformed it into a natural history library second to none outside London, impeccably conserved and catalogued. She also had responsibility for editing the Society's publication, *Transactions*, which still enjoys an international circulation. In 1974 she was awarded the MBE for "services as secretary of the Northumberland Natural History Society, and in 1980 the Society elected her an honorary member.

Following Russell Goddard's death, Grace continued his work on the Farne Islands. She turned his notebooks into a diary and continued her own observations. Her legacy was 22 volumes packed with information about the wildlife of the Farnes, essential material for future researchers. Through her field work on the Farnes her name became synonymous with the islands, and in 1951 she published her first book, *The Farne Islands: Their History and Wildlife*. (Watt 1951), which she dedicated to her friend Russel Goddard.

In April, May and June it was the birds that drew Grace to the islands, because, from 1949, the NNHS was the only body allowed to ring birds on the Farne Islands and Grace was the named "A" class ringer responsible for directing the ringing and sending all the paperwork back to the British Trust for Ornithology. Under her direction, a staggering total of 187,600, seabirds were ringed, many of which, particularly terns, she ringed herself.

Every year she prepared the report for the National Trust and was always very excited to hear of "her" birds being recovered from all corners of the world. For her services to bird protection, she was awarded the Silver Medal of the Royal Society for the Protection of Birds in 1959.

During their calving period, in October, November and December her attention turned to the grey seals. In 1951 Grace, along with Dr Ian Telfer, initiated the numbered tagging of seals and it was only 15 days later that the first tagged seal turned up in Oslo. They were delighted and a new branch of seal study was begun. From then onwards, every year Grace ensured the counting, weighing, measuring, tagging and general research on seals. She became an international authority on seals and, in 1962, published her second book, *Grey Seals and the Farne Islands*. (Hickling 1962).

The crossing to the Farne Islands is not for the faint hearted, especially in winter and sometimes the weather was so bad that it was necessary for Grace to travel by helicopter to maintain the continuity of her research. Grace also served enthusiastically on the Farne Islands Local Committee of the National Trust, which enabled her to contribute to their protection.

Grace Hickling played a major role, over seven years in negotiations leading up to the establishment in 1964, of the Lindisfarne National Nature Reserve and from that date she was the naturalists' representative on the Wildfowl Panel that advised the Nature Conservancy Council.

Somehow Grace did manage to have other interests outside natural history. Always proud of her Cambridge degree, she was chairman of the Northumbrian Cambridge Association. At one time she served as chairman of Gosforth Urban District Council. She was a governor of three schools, as well as a vice-president of the Literary and Philosophical Society of Newcastle, the distinguished parent body from which the Natural History Society had emerged in 1829.

Grace's work was her life and she left little time for what is now called downtime, or personal recreation. She lived with her widowed father until his death in 1969, from which time she lived alone. She enjoyed driving but never wanted to have a television set. Her holidays were spent either on her black and white photographic studies of great English houses or visiting Scarborough with her cousin. It was not until her 70th year that she could be persuaded to take a holiday abroad, and unsurprisingly she chose an island, Madeira, to which she returned several times.

Whilst in Madeira in 1982 she became ill and required a major abdominal operation, from which she recovered but which seems to have weakened her. In June 1986 she had a fall when visiting the Farnes and brushed it off as nothing but complained subsequently of headaches. In December that same year she collapsed at home and died there, alone.

In accordance with her wishes, Grace Hickling's ashes were scattered on the sands of St. Cuthbert's Cove on the Inner Farne on March 20th 1987, the 1300th anniversary of the death of St. Cuthbert in that same place. In 1988 the Natural History Society of Northumbria, placed a bronze plaque into the rock face at St Cuthbert's cove in memory of Grace. It depicts arctic terns in flight and states simply: "Grace Hickling 1908-1986 protector of Northumbrian wildlife." A very well-deserved accolade.

Dr Marie Victoire Lebour (1876 - 1971)

Marine biologist of enduring influence

A rare photograph of Dr Marie Victoire Lebour.

At the end of the obituary of Marie Lebour that appeared in the *Journal of the Marine Biological Association of Great Britain* in 1972, the list of her published works - 175 in total - took up five pages. The earliest was dated 1900 and the most recent 1959. As well as articles of varying lengths the list contained important books and standard reference works. There is no doubt that Marie Lebour was a scholar and an expert who, by general agreement, managed to combine in her extraordinary output both astounding quality and quantity.

Marie was born in West Woodburn, Northumberland, in 1876, the youngest of three daughters of Professor George Lebour and his wife Emily. Professor Lebour, born in St. Omer in Northern France and the son of an artist, had studied at the Royal College of Mines in London and then came to Durham University's Science College, (later Armstrong College, Newcastle) in 1873 to take up a lectureship in geology. He became Professor six years later, a post he would hold for 39 years until retirement in 1918. He wrote *Handbook to the Geology and Natural History of Northumberland and Durham* which was published in a number of editions from 1879 onwards.

Marie's childhood seems to have been a happy one and, no doubt through her father's influence, her interest in natural history and in the plant and animal life of the Northumberland countryside where she was growing up was awakened at an early age. She also showed early on a talent for drawing, perhaps inherited from her French artist grandfather.

Indeed it was to study art that she first enrolled at Armstrong College as a student but at some point switched to zoology where she achieved an Associate degree in 1903, her B.Sc in 1904 and a Master's Degree in 1907. From these dates it would seem that she began her university studies when she was already in her 20s - this late starting date perhaps explained by the fact that in those days it was unusual for a woman to enter higher education at all and the opportunities for them to do so happened only slowly as more institutions decided to admit women alongside men and as more courses became available to them.

Marie's interest in marine biology was evident even before her formal studies in zoology began as her first published article about molluscs in Northumberland "collected chiefly at Corbridge-on-Tyne and on the lower Tweed" appeared in 1900. This was followed two years later with an article on "Marine Mollusca of Sandsend, Yorkshire". These articles were a sign of things to come since it was her later discoveries about the life-histories of molluscs that advanced human knowledge of them significantly.

Marie was appointed to the staff of Armstrong College when she obtained her B.Sc in 1904 and then in 1906, when still studying for her Master's Degree, took up the post of Junior Demonstrator in Zoology at Leeds University. She became an Assistant Lecturer at Leeds in 1909. During her time there she also began working on her Doctorate, which she would eventually be awarded in 1917. Before that, however, in 1915 her services were offered by Leeds, with her agreement, to the Marine Biological Association's Laboratory in Plymouth, where staff numbers had been severely depleted because of men enlisting to serve in the First World War. The transfer to Plymouth was to last for the duration of the war, although the widespread expectation at that time was that the fighting would be over by the following year. Whether Marie preferred Plymouth because it was near the sea and, or whether, the laboratory work there suited her research interests more - or both - is not known, but it is on record that although she was offered a permanent post by Leeds in 1917 she opted to stay in Plymouth and indeed would remain there for the rest of her long career.

Marie's father died in 1918 and after that her widowed mother came to live with her, and her sister Yvonne, in the Mannamead area of Plymouth. Sadly it seems that only a short time after the move Marie's mother became an invalid, and both Marie and Yvonne became her carers. Marie reduced her hours at the laboratory from full time to two-thirds but continued to publish articles and conduct research at what appears to have been a breakneck rate! The role of carer did prevent her from travelling to faraway places, although it is clear that Marie's interests in the marine environment were not restricted to the waters around the south-west of England but were global.

Marie seemed to have been devoted to her family. She also found time to keep up with a circle of friends and she loved the company of children. One of the daughters of Professor Walter Garstang of Leeds, who had appointed Marie in 1906 and who became a lifelong friend and colleague, recalled, charmingly, how Marie would make paper animals "for Zoos and for Noah's Arks" for her and her sisters and what good company she was. Marie and her sister also liked entertaining friends, and the children of friends, in their flat where the cakes were always home-made.

The time from the end of the First World War up to the start of the Second World War was a particularly productive period of Marie's career and, although home commitments did not allow much travel, she did attend conferences and events in order to deliver papers and speak about her work. These occasions aroused interest in Marie and her research. Organisations such as the Women's Freedom League were always interested in women excelling in new roles and disciplines. In their publication *The Vote* of 29th August 1919 it was reported that Marie would be presenting a paper at the annual meeting of the British Association of Science, taking place in Bournemouth under the chairmanship, coincidentally, of another eminent Northumbrian, Sir Charles Parsons. In an issue in 1923 *The Vote* again reported Marie delivering a paper at the same organisation's annual conference, on that occasion in Liverpool.

Other newspapers and publications also profiled her and her work particularly in her discoveries about aspects of marine life. In a piece in the *Illustrated London News* of March 1933 about the discovery of the fascinating world beneath the ocean waves the reporter enthuses "Dr Marie Lebour is one of the wizards engaged in the discovery of these marvels. She always has something new to tell us."

Marie could never resist any opportunity to widen her research and if she could not travel herself found ways of using other peoples' travels for her benefit. In an article in *Science Progress* in 1933 she told how she had persuaded her brother-in-law, who was travelling to Ceylon (now Sri Lanka) on a cruise ship that had a running seawater bath to carry out experiments and collect samples of plankton for her. This involved a procedure of fitting bags and tubes containing a small amount of formalin over the bath taps for around an hour each time. It resulted in her detailing and illustrating a variety of life-forms found in the plankton of tropical seas.

Marie's articles and publications mostly contained her own illustrations. These were in her own distinctive style and were described as "more like sketches, but they never failed to emphasize the important critical diagnostic characters." The nature conservationist Dame Miriam Rothschild, who had worked with Marie, admired her drawings immensely and spoke of "the subtle quality of her marvellously gifted pencil" and "how her sketches embodied the 'feel' of the creature in question, possessing the quality of affectionate portraits as well as that of scientifically accurate diagrams."

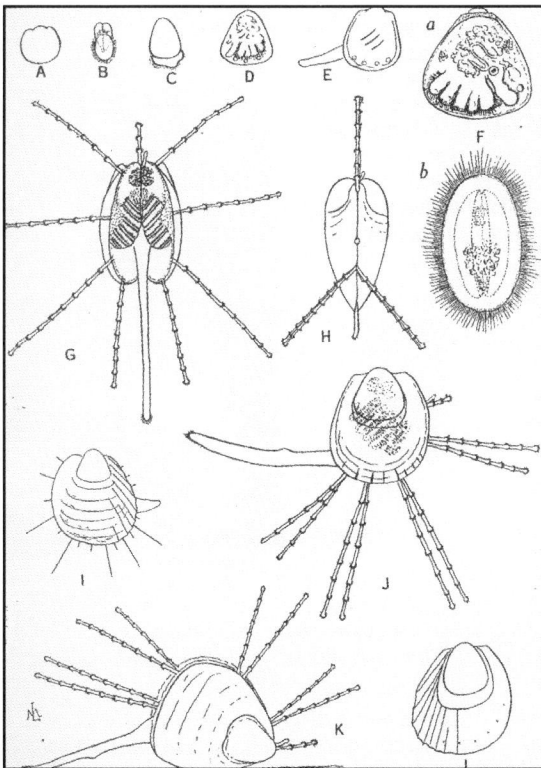

Illustrations from Dr Marie Lebour's paper: Larval and Post-larval Lima from Plymouth (Journal of the Marine Biological Association of the United Kingdom).

With the death of her mother in 1937, Marie returned to working full-time at Plymouth Laboratory and also was free to travel, accepting, in 1939, an opportunity to go on an expedition to Bermuda with two longstanding colleagues and friends, Professor Garstang and Dr Robert Gurney. Also joining them from America on the trip would be Dr Jaques of the Rockefeller Institute. All started well but tragedy struck. Marie and her colleagues had been taking every opportunity to go collecting marine samples and she and Dr Jacques went out one evening in failing light in a small dinghy and, while dredging for samples in the bay, their boat capsized. It turned out that neither of them could swim and while Marie managed to cling to the side of the boat and eventually, in a very distressed and semi-conscious state, was rescued, Dr Jacques disappeared into the water and was drowned. The incident was widely reported in the British press and understandably completely overshadowed an expedition that had begun with such optimism and eagerness.

Also in 1939 there was a happier occasion for Marie when she received a medal from the King of Belgium for her help in classifying natural history collections that had been made during a voyage he had undertaken to Asia in 1928-29.

Marie and her sister, after their mother's death, moved to a bungalow in Cawsand in East Cornwall across the water from Plymouth. Cawsand has been described as "Cornwall's forgotten south-east corner, a beautiful landscape of tidal creeks, sandy beaches, lush farmland and country parks". Marie and her sister apparently had a steep garden that they tended lovingly, climbing about it "like mountain goats". They loved the location and delighted in receiving visitors there.

In 1945 Marie formally retired from the Plymouth Laboratory but in practice continued much as before, visiting the laboratory regularly to carry out research and continuing to publish articles until her late eighties, thwarted only from continuing by failing eyesight.

Marie died on 2nd October 1971 at the age of 95. The obituary of her by Sir Frederick Russell, Director of the Plymouth Laboratory, contains many heartfelt tributes to her, both for her many achievements in marine research and for her many personal qualities. Sir Frederick himself says "She worked with great enthusiasm and energy and was never still; she walked always at a little jog-trot and I can well remember the sound of her footsteps as she pattered back and forth from her cubicle to her plunger-jars."

For Miriam Rothschild, her first impression of Marie was that "everyone came out of her room looking happy" and her "charming and welcoming smile continued, unfailingly, to dispense a lift of the heart."

Marie's academic standing and her research achievements continue to influence today's marine scientists and ecologists. In an article in the *Journal of Plankton* research, from October 2021, John R Dolan wrote "Marie Lebour was not only a pioneer of plankton research, but also a public proponent of the importance and beauty of the plankton". Many other aspects of Marie's marine studies also continue to influence and inform those following in her footsteps today.

Above all Marie's work is relevant to many concerns about our marine environment, in an era of global warming. This includes such issues as how global warming may affect the availability of some plankton that are a primary food source in the marine supply chain and what amount of plankton in the future may be able to help reduce atmospheric CO_2 levels.

Although Marie, by all accounts, was never given to boasting perhaps she had some inkling of how long lasting her legacy would be. There is no doubt that from all that we know of her she deserves to be remembered and honoured.

Dr Marie Victoire Lebour.

Constance Leathart (1903 - 1993)

Pioneering aviator and brave wartime pilot

Constance Leathart was a remarkable woman, one of the first women aviators and the first woman in the UK outside London to get a pilot's licence. She never courted publicity and surprisingly little has been written about her but her place in aviation history fully deserves to be recognised, especially so in the North East of England, her home area.

Constance (Con) was born in Low Fell, Gateshead, in comfortable circumstances. When she was three years old the family moved to Low Angerton, near Hartburn in Northumberland. An only child, she was educated at the boarding schools Cheltenham Ladies College and Queen Ethelburga's Collegiate, near York. One of her contemporaries at Queen Ethelburga's - and a close friend - was Susan Slade, another early woman aviator who obtained her pilot's licence a year after Con. Sadly their long friendship would come to a tragic end with Susan's death in an air crash during war service in 1944.

Con's photo albums are held in the Northumberland County Archives at Woodhorn and reveal what seems to have been a happy childhood in the Northumberland countryside with an obvious attachment to dogs, horses and country pursuits. She also seems to have had an interest in flying from an early age, perhaps because her childhood coincided with some of the key and exciting early developments in aviation history.

By 1925, aged 22, she had become one of the pioneering members of the Newcastle Aero Club based in Cramlington. When she first applied to join the club she gave her name on the application form as C R Leathart and was accepted before it was known she was a woman. She managed to convince the members of her seriousness about flying and of her determination to succeed on entirely equal terms with male colleagues. She obtained her pilot's licence in 1927 having persisted in her commitment to flying despite a crash landing on her first solo flight and also following the tragic death of her former instructor in a flying accident. She overcame physical challenges being short and stocky in build, and short-sighted. At the time a newspaper report described her as "a vivacious Eton-cropped girl, she probably knows more about the innards of a plane than many male pilots." Con's family were surprised at her enthusiasm for flying and she recalled many years later how they had said to her "What are you doing with all this silly flying? It will never be any good to you" - a prediction which turned out to be entirely false given Con's later wartime service. Con herself wrote that she thought she would get bored by it but became "keener than ever" as time went by.

During the late 1920s and 30s Con became friends with the other pioneer women pilots including Amy Johnson, who gained her pilot's licence in 1929. Con's albums contain photographs of some of the early women aviators and reveal an obvious camaraderie as they sought to prove their value in what was very much a man's world. They attracted considerable publicity. As John Sleight put it, "Long before the dawn of equal opportunity, a small band of women in the 1930s set countless hearts beating with their daring exploits in aviation." Con herself described her friend Amy Johnson as "having plenty of guts" and as "a very nice person". Poignantly, she was to spend time with Amy Johnson the night before Amy died in a wartime crash in 1941.

Press clippings from the 1920s and 30s reveal just how exciting - and frequently precarious - Con's aviation experiences were. She took part in many competitions - some in wretched weather conditions - on equal terms with men and won a number of prizes in races with her name being recorded on the honours board of the Woolsington clubhouse in Newcastle. There is a delightful account in Newcastle's *North Mail* in 1927 by a journalist accompanying Con on one of her flights, who described her piloting skill as "already a by-word at the club" and that she had done "some of the finest stunt exhibitions ever performed by a club member." The same article describes flying over the River Tyne and looking down at the unfinished steel work of the new bridge (the Tyne Bridge) which was to be completed in 1929.

The dangers of flying were ever present in those early years. In 1928 Con was amongst those pilots searching for a missing airman in the Scottish Borders. She herself survived further crash landings; in 1930 - when her plane did a somersault on landing - and again in 1931, when she had to crash land in a meadow near Munich. On this second occasion it was reported that she subsequently "strolled to the hangars and supervised the dismantling of the machine" obviously undaunted by her ordeal.

Con was the first woman in Britain to design and fly a glider, which she did at Cramlington in 1930. She participated in gliding competitions at home and in Germany. She was also, in her Tiger Moth, one of the first women to fly over the Alps. She described how spending four hours in a cockpit in those early planes left you "pretty stiff" and also recalled in later life how "in the old days you flew with only a compass and followed the line of the railway tracks" and how "it was very nice because you got to know the country very well!"

Con preferred, as did many women pilots, to fly solo. As Amelia Earhart put it after her flight across the Atlantic - "I had made up my mind to fly alone, because if there is a man in the machine you can bet your life he wants to take control, and I was determined that if I did it again I was the one who was going to control the machine."

Not restricting herself to flying, Con also started an aircraft repair business at Cramlington with Walter Runciman, a dashing and handsome fellow Northumbrian and obviously a great friend given the number of photos of him contained in her albums. Working together they both acquired business experience and knowledge of aeroplane mechanics.

Contemporary descriptions of Con vary. From "petite" and "vivacious" in early newspaper articles to "very short and extraordinarily square", which was the later description of Molly Rose who served under Con in wartime. Molly also said that she was "amazed that she was tall enough or agile enough to cope with flying" All, however, recognised just what a dedicated, fearless and able aviator she was.

She was also remembered as "mannish" with a liking for Woodbines, cigars and whisky - particularly between bouts of flying! Photographs, particularly when wearing her aviation suits - do indeed show Con as "mannish" but, not surprisingly, women aviators in general took care not to dress in feminine or what would have been seen as unsuitable clothes, risking male derision, and they often favoured the Eton crop hairstyle more suited to flying than having long flowing locks! In her photo album Con occasionally comments ruefully on her less than glamorous appearance but in a no-nonsense and down to earth way gives the impression of being thoroughly comfortable in her own skin, an impression confirmed by those who knew her and who were part of her wide circle of friends, both male and female. She certainly didn't want being a woman to stop her from participating in male-dominated occupations and pastimes. As a child she had been a tomboy and clearly continued to enjoy sporting and adventurous activities as an adult. It is not known if she had any romantic attachments but one of her friends remembered her talking about a man she had met, but where she confessed that the relationship "had never got beyond a trot!".

By the start of the Second World War, Con, aged 36, was already a hugely experienced aviator having flown 16 different kinds of aeroplanes and clocked up hundreds of flying hours. This level of experience was indeed greater than many of the young male pilots, including those who were destined for bombing missions. Con, along with other women aviators volunteered her services for the war effort straightaway and, after a short spell in the

map room at Bristol, was accepted to take part in the Air Transport Auxiliary.

At the beginning of the war, the role that women pilots could play was not at first fully appreciated. It was recognised that qualified women pilots could play a useful part in flying planes within the UK, delivering them to different air bases for onward missions, or for maintenance and refuelling. But women pilots, however experienced, would not be used for combat and there were limits on the number of hours they could fly and the speed at which they could fly. They were also not to be allowed to fly solo. Before long, some of these restrictions were recognised as being unrealistic, not least through the determination of the women concerned to show just how capable they could be at the controls. With regard to the speed restrictions imposed on women of not exceeding 250 miles an hour when flying a Spitfire, the aviation historian Richard Poad commented "you tell that to a hot-blooded woman or man in a plane that will do 400. They weren't supposed to go low flying - they did. They weren't supposed to do stunts - they did." Con herself described the Spitfire as being a very easy plane to fly and the technical side of her work seemed to offer her no new or difficult challenges.

Overall Con's war record was impressive. She rose to the rank of flight captain and was involved in flying many aircraft, including heavy bombers, to airfields in many countries. However, she describes how, after four years' service towards the end of the war, she was unable to continue as a pilot because "of reacting the wrong way to a flu jab" and becoming seriously ill as a result. She eventually recovered and in the aftermath of war was able to resume flying as part of the United Nations Relief and Rehabilitation organisation, work that was also challenging and dangerous at times. A telling example of Con's bravery and resourcefulness when undertaking such missions - was her flight, carrying much needed provisions, to the Greek island of Icaria which had been all but destroyed under Nazi occupation. The islanders, traumatised and near starvation, feared that Con's plane was part of yet another enemy attack and were hostile and highly suspicious of her when she landed there. Keeping her cool in a dangerous and volatile situation she managed to win the people over by talking reassuringly and explaining that she was bringing in vital food supplies and other necessities. Con was especially touched by the plight of the children on the island and on her return lobbied for more assistance to be given to them urgently.

Following her involvement in this work Con was given the award of merit by the International Union of Child Welfare. She was also hailed as a "British heroine" in an effusive letter from the Greek Government commenting on her international post-war relief efforts.

By the time Con returned permanently to her Northumberland home she had been away for seven years on war and post-war duties. She continued to fly for a few years afterwards and was remembered by Jim Denyer (Mr Newcastle Airport), himself a distinguished pilot in peace and war. He admired Con greatly, describing her as a "lovely lady" and recalled her flying her own plane "with great expertise" when he arrived in Woolsington in 1951. For a few years after the war, she continued to run her Cramlington aircraft repair company, but closed the business and retired from flying in around 1958.

After retiring from aviation - after 30 years flying - she spent the rest of her life in her Northumbrian farmhouse near Little Bavington, running her cattle and sheep farm. There she also cared for rescue donkeys. Her friends and family, including her cousin Eileen Burn, remember her sending donkey charity Christmas cards each year.

Some descriptions of her in her long retirement have portrayed her as being something of a recluse but this is hotly contested by many who were close to her. They describe a very sociable woman who enjoyed company and gave wonderful picnics and parties with "lovely stews, keeping hot in old fashioned vacuum flasks". She also liked playing poker - and usually won! A friend, Mary Gray, related a charming anecdote about Con and her mother Ruth who gave a party on a train in 1953 on the Wannie railway line which ran from Morpeth, through Scots Gap to the Borders with a branch line to Rothbury. The line had been closed to passengers the year before and was restricted to occasional freight service. However Con and her mother managed to hire a train to host the party and apparently their friends got on the train at the various stations nearest to their homes, between Morpeth and Rothbury where they all enjoyed food and champagne and where they alighted at various points to admire the scenery, finally arriving at Rothbury to a formal welcome by station staff!

Con died, aged 89, in 1993, a month before her 90th birthday. Her loyal friends and admirers were torn between respecting her wish for little publicity while wanting to make sure that her remarkable and inspirational life should not be forgotten. Her funeral was a very simple one, in accordance with what she had wanted, but even so a number of people were present for the internment in Thockrington Churchyard - a lovely, remote, Northumbrian churchyard not far from Con's home. She did not want a formal headstone but her friend Derek Ions, who with his wife Dora cared devotedly for her in her later years, discreetly carved her initials into the stepping stone that she used to get in and out of her "rather leafy" swimming pool at her farm, and placed the stone in the churchyard.

Given that she had died just before her 90th birthday her close friends, after the funeral, returned to her home and ate the cake that had been prepared for her birthday celebration. Along with some champagne they toasted her memory and hoped in doing so that Con would have appreciated and enjoyed this gesture of friendship and affection from those people she held most dear.

Sarah Losh (1786 - 1853)

Architect, philanthropist and visionary

The small and exquisite Church of St Mary in the hamlet of Wreay near Carlisle, is recognised as one of the hundred best churches in England. A masterpiece of English Art, it is classified as a Grade ll * listed building. This beautiful, unique, eccentric church is the creation of Sarah Losh, who, between 1839 and 1842, designed and commissioned it. She alone was its architect.

The Losh family were Cumbrians from Wreay, a hamlet five miles South of Carlisle, very close to the Northumbrian border. In the mid-19th century, the Laird of the family seat, Woodside, was John Losh. He produced four sons, who set out to make their fortunes in the new industries on the Tyne. All four men achieved eminence and became identified with the public and industrial life of Newcastle. John, Sarah's father, founded the Walker Alkali works, which became one of the most successful manufacturing establishments in the country. James, a lawyer, became Recorder of Newcastle, the highest legal office in the city, and a founder member of the Literary and Philosophical Society. George was a chemical manufacturer and William started the ironworks of Messrs Losh, Wilson and Bell which was also very successful. They were a close family, radicals, free thinkers, scientific experimenters, friends of the Lakeland poets, they campaigned against slavery and for toleration and reform.

Sarah was the first child of John and his wife Isabella. The second child, died in infancy. Katherine was born in 1788, and finally, Joseph, was born in 1789, but he had severe learning disabilities and had to be looked after all his life. This meant that the two girls would inherit the family estates.

The girls, educated at home, were eager and bright scholars, Sarah being the cleverer, more studious and reserved of the two, Katherine more outgoing and easy. Their father and uncle James were Cambridge men, and uncle James was passionate about women's education and ensured that when he couldn't teach Sarah and Katherine himself, the best tutors would be engaged.

Sarah was exceptional in her mastery of Greek, Latin, Italian, French, mathematics and music. After the unexpected death of their mother in 1799, James was even more conscientious in his care for them and for Robert. Throughout their lives, the girls moved between Woodside, Carlisle and Newcastle, staying with aunts and uncles and cousins. They routinely visited London, Bath and Bristol and of course the Lake District, all the time mixing with intellectuals and friends like the Wordsworths, and the Edgeworths. Both

sisters attended "coming out balls" in Carlisle when they came of age and, though they were the Belles of the Ball in every sense, marriage and family life did not appeal to the sisters. They were handsome, charming and rich but they rejected all proposals of marriage preferring each other's companionship and life as the accomplished daughters of John Losh.

Sarah and Katherine lived uncomplicated lives at Woodside. They engaged in good works, they gardened, sketched, read the poetry of Byron and the novels of Scott, they read books on history, architecture, religion, science and geology. Sarah was a voracious reader throughout her life. They walked the fells, explored the Solway and discovered for themselves old churches and buildings, like St Bridget's church in Bridekirk, Naworth Castle, Lanercost Priory, Hadrian's Wall and the Bewcastle cross.

When their father died in 1813, the sisters became independent young women of very considerable means. No doubt to distract them from their grief, they spent three months travelling in Holland and France in 1814. Then in 1816 they set off on their own Grand Tour, visiting France, Germany, Switzerland and Italy. Sarah filled seven notebooks with comment and sketches of everything that struck her strongly, particularly in Rome, Naples and

Pompeii. Sarah had become very interested in architecture in her 20s and this European tour certainly stimulated her interest and ideas.

After their European tour the sisters embarked on a number of quite major architectural projects. They greatly enlarged Woodside, creating more light and space. They completely replaced the Georgian facade with a Tudor-style facade. They installed mullioned windows with Gothic style inner frames to complete the Tudor look. No architect was involved, this was all their own work. It was at about this time that Sarah set up a studio-cum-workshop and invited local carpenters and stonemasons to teach her some of their skills. Her library was enlarged with all sorts of learned tomes on architecture and world religions, books that she read with great pleasure and fervour.

Because they owned virtually the whole village, the land, the houses and the shops as well as the Plough Inn, and because they took their responsibilities seriously, they built a little Dame school for the girls of the village, and later they built a new school for the village that was completed in 1830. While it was not uncommon for the women of landowning families to fund and supervise the building of schools, it was unknown for them to design them and work as architect and site manager, as was the case here. They also built a schoolmaster's house nearby in a style copied from their visit to Pompeii.

Disaster struck Sarah's personal life when, in 1833, Uncle James Losh died from a stroke and tragically two years later, Katherine became ill and died aged only 47. Sarah was utterly inconsolable in her grief. These were the two people closest to her and Katherine had been the light of her life. Although she wore the dark colours of mourning for the rest of her life, she did eventually recover. Sarah was 50 years old at the time and when her period of deep mourning was over she must have woken up and decided to channel her creativity and her knowledge and skills, all she knew of architecture and art into a church to commemorate her parents and Katherine. But first she built a Mortuary Chapel for the village, loosely copied from a centuries old ruin, recently uncovered among the Cornish dunes at Perranzabuloe.

She then approached the Twelve Men of the village, who were responsible for the roads and fences, the church and the people, and offered to build a new church to replace the existing dilapidated chapel.

She offered "to furnish a new site for the chapel and defray all the expenses of its re-erection, on condition that I should be left unrestricted as to the mode of building it".

They agreed, and a faculty to rebuild Wreay chapel was granted on 20th May, 1841. It allowed Sarah to take down the existing structure and build a "more commodious" church within 30 yards of the old one.

A brief word about Sarah's financial position. When their father died in

1813, Sarah and Katherine each inherited an equal half share of his wealth; the family seat and estates and the very lucrative Walker Alkali Works. (Alkali was essential to the weaving industry, the manufacture of soap and glass production, and throughout the century, provided an excellent dependable income). When Katherine died in 1834, all this passed to Sarah, who retained control of the Alkali works until 1847 when she sold them to her uncle. As the years passed, Sarah's wealth increased to include shares in her uncles' iron works and the family investments in the rail industry. The money for Sarah's church came at least in part from business interests in Newcastle.

Work began in 1841. The new St Mary's was built by a team of local builders, led by William Hindson - a gifted stonemason. So popular were both Sarah and the project that local people gave their labour free when they could. It was constructed using local stone, local timber and local glaziers, and Sarah was on site nearly every day directing the workmen in their operations.

The style of the church is simple and rustic, Sarah described it as very early Saxon or modified Lombardic. The shape is a rectangular nave, with rounded arches and a chancel apse, not unlike a small Byzantine basilica but unique in Britain at the time.

The Church is decorated as no other, with a wealth of symbols drawn from earlier religions and nature, it is a celebration of the creation and is not in many ways specifically Christian, for unusually there is no cross any where in the church. On each outside elevation is carved a monstrous gargoyle. The window embrasures are decorated with larger-than-life carvings of flora and fauna. Motifs include the caterpillar, chrysalis and butterfly, symbols of life death and resurrection. There are carvings of ammonites, wheat, coral and poppies and other items.

Inside the nave is plain but the light is filtered through lovely stained glass; bright leaves on black backgrounds, mosaics and cut outs of fossils. The larger windows were made by William Wailes of Newcastle and transported by train. The chancel arch has an elegant frieze of angels and palm trees. The chancel itself is quite remarkable with its arcaded apse and closely spaced columns and painted surrounds.

The furnishings are superbly executed. The font is adorned with butterflies, and pomegranates and was carved by Sarah herself. The pulpit is a hollow tree-trunk made from black oak dug up from a nearby bog. The lectern is supported by an eagle and the reading desk by a stork. Both were carved by a crippled man, John Scott from Dalston. Instead of a cross on the altar there are two lotus-shaped candlesticks, symbols of light and continuity, these were carved in rose-pink alabaster by Sarah assisted by William Septimus.

No description of St Mary's church, Wreay, would be complete without

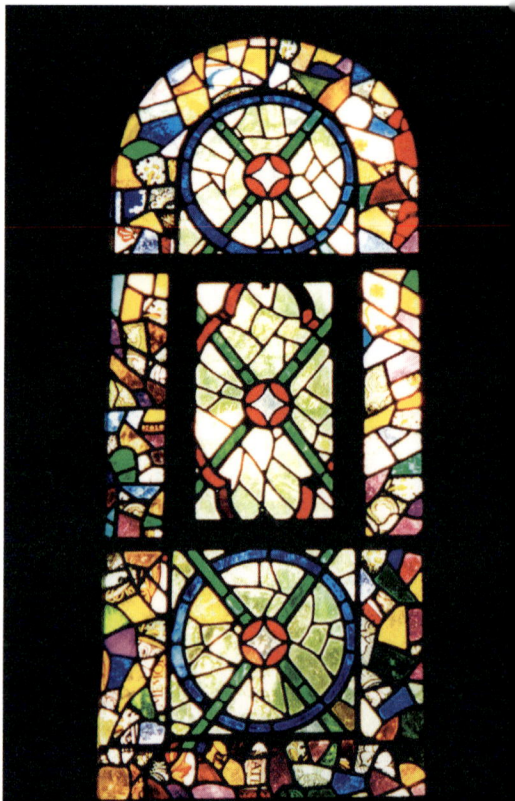

Clockwise from top: The interior of the church of St Mary in Wreay, with its winged-turtle gargoyle, a window by William Wailes and octagonal alabaster font.

Photos courtesy of the Friends of St Mary's Church.

mentioning the pine cones. They are everywhere, carved into the roof beams, as corbels for the door arch, on the walls and used as doorhandles. There are two reasons for this. Sarah loved the idea of the pine cone as an ancient symbol of regeneration and enlightenment, and the idea that mathematicians, like herself, reverence the pine cone as a graphic example of the "Sacred Geometry" of nature. But there was a more personal reason too. Major William Thain was a family friend who often came to stay at Woodside. Sarah and he were friends for many years until his death. A gallant soldier, he fought at Waterloo but died on the Afghan frontier in 1842. The last missive William had sent to Sarah was a pine cone, and the news of his death reached her as she was building her church.

William Thain's death may also be the explanation for the mysterious single arrow that can be seen in the church, piercing the wall above the baptistery. Sarah never offered any explanation of it. Perhaps it was a symbol of unexpected death, or of a heart pierced with grief.

The church was consecrated in December 1842, to great local acclaim, but while the church of St Mary may have been finished, Sarah had more to do. She went on to make a reproduction of the Bewcastle Cross as a memorial to her parents. On the base of the cross the Latin inscription reads, "Two daughters proposed that this stone be set up: one, greatly sorrowing performed it." And then in 1847 she built a mausoleum, a memorial to Katherine herself. She could see nothing beautiful in Katherine's death and deliberately created quite an ugly building and commissioned the local sculptor Dunbar, to make the serene white marble statue of Katherine to place within it, trapped forever in a sunless box of stone. Katherine is depicted sitting, her head bent as if reading, but it is not a book, but a pine cone she holds, with its promise that life, art and creation will go on.

In her final years Sarah continued her quiet philanthropy, helping the poor wherever she could. Her name appears on many subscribers lists, and as always she entertained her family and friends and continued to read widely. She did undertake one last building project, begun in 1843 and completed in 1849, she restored the Anglo-Norman church at Newton Arlosh on the Solway plain, at her own expense. (Her family hailed from Newton Arlosh.) However, in 1849, she became very ill and although she recovered she began to suffer increasingly from bouts of bronchitis, which greatly weakened her. In March 1853, aged 67, Sarah died from dysentery.

Sarah is buried with her sister in Wreay churchyard. The gravestone, decorated with scallop shells and plants, says simply, "Katherine Isabella Losh, died February 1835 aged 47. Sarah Losh died March 29 1853. And in Latin, - Parted in life, in death reunited. Lord let thy Mercy lighten upon us."

Upon her death, Henry Lonsdale, who dedicated a chapter to her in his *Worthies of Cumberland* described Sarah as, "unassuming, generous and impressively intellectual, well informed in architecture, and history and English lore - the beautifullest of women - a study for the historian and philanthropist."

Sarah's work is wonderful and groundbreaking and without any forerunner. Historians have failed to find any pattern book from which Sarah could have derived her ideas. In 1860, Gabriel Rossetti, wrote, "she must have been a really great genius and should be better known". Rossetti described the Pompeiian cottage, the cemetery, the mortuary chapel based on the lost church in the dunes and the Tudor wing at Woodside: "all these things are real works of genius, but especially the church at Wreay, a most beautiful thing. She was entirely without systematic study as an architect, but her practical as well as inventive powers were extraordinary."

Of course no training was available to women at that time. The institute of Architects (founded in 1834) was a male preserve, and the RIBA would not admit women until 1898. Sarah was deemed a mere amateur.

When William Pevsner saw the church in 1967 he was dumbfounded at her, "amazingly forward-pointing building." He wrote that, "it has a solidity all of its own ... its symbolic carvings have no parallel at all, in fact one might make the mistake of dating St Mary, Wreay, as one example of the Byzantine revival which took place about 1900 and its carvings as Arts and Crafts". Simon Jenkins, in his book *England's Thousand Best Churches* describes Sarah as a "Charlotte Bronte in wood and stone. All of this wonderful work is the work of an individual genius and the Arts and Crafts Movement took half a century to catch up with her."

And finally Pugin's biographer, Rosemary Hill, asks how important is Losh's work? Her answer is, "If artistic feeling is to be measured by an ability to seize the currents of thought and feeling that flow through the age and give them fresh and vital expression, Sarah Losh and her church are very important indeed."

The beautiful church of St Mary Wreay is still in use and should be on everyone's bucket list.

Church of St Mary in Wreay, near Carlisle

Mary Ann Macham made a remarkable journey to arrive in the North East.

Mary Ann Macham (1802 - 1893)

Escaped slavery and lived in North Shields for 60 years

For 40 years Mr and Mrs James Blyth lived a quiet and upright life in North Shields, he a rope maker, she a domestic servant, an unremarkable couple at first glance. However, Mrs Blyth, was an escaped slave, a fugitive from a sugar plantation in Virginia in the United States of America, where, as Mary Ann Macham, she had endured a life of unspeakable hardship, degradation and cruelty. She arrived in North Shields completely alone on Christmas Day in 1831, a 29-year-old single mixed-race woman, met by two Quaker women, Mary and Sarah Spence, abolitionists, who welcomed her into their community.

Mary Ann, the child of a white slave owner and a black slave, was born in 1802 in Virginia and seemed destined for a life of cruelty and hardship. She was taken from her mother, Judy, at only 15 months old, and looked after by her father's sister until she was sold into slavery to pay a debt. She was badly treated for many years and then as a 12-year-old girl, was taken with 150 other slaves to be put up for sale at Richmond Slave Market, no better than a cattle market, where the slaves were subjected to humiliating physical examinations to ensure they were a "good investment". At the tender age of 12, Mary Ann fetched a price of $450 and was taken to a large plantation in Richmond, where she was to remain for the next 17 years of her life.

In later years Mary Ann dictated an account of her life as a slave. She was regularly whipped with cowhides which left permanent scars. All slaves, old and young, male and female, were whipped regularly for minor offences, usually naked, tied to something to keep them upright and avoiding their faces lest the damage would disfigure and reduce their market value. Another favourite punishment was solitary confinement, slaves were locked up alone from Saturday to Monday. Mary recounted that she was often locked up, once for helping a young girl who was learning to knit to pick up a dropped stitch!

Conditions for slaves were particularly difficult in 1831 because sugar was becoming less profitable, so slaves were made to work even harder to keep profits up. The year Mary escaped there was a black rebellion, "Nat Turners Rebellion," in Virginia. Slaves rose up and killed more than 50 of their white enslavers, before being defeated and suffering terrible reprisals.

In her account, Mary explained that her escape was assisted by a friend who hid her until she could get on board a vessel to take her to Holland then on to England. For days she hid in trees to avoid the bloodhounds. It was impossible to sleep up a tree and she was cold and terrified, not just of capture but of deadly snakes. When it became too cold, she hid in a hayloft. Because she was considered "valuable property" a reward had been offered for her return, dead or alive and so the search was intense and prolonged. For days she was petrified by the shouting, the baying of bloodhounds and the hullabaloo of the persistent search.

After many terrifying days, when she was so desperate she almost gave herself up, the boat arrived. She was smuggled aboard by the second mate, but it was a further 10 days before the vessel, the *Atlas*, was laden and ready to go, during which time local police and customs officers came aboard several times searching for her but miraculously she remained undiscovered. The first mate undertook to conceal her through the long sea voyage to Flushing. She was hidden among the water casks in the damp hold, where the smell was foul and she became stiff with the cold.

The *Atlas* left Cape Henry in August and reached Flushing 60 long days later due to very rough seas, during which time she had only biscuits and water to sustain her. Because the Dutch and Belgians were at war in 1831, it took a further six weeks to find a buyer for their cargo. During this time, a stevedore hid her away in lodgings in Flushing, pretending she was his American cousin. The ship eventually left Flushing for Grimsby and from there they sailed to Hull. The rest of her journey was by coach, to York, and on to North Shields, arriving on Christmas morning, 1831. Her traumatic, life-threatening journey was over. She was safe.

Mary Ann knew little of the world she had arrived in, or of the huge effort that was being made by so many to abolish slavery. Although the slave trade had been abolished in 1807, slavery itself still flourished and evidence of the horrific treatment of slaves was piling up, so that by 1831 the abolitionist campaign had intensified with a torrent of anti-slavery propaganda and petitions presented to parliament. 35 petitions were sent from the north east, including both North and South Shields. When news of the 1831 rebellion in Jamaica and the wicked reprisals that followed it reached Britain, as many as 40,000 people attended a rally in Newcastle and more than a million signatures on petitions demanding immediate emancipation reached Parliament from all over the country.

So it was that *The Abolition of Slavery Act* made slavery illegal throughout the British Empire in 1833, amid great, if qualified, rejoicing amongst abolitionists up and down the land. However, slavery was still widespread elsewhere, and the abolition of slavery in America became the new target for abolitionist activity until 1865, with the final emancipation of American slaves. Mary Ann's life in North Shields spanned these same years and throughout them the quiet generosity of the whole Spence family supported and concealed her.

There was a long tradition of Quaker-led anti-slavery activity in the North East, dating back to the 18th century, and North East abolitionists became deeply engaged in the campaign to end slavery in America. Mary had arrived in a town that was a hive of abolitionist activity. The North Shields Anti-Slavery Society was spearheaded by the leading Quaker families of the town, notable among them the Spence family. Robert Spence, father of the young women who had first welcomed Mary Ann to North Shields, organised and chaired the abolitionist meetings, meetings that attracted audiences of 500. Ann Spence, a younger daughter often hosted the Afro-American abolitionists and fugitive slave speakers at her home, Low Light Tannery House.

There was a stream of charismatic African American visitors to the town, fugitive slaves and dedicated abolitionists who addressed meetings. A delegate from North Shields attended to the first World Slavery Convention in 1840.

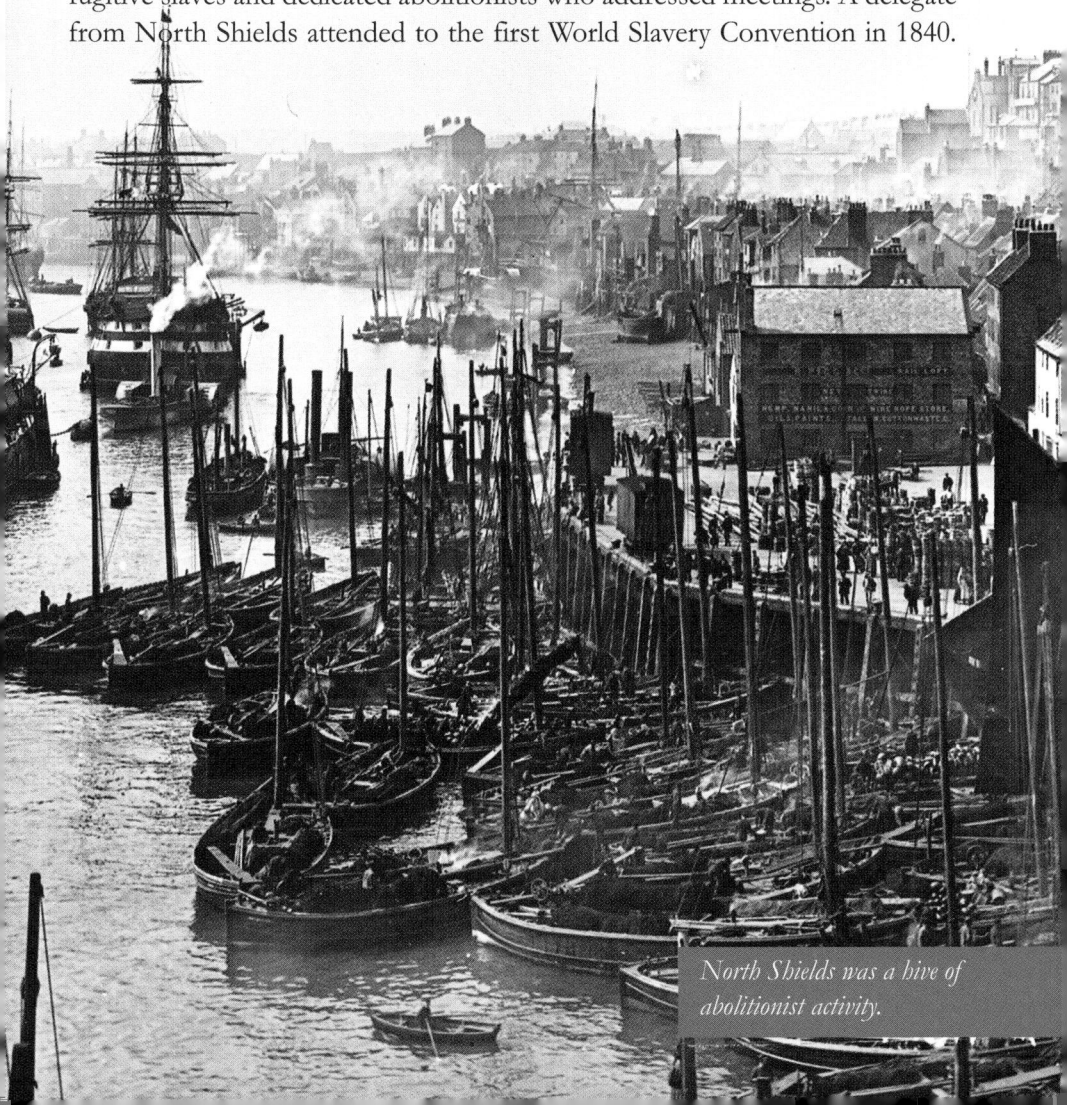

North Shields was a hive of abolitionist activity.

During the 1840s and 1850s there was a Ladies Free Produce Society in the town and Harriet Beecher Stowe's visit to the area had such a profound effect that the owner of the Railway Tavern in Bedford Street, changed its name to "Uncle Tom's Cabin". During the years 1840 to 1845 Harriet Martineau, that staunch opponent of slavery, was living only 10 minutes' walk away in Tynemouth Front Street.

Given that Mary Ann lived with and worked for the Spence family in North Shields during this period of intense anti-slavery activity, it seems likely that she would have met some of the speakers personally, especially those who, like herself, were escaped slaves from America. They included Frederick Douglass and William Wells Brown. Perhaps she was involved in the Ladies' Free Produce Society. She may have watched black entertainers in local theatres. North Shields was, of course, a major port and its residents would have been used to seeing black sailors from the merchant ships and ships of the Royal Navy but there is no record of any other black women in the area at this time.

Her own life in North Shields as a domestic servant and home maker was below the radar of the public gaze. The little we know of Mary Ann's life in North Shields has been gleaned from official public records, from censuses, certificates and directories. The lack of any other information about her, in the local press or in minute books, is because the Spence family were protecting her privacy. Mary Ann had already suffered the horrific physical and mental traumas of her early life in slavery, followed by a perilous escape and clandestine entry into this country. She must have lived in constant fear of being recaptured, fear which would have diminished as the years passed but which never fully left her. The last thing she wanted was publicity.

What we do know is that, soon after her arrival and by 1834, Mary Ann lived with the Spence family in their own home, 109 Howard Street, the premises of the Proctor Spence Drapery business. She worked for members of the Spence family as a paid domestic servant throughout her working life. In August 1841, aged 38, she married a local man, a widower, James Blyth, in the Anglican Church in Wallsend. It seems she never became a Quaker. Their first home was in Charlotte Street but by 1851 they lived in a flat in 57 Howard Street. The 1851 census shows that by this time Mary Ann had ceased working and lists her as a British subject born in Virginia, in America. The couple had no children, and the 1861 census shows them living, still in Howard Street but in number 70. The 1871 Census describes James as a banker's porter, probably at the Spence family bank, and probably an "honorarium," a retirement job, for he was 68 by then. Six years later James died and was buried in Preston Cemetery, with a fine gravestone next to the Spence family plot, surrounded by the graves of eminent North East Quakers such as the Richardsons and the Watsons. No doubt these arrangements had been made by the Spence family.

In 1881 Mary Ann moved to 39 Nelson Street, North Shields, and was "rooming" with the family of William Irwin, a sail maker. Sometime before the next census in 1891, Mary Ann moved away from North Shields for the first time, and is shown living at 244 Clara Street, Benwell, in a self-contained residence in the household of Mr and Mrs Ardus. Mrs Ardus was James Blyth's niece. The census also states that Mary Ann was "living off her own means."

It was while she was in Benwell, that Mary Ann Macham died, aged 91. If she had remained as a slave in America her life expectancy would at best have been half that age. Mary Ann is buried next to her beloved James in Preston Cemetery, in a recorded, but until recently, unmarked grave.

In 2020 a group of volunteers based at the Low Lights in North Shields raised sufficient money to place a memorial on the grave she shares with her husband. It reads: "MARY ANN BLYTH, nee MACHAM 1802-1893 Rests w. her husband James. Escaped from slavery in Virginia USA. Arrived in N. Shields on Christmas Day 1831.Welcomed into freedom by the Spence family. Supported in her new life by the Quaker community."

Mary's grave alongside the resting place of her husband James, in Preston Cemetery, North Shields.

Teresa Merz (1879 - 1958)

Pioneer of social services

Teresa Merz visiting The Boys' Migration Hostel in the east of Newcastle, in 1928.

In 1965 a new engineering and mathematics building was opened in Newcastle University by the then Prime Minister Harold Wilson. The building was named Merz Court in honour of Dr John Theodore Merz and his sons Charles and Norbert. Theo Merz had been a long-serving member of the Court of Newcastle University and had made a huge contribution to Newcastle life as a scientist, industrialist and academic. His sons Charles (who pioneered the electrical supply system that became the model for the National Grid) and Norbert (an accountant) played key roles in the family firm, which later under Charles became Merz and McLellan. However, no mention was made in the dedication of Merz Court of Teresa, the only daughter in the family. Yet Teresa was a remarkable woman whose contribution to Newcastle life was also hugely significant - albeit in a very different way - and she should certainly be commemorated for all she did.

Teresa's life and achievements had been mentioned in a book published two decades earlier than the opening of Merz Court by a local journalist, James Spencer. His book *Northern Pageant* contains a chapter "They Do Good Quietly" and the subject of it is Teresa, whom the author obviously admired and felt deserved to be much better known and acknowledged. In more recent times Teresa has also been profiled in an excellent article by Elizabeth O'Donnell in the Spring 2017 issue of the *Women's History Journal*, the publication of the Women's History Society. Her work on Teresa has been publicised through the website "Quakerstrongrooms" by the Quaker Library in central London, where many other Quaker women of significance to the history of the North East of England have also been highlighted. The organisation Connected Voice, formerly the Council for Voluntary Service in Newcastle today proudly proclaims Teresa as one of its founders. Philanthropy North East likewise pays tribute to her as an inspiration for their work.

Teresa Merz was born in Gateshead in 1879 to John Theodore Merz and his wife Alice Mary Merz. The Merz family was of German descent although Theo had been born in Manchester. Alice, his wife, was Newcastle born and bred, and was part of the Richardson family, who were well known Quakers in the city and whose women members included campaigners against slavery, advocates of women's higher education and of women's suffrage. Teresa and her three brothers were brought up as Quakers although their father Theo never formally joined, having doubts about the commitment to pacifism that Quakers espoused.

Teresa as a young girl.

Teresa grew up in a happy, comfortable and caring family in a house called "The Quarries" in Grainger Park Road in Newcastle's west end. The family were also very much part of a wider circle of Quaker friends and relations and were particularly close to Alice's sister Elizabeth Spence Watson, her husband Robert and their children. Being comfortably off the families were able to enjoy outings and holidays, and meet on many sporting and social occasions. It was also an environment that exposed the children to much intellectual and

informed discussion about the issues of the day, given the political, religious and cultural interests of the families, their friends and acquaintances.

Although Teresa was obviously an intelligent child, she was not offered the same educational opportunities as her brothers. This seems surprising and marks the Merz household as rather different in its views on women's education from the wider Richardson clan and indeed from the approach taken by many Quakers. Teresa, unlike her brothers, was mostly educated at home with the help of a governess, with only a short period of attendance at a day school. Furthermore, she was neither expected - nor encouraged - to go to university, again in contrast to her brothers. She was firmly domestically based, helping to look after the family home, including assisting her father with his collection of books in the family library. Her mother described her in one of her notebooks as "a rare girl - studious and competent in every way - quite unconventional, full of interests and bright and charming and loving." She also in another note said that Teresa was "clever at work and in all practical ways and an immense help and comfort."

While not openly rebelling against the family expectations, Teresa gradually took a number of opportunities to show her academic and intellectual potential. She took some art classes and was also said to be good at mathematics and history. In her early twenties, and apparently encouraged by some local academics, she entered a history essay she had written to be considered for the annual Gladstone Memorial Prize, given by Armstrong College, Newcastle, and won! Her chosen subject "The Junto" was about a group of leading politicians of Queen Anne's reign who were determined to ensure the Protestant succession after her death. This essay was later turned into a book. It is a lively historical account - which although clearly well-researched - also contains the author's own views and perspectives.

Teresa's much loved younger brother, Ernest, was obviously struck by his sister's intelligence and scholarship and pleaded with the family for her to be allowed to study at Newnham College, Cambridge, which she did for a year from October 1904. Her subjects there were philosophy, ancient Greek history, and economics. She excelled and enjoyed the company of her fellow students who were keen for her to undertake a full degree course, even to the extent of sending a "round robin" letter to Teresa's parents, urging them to allow this to happen. However, at her parents' urging, Teresa returned home. Alice, her mother, wrote "It is a luxury to have Teresa at home ... tho Newnham will miss her." Alice also wrote that her daughter "has a gift for philanthropy, which she carries out with zest and love and great tact". This may be the first family written mention of what must have already been a keen involvement in charitable work and of her efforts to alleviate some of the problems of poverty and poor social conditions which she had become aware of in her home area. From her late twenties onwards it would be this commitment to philanthropy that would dominate her life and involve her in constant work and activities of an astonishing volume and variety.

An early preoccupation was with the hardships experienced by many mothers trying to earn enough money to live on while looking after their babies. This led to the establishment of a home "The Rose Joicey Home", a convalescent home for mothers and young children who needed rest and recuperation. Teresa was to manage this home, often virtually single-handedly, from before the First World War for at least 30 years. Records of the minutes of the management committee, held by Tyne and Wear Archives, show how central Teresa's role was and how she worked with others - for example by forging a partnership with the Mothers and Babies Welcome Society. The records also contain some of the tributes paid to her by patients. One woman wrote "thank you for the wonderful fortnight's holiday you gave me, the food was beautiful ... I got that rest and my meals were all cooked for me, which meant a lot to me ... God bless you for doing all the wonderful work for all of us, the way you do it ...". The Rose Joicey home continued in existence until the 1960s and survives today in the form of a fund providing grants for much needed respite breaks.

Besides the convalescent home, Teresa also opened Hope House, which provided accommodation for working women who would otherwise have been homeless or living in slum conditions. She also used some family money to purchase a country cottage for the use of some of the poorest people so they could "be refreshed" in the country.

By January 1913, her mother was writing that Teresa was on so many committees that she was never at home and it is true that in addition to the schemes she herself had set up, and was responsible for, she was also active in many other projects through her work for the Charity Organisation Society (COS). She was also undertaking a number of speaking engagements to raise awareness of social and economic problems and of the rights - and needs - of women. The opening of Hope House, for example, was accompanied by statements and lectures by Teresa and others about the importance of giving women a voice in the corridors of power and how, as citizens of the country, their needs should be considered as of equal merit to those of any other section of society. Indeed, in the previous year, 1911, Teresa had taken part in the Women's Suffrage Coronation Procession in London to show her support for equal voting rights.

While concern for the welfare of women was a vital part of her work, Teresa also supported charities providing relief for men in local industry particularly at times of strikes and lockouts. She actively engaged in efforts to help unemployed men retrain or take up activities to build confidence and boost chances of re-employment.

Her own family continued to be important to her in these years before the First World War. A very happy short holiday with her brother Ernest in London in 1908, where he was studying law, was followed a year later by the devastating news that he had committed suicide, something that was never explained or understood but left Teresa (to whom he had always been very close) understandably grief-stricken and bereft. Throwing herself so entirely into charity work, to which she was obviously committed anyway, may also have been a way of seeking to overcome this tragedy.

While Teresa felt the work she was doing was useful and worthwhile, she was conscious of its limitations and aware that views were changing about the role of social work and the provision of social services. In June 1914 she played a role in planning a national conference of some 400 delegates from the COS, the Guilds of Help and the Councils of Social Welfare, held in Newcastle with the aim of getting better co-ordination between different charities and pooling their efforts to achieve a more efficient service. She also understood that, while it might be commendable for wealthy citizens to donate money to charities, it was also important that society as a whole should take responsibility for providing decent living and working conditions and ensuring the necessary resources for proper social services. Looking through the records of some of the organisations she was involved with, it is striking how she was able to combine practical involvement with producing the necessary paperwork which alone must have consumed a large amount of time. It is also obvious that her approach was very professional despite being an amateur in the sense of being voluntary and unpaid.

Such was Teresa's life before the first world war broke out in 1914. For her, as for most others, that conflict would have a profound effect and involve new priorities and experiences. Early in the conflict the Hope House accommodation for working women became available for munitions workers. Teresa also helped set up a nursery for the babies of women working in the factories and was involved in a "Patriotic Club" for wives and mothers in order to help them cope with some of the daily challenges of wartime.

Courageously, particularly in view of her own part-German descent, Teresa also took up the cause of women married to Germans and the children of Germans who had been labelled "enemy aliens" and deemed ineligible for any help or financial assistance. She persisted in supporting these families even when criticised and obviously felt that the unfair scapegoating of people, many of whom had lived in Britain happily and usefully for many years, was entirely unacceptable.

Teresa also drew attention to the need for more women police officers to protect women in unsafe neighbourhoods and, as ever willing to get directly involved, took part in some police patrols herself.

Later in the war she also experienced some service overseas, through her work with the Friends War Victims Relief Committee (FWVRC). Initially she had turned down their invitation to do some work in Holland but later was asked to help some of the Serbian refugee victims of war whose plight was such that they were described as "living skeletons". Teresa sailed from Liverpool to Greece (via Malta and Alexandria) and then ended up taking 350 Serb refugees from Greece to Corsica where they had been given asylum. She told subsequently how on the way to Corsica, their ship had been chased by U-boats and how Allied guns had saved them. "Quite an exciting time" was her description. In Corsica she was in charge of a hostel with 50 Serbs. Her experience in running charitable homes in the North-East proved useful, as she set up workshops and organised activities aimed at helping the hostel residents to be self-governing and gaining a sense of purpose. Her fine record in helping Serb refugees was recognised by an honour conferred on her by Serbia's Crown Prince. Also during the war she was given an award for her work with the Red Cross.

When the war ended, Teresa's own sense of purpose and commitment to her work was undimmed and indeed the quantity and quality of her work increased unceasingly. Her stamina was astonishing. All of her previous activities continued with several new ones coming to the fore. She became one of the first women magistrates in Newcastle, appointed in 1921, and eventually would become the longest serving. With the economic downturn of the 1920s, which became full-blown depression of the 1930s hitting Tyneside particularly hard, she threw herself into efforts to tackle the effects of unemployment and provide needed accommodation for jobless men through the creation, in 1929, of the Newcastle Housing Trust. The former home of her aunt and uncle, the Spence Watsons, - Bensham Grove in Gateshead - was also put to use as a fellowship centre providing support to both men and women from families in need. Later on Bensham Grove also provided health monitoring for the babies of such households.

The shortage of work at home was also leading to initiatives to resettle people, particularly young men, in parts of the British Empire, including in Canada and Australia. Teresa felt that such resettlement often involved family breakups and forced emigration. She set up a boys' migration hostel to help prepare those who wanted to emigrate and to do what she could to ensure that they would be helped and well-integrated when they arrived at their destination.

For this work she was awarded the OBE in 1928, which was well-deserved, but might have been considered overdue given all her previous charitable roles and efforts! The success of the men's hostel led to the establishment of a similar facility for women. This gave training in a variety of domestic-type services to "spinsters or childless widows", who asked to emigrate. The language describing this hostel is very dated but there were a number of women who felt that work in "British Dominions" overseas would represent an opportunity for a better future.

Perhaps most significant of all however was the role Teresa played in laying the foundations of the extensive network of social services that exist today and have existed in some form or other since the emergence of the welfare state in the aftermath of the Second World War. Having for a long time been convinced of the need for proper co-ordination between charitable social services, in 1920 she played a key role in founding the Newcastle Citizens Service Society. In 1925 she was an initiator in the creation of the Bureau of Social Research for Tyneside, which fostered research into the nature of social problems and disseminated the results of that work in order that future services could address real needs, based on evidence. This work led to the formation, in 1929, of the Tyneside Council of Social Services, now approaching its centenary, and known today under the name of Connected Voice.

In the 1930s Teresa seems to have consciously and increasingly adopted a thriftier and simpler lifestyle. In 1935, after the death of both of her parents, she converted the family home into a nursery for illegitimate children. She had long been horrified at the way illegitimacy stigmatised innocent children and had sought various ways of helping and supporting them. The nursery did well, helping the mothers of the children to obtain employment knowing that their children were being looked after. In the Second World War it was evacuated to Grasmere in the Lake District. Those mothers who were able to did contribute towards the nursery costs, but Teresa, as ever with her various ventures, frequently helped out personally, to relieve any hardship.

Sometime after the war Teresa donated the family home to St Nicholas Cathedral for continued use as a school while she moved out and found smaller accommodation for herself. Eventually that school moved to newer premises and the house then became a nursing home. Today it has a new role having become a mosque.

Such memories as exist of Teresa in her last years are mixed. One neighbour's account is of someone "spinsterish", "gaunt, thin and reserved." Great-nieces and nephews sometimes felt when visiting her that they were being presented to "a royal personage" rather than a relative. But given that she was the last surviving member of her generation of her family, such descriptions from the very young of people they think very old are not surprising. Most remember her with great warmth as "Auntie Teresa" who, despite her preoccupations, always remembered birthdays with cards and nice presents, someone for whom family always remained precious. The few photographs publicly available of her always seem to show her smiling and cheerful, amongst fellow workers and colleagues. Perhaps the best and most charming description of her is the contemporary one by James Spencer in *Northern Pageant*. Writing about her nursery for illegitimate babies he recounts, "All the children love Miss Merz. Wherever she goes she is followed by several toddlers, tumbling over one another in their eagerness to seize her hand or a bit of her dress".

Teresa died at home in November 1958. She had apparently been working until a couple of days before her death. While the Merz family has left an important legacy with its contribution to Newcastle's industrial and economic life, a key part of the Merz legacy must be to recognise Teresa's own role in working tirelessly to combat poverty and unemployment, in supporting women sometimes in dire circumstances, and, vitally, laying the basis for a proper coordinated range of social services, based on a thorough understanding of the problems to be tackled and the circumstances which had created them. Surely her life is very much to be remembered and treasured.

The Sandgate area of Newcastle at the turn of the century. Teresa worked tirelessly to combat poverty and unemployment in these parts of the city.

Mary Midgley in 2014 talking to the Guardian
newspaper about her latest book and, inset,
Mary, in 1949.

Mary Midgley (1919 - 2018)

Philosopher of growing reputation and renown

Mary Midgley moved to Newcastle with her husband Geoffrey from Reading in 1950 and never moved away, living in Jesmond for some 68 years until her death aged 99, in 2018. In her autobiography she says, "we both took to Newcastle right away" and "that we liked the place too much to leave it." It was in Newcastle where she and Geoffrey brought up their family of three sons and it was as a Lecturer in Philosophy at Newcastle University from 1962-1980 where her reputation first emerged and became established. Today her work and contribution to philosophy make her one of the preeminent thinkers of our time.

When Mary arrived in Newcastle, she was not aware that she had any family links with the city but subsequently discovered that her grandfather David Hay had studied engineering at Armstrong College - the forerunner of what would become Newcastle University. And it was at the library of the Literary and Philosophical Society in the city that he met his future wife, Beatrice McCallum, who was living with her family in Jesmond. David and Beatrice moved to London in the 1880s but the connection with Newcastle was certainly not lost as David became one of the partners in the firm that designed Newcastle's most recognisable landmark, the Tyne Bridge, completed in 1928.

In her fascinating autobiography *The Owl of Minerva*, Mary describes what would seem to many as a rather grand upbringing in a rectory with servants - a housemaid, cook, charlady, nanny and gardener. Mary's father was a Church of England clergyman and when Mary was born, he was a curate in Dulwich, London. Following a short spell as a chaplain at Kings College, Cambridge and when Mary was five, he was appointed Rector of Greenford, then a village to the west of London and it was the rectory there which Mary remembered vividly for its wonderful garden, grounds and outbuildings, perfect for children to explore - a place which left her with many happy and long-lasting memories. Her early education was provided by her nanny and by a governess at the neighbouring grand house where she, her brother, and the children of that house learned and played together. The Greenford of today is very different from Mary's childhood days as its population has greatly increased through the relentless expansion of London and the proximity of Heathrow Airport.

When Mary was 15 the family moved to Kingston, by which time she had become a boarder at Downe House school near Newbury. This school was so named as it had originally been located at Downe House in Kent, coincidentally the home of Charles Darwin whose evolutionary theories would become so familiar to Mary in her later career. School was not an unhappy period in Mary's life as she made some good friends and found much of the teaching, and the atmosphere, to her liking but she felt less well prepared for Oxford University, to which she won a place in 1937, than many of her contemporaries "from more highly organised girls' schools." At least she was pleased that the school had given her the chance to study Greek and she was also grateful to one teacher who dissuaded her from applying to study English at university by saying that "English literature is something that you read in any case, so it is better to study something that you otherwise wouldn't!" Having been drawn to the works of Plato, Mary then decided to study Classics, which included philosophy - a decision she took without realising quite how her life would be influenced as a result.

In the year after leaving school and before going to Oxford, Mary wanted to spend some time abroad and travelled to Vienna to improve her knowledge of German. The visit turned out to be much shorter than expected, coinciding, as it did, with the take-over of Austria by Hitler, the "Anschluss". Mary, who was staying with a Jewish family to whom she had become very attached, witnessed some of the appalling acts against Vienna's Jewish population. She left Vienna after one month, having originally hoped to spend at least three months there. She was relieved to hear that the family with whom she had stayed had, despite being targeted by the Nazis, managed to escape and eventually settled in Israel.

Mary's arrival at Somerville College, Oxford, coincided with the ever-worsening world situation leading up to the Second World War. When war was declared she debated as to whether she should join the war effort straightaway, but she was persuaded, that with the absence of male students, there would be a need for women graduates as soon as the war was over.

In an article in the *Guardian* (3/10/05), when she was 86, she wrote of her Oxford days that "Things had been far from normal during my undergraduate course. A lot of the men were away at the war. Classes were small and they contained about as many women as men. The loud contests of competing male voices were not there. This was helpful, and I think it had a lot to do with allowing me, along with the other women, to be heard and work out our own ideas - an invaluable experience."

Mary's closest friend at Somerville was the philosopher and celebrated writer Iris Murdoch and their friendship was to prove deep and lasting. Iris was Mary's bridesmaid, and their friendship survived both geographical distance and Iris's stark changes in political outlook, from fervent Communist to ardent Thatcherite - in contrast to Mary's constant attachment to left-leaning social democracy.

Indeed, at Oxford Mary formed part of an astonishingly gifted quartet of women philosophers. As well as Mary and Iris there were Elizabeth Anscombe and Philippa Foote and interest in them as a significant and influential group of women philosophers has intensified in recent years, particularly through the "In Parenthesis" initiative. Mary, in particular, is celebrated in the "Notes from a Biscuit Tin" initiative, so called because of the unending supply of biscuits Mary always had for her countless friends and visitors.

Some aspects of philosophy at Oxford inspired and motivated Mary. She particularly valued the courses taught by her tutor Donald MacKinnon whom she described as "an amazingly good teacher". Other aspects of the teaching she found off-putting and seeds were sown there that explain some of her later views and writings. She came to reject doctrines that seemed to her exclusive and "reductionist", which sought, in her view, to impose a single approach, intolerant of others. She felt that such theories often ignored the realities of the world around us and the social context within which human beings operate.

Mary graduated with a First in 1942 and, given that this was in the middle of the war, she deferred any further study in order to try to help to support the war effort. Wryly she would observe afterwards that she was not sure how valuable her contribution to that cause had been but she worked hard at the - often bureaucratic – tasks to which she was assigned.

At the end of the war she returned to Oxford and worked for a while as an assistant and secretary to Professor Gilbert Murray and then was tempted to begin working on a doctoral thesis on the philosophy of the Neo-Platonist, Plotinus. This proved impractical for her to complete, partly because she felt her knowledge of Greek inadequate and partly because of the never-ending ramifications of the topic. Furthermore she was encouraged to apply for a position as Lecturer in Philosophy at Reading University, a post that she accepted in 1949 and which absorbed her in teaching responsibilities and intensive course preparation and marking.

It was around this time she met Geoffrey Midgley, also a philosopher and Oxford graduate. By the end of the summer vacation in 1950 they had decided to marry. Geoffrey was already a lecturer at Newcastle University and Mary, who had always wanted children, chose to join him there and start a family. In the years following, their three sons, Martin, Tom and David, were born and Mary busied herself with motherhood, wanting to spend time with her sons during their formative years. She also continued to read voraciously, both in the field of philosophy and more widely. She began reviewing books, particularly novels, mostly for the *New Statesman* and this led to other journalistic and broadcasting opportunities.

It is often pointed out that Mary did not begin writing the philosophical books upon which her reputation now rests until she was fifty or so, but she had absolutely no regrets about this as she felt that by that time she had learned more about life and this had enriched her thoughts while keeping her rooted in reality. However once begun she never stopped, with her book *What is Philosophy For* being published only one month before she died aged 99!

She was appointed Philosophy Lecturer in Newcastle in 1964, initially working part-time and eventually progressing to Senior Lecturer. Both she and Geoffrey were strongly committed to supporting and nurturing their students and both disliked the increasing stress by UK universities from the 1970s onwards on academic staff producing papers and publications, feeling that it led to a "quantity not quality" outcome and a box ticking mentality. Mary also strongly criticised in later years the tendency in universities to close smaller departments and concentrate on "centres of excellence", often simply for financial considerations, and which she felt diminished the possibility of cross-departmental working between colleagues from different disciplines. At many key points in her career she had treasured the contacts with fellow academics in other disciplines, feeling that they enriched her own work and brought new aspects to bear on her thinking.

Mary and Geoffrey were well known for their sociability and hospitality. As Jane Heal (an academic colleague at Newcastle and later Professor of Philosophy at St John's College, Cambridge) put it in her authoritative, and affectionate, obituary of Mary in the *Guardian*, "for nearly half a century, she and her husband Geoffrey kept open house in Newcastle for friends, colleagues and pupils. At parties and frequent informal gatherings, tea, homemade beer and good whisky were freely dispensed while robust discussion flowed."

In her autobiography, Mary confesses to being "messy" all her life, and the house in Jesmond seems to have been a scene of cheery chaos. Friends remember, at a time when the street where they lived in Jesmond had suffered a number of burglaries, that a neighbour, when Mary and Geoffrey were away, looked through their window and was certain that burglars had broken in because of the general disorder.

Mary's first book entitled *Beast and Man* (1978) formed the foundation stone of her reputation. It was described as a "classic study of humanity's place in the order of things" and "as a brilliant and persuasive attempt to set us in our animal context." Indeed this work would chime in with the growing interest in animal rights, and in seeing the connections between humans and animals as sentient beings. The book's central thesis is that natural selection is not the only basis for evolution in both the human and animal worlds and other factors need to be taken into account. This theme would be expanded in subsequent works such as *Are you an illusion* (2014) where she rejected as unproven determinism scientific theories seeing the human brain as "just a lot of cells" meaning that humans were nothing more than robots entirely at the mercy of their genes.

Mary also argued that the natural environment had to be taken into account as a factor influencing the evolution of humans and animals and in this respect, too, she comes across as a philosopher of our time with its concern about climate change.

The title of the book *Beast and Man* was not Mary's choice. She preferred "Beastliness" but was persuaded by American colleagues, particularly at Cornell University where she had many admirers, that the connotations of that word in American English were entirely pejorative, equating it solely with bestiality.

Beast and Man, as is the case with her other books, is written in clear language and the arguments are rooted in experience of the real world. Mary emphasised the importance of "sticking as close as possible to everyday language, not in the interest of dumbing-down but so as to show how the topic arises out of its context."

Another important and well-received work was her book *Wickedness* on a timeless subject, the nature of evil. From a humanist perspective she wrote of wickedness as being part of human nature and the importance of understanding it, not least in order to mitigate its effects.

In total Mary published 16 books, alongside numerous articles, and their impact was such that she became a contributor to many radio and television programmes dealing with moral and philosophical challenges, such as Radio 4's *The Moral Maze*. Her lucidity in her TV and radio work shines out and, as Professor Heal expressed it, "the drive of her thought is throughout sane and humane". Many of her televised or broadcast interviews are still available to download today and are widely accessed. They include a televised discussion with the writer and comedian Rob Newman, a self-confessed fan of Mary's, in 2014, when she was aged 95 and where she shows an awe-inspiring command of her subject conveyed with outstanding clarity of expression.

A measure of her importance to philosophy generally is evident in the fact that Routledge produced *The Essential Mary Midgley*, edited by David Midgley in 2005. Not surprisingly Mary's achievements have been recognised in other ways, through, for example, having been awarded Honorary Doctorates from Durham University (1995) and from Newcastle University (2008).

In conclusion, it is clear that the North East has many reasons to be immensely proud of this adopted daughter, whose legacy is turning out to be so deservedly acclaimed worldwide.

Dr Muriel Morley made a huge contribution to the development of speech therapy.

Dr Muriel Morley (1899 - 1993)

Pioneering speech therapist

Muriel Morley was a pioneering speech therapist who, in 1959, established the first ever academic department of speech, at King's College Newcastle, in the University of Durham. Later in 1964 she developed Britain's very first degree course in speech. In 1958 she was awarded the degree of Doctor of Science by the University of Durham in recognition of her book, *The Development and Disorders of Speech in Childhood*, which was seen as a landmark in speech pathology. In 1980 she received an OBE in acknowledgement of her massive contribution to the development of Speech Therapy. Thanks to the seeds she planted, Newcastle remains a centre of excellence in speech therapy to this day.

Muriel Morley came to her chosen field of speech therapy in an unusual way. She was born in Halifax, the eldest daughter Samuel Edwin Morley and Helen Ann Monk. The family moved to Tyneside in 1913. Muriel attended High Schools in Halifax and Monkseaton, and then went on to read physics and biology at Armstrong College, the Newcastle division of Durham University.

She graduated with a B.Sc. and having decided to teach she gained a certificate in education in 1920. She then taught physics at the Church High School in Newcastle for 10 years before going out to India to teach. She was captivated by Indian culture and by the people and was very happy there, but sadly while in India she contracted dysentery and had to return home after only a year. Over the next few months she was unwell and faced an uncertain future having been told that she was no longer strong enough to teach. She would have to find a new profession. In fact she did recover completely and regained her drive and energy.

And so it was that in 1932 she responded to an unusual advertisement. A Newcastle plastic surgeon, William Wardill, had devised an operation, a new type of pharyngoplasty, for children with cleft palate. He was seeking "an educated" woman who could assess the child's speech skills before and after the operation and help evaluate the effectiveness of the procedure. Muriel applied, Dr Wardill liked her and engaged her services. She was offered one guinea per session and was initially engaged for two sessions per week to work at the Royal Victoria Infirmary in Newcastle. She was immediately fascinated by the work and it seems that she quickly became an expert photographer of both the inside and the outside of the mouth. She was able to depict changes in patients' condition. Equally she had soon read everything she could find about cleft palates and their management. Miss Morley had no previous formal training in speech therapy because little was available. Self-taught and using her background in physics and biology with some knowledge of phonetics, she continued working in her new-found specialism for the next four years. In 1938, realising she needed to know more about the full range of speech and language disorders she trained formally working with colleagues in London and Liverpool, and in 1938 gained the diploma of the British Society of Speech Therapists. By the end of the war she had made a detailed analysis of her work with Dr Wardill and this was published in 1945 as *Cleft Palate and Speech*. It became a standard textbook on the subject.

Not only had Miss Morley discovered a rewarding, new role, but her collaboration with Dr Wardill, which started in 1933, marked the absolute beginning of speech therapy work in Newcastle.

During the 1940s medical professionals and schools alike were increasingly aware of the value of speech therapy in all its aspects and the *1944 Education Act* placed a statutory responsibility on LEAs to provide special educational treatment for children with speech defects. Provision expanded nationally and in Newcastle a clinic was opened at the Fleming Children's Hospital in 1940. In 1941 the General Hospital began to make provision for adult patients. Muriel's case load expanded to include men suffering from aphasia and other speech disorders due to head injuries inflicted in the war. By the end of the

Cleft lip is when an opening or split in the upper lip occurs when facial structures in an unborn baby don't close completely. Some children also have a cleft in the roof of the mouth this is called a cleft palate. It seems that every three minutes a baby is born with a cleft. The impact of this condition is disfiguring and it adversely affects the development of speech, as well as impeding feeding. Today the condition can be corrected with surgery restoring normal function with minimal scarring. In 1930 this was pioneering surgery.

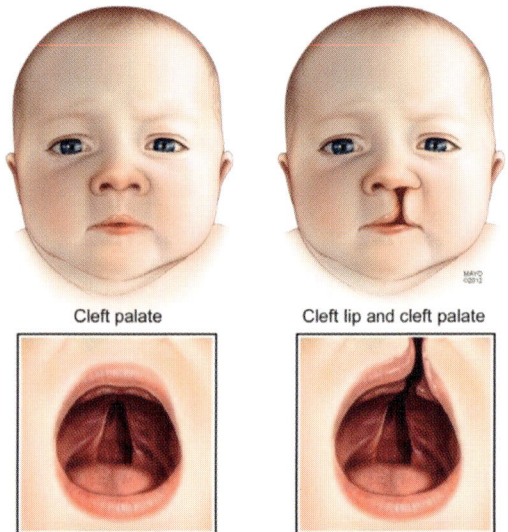

Cleft palate

Cleft lip and cleft palate

war Muriel Morley had set up the Newcastle Hospitals Speech Therapy Service and was working full time in three hospitals on the basis of 10 sessions per week. She was joined by a second speech therapist in 1949 and by 1962 the service employed four full-time speech therapists. Muriel Morley said that until 1932 she had never even heard of the profession of speech therapy (in fact the term was a new one first coined in 1926).

In 1949 Muriel Morley developed a relationship with the university Department of Child Health and began to work closely with Donald Court, later Professor Court. They were joined by Henry Miller the Dean of Medicine and later Vice-Chancellor, then Roger Garside, an Applied Psychologist. This strong and influential academic quartet held weekly meetings over a period of seven years during which a wide range of children with language and speech disorders were seen. Not only were the children being seen by the best in their field, but this quartet also produced important guidance in the form of papers for other practitioners.

Muriel's close association with colleagues in the Department of Child Health in the university, coincided with the Newcastle Family Survey (1947-62) and enabled her and her colleagues to study a representative survey of 847 children and record the development of language and speech, and the frequency and character of disorders at ages four, five, six and 15 years. Again, this was ground-breaking work and she wrote the research up in a book, *Development and Disorders of Speech in Childhood*, for which the University awarded her the degree of Doctor of Science in 1958.

By 1958 speech therapy had been a respected discipline in the hospitals and school clinics of Newcastle for 25 years, and the university been a major contributor to the quality of the provision through the Departments of Child Health and Medicine. It was at this point that Dr Morley suggested the university consider establishing a Department, or a sub Department of Speech Therapy, so that instead of just holding clinics, they could also offer training and research facilities. She wanted to develop a university degree course in Speech Therapy and there is no doubt that Muriel Morley was the driving force behind the initiative. It was her insistence on the personal and social importance of speech and the need for its academic study that led to the establishment in 1959, of the Sub-Department of Speech in the Department of Child Health. Dr Morley was appointed to develop this sub-department, establish research priorities and prepare the degree course in speech therapy. Her insistence on a degree level course was inspired by her belief in the highest academic standards and her concern for the status of her profession.

At the time speech therapists qualified by gaining a diploma from the College of Speech Therapists. But those who wanted to study their subject to degree level had to go abroad to find a degree course, usually America. Unfortunately, some remained there and were lost to this country. She wanted to stop this flow of good people and keep them in this country. She was sixty by this time and had intended to retire however she was easily persuaded to stay on for a further five years and by 1964 a three-year under-graduate course in speech and speech pathology was ready. Successful candidates were awarded a BSc (Speech). Since then literally hundreds have graduated as professionally qualified speech therapists in Newcastle. In 1983, long after Dr. Morley's retirement the sub department became a full Department of Speech in the Department of Child Health in the University of Newcastle.

We have already noted Dr Morley's concern for the status of this relatively new profession, and she became a founder member of the College of Speech Therapists, first formed in 1945. Between 1947 and 1963 Dr Morley served for several three-year periods on the College Council. As a Council member she would always support the demand for higher salaries, improved status, and a better career structure. In 1959, for example, the Government of the day decided to bring together a number of disciplines under the *Bill for Professions Supplementary to Medicine*. This was supposed to include speech therapy but Dr Morley and the College reacted immediately. They refused to accept that speech therapy could be described as "supplementary" to any other profession. Muriel contacted the minister responsible and explained this. A national referendum of speech therapists was organised to protest and the whole profession stood firm, and, despite government anger, speech therapy was removed from the Bill. If this threat to the integrity and independence of a young profession had not been removed, the academic development of speech therapy would have been prevented or at least delayed for a very long time.

Throughout her life Muriel was an avid reader of books and journals especially the *American Journal of Speech Disorders* to which she often subscribed. From 1966 for six years she was editor of the College of Speech Therapists Academic Journal, during which time she increased the content, improved the style and widened the circulation. In 1971, she became third President of the College of Speech Therapists.

Dr Morley travelled widely in the English-speaking world as as a visiting professor. She travelled to Australia and New Zealand and between 1951 and 1970 made five visits to the USA. These visits established the twin pillars of her professional philosophy; that speech and language must be studied and taught in universities and that academic excellence must be complemented by the highest standards of clinical work.

Dr Morley never married and retired in 1964. In retirement she lived in Northumberland enjoying the photography that she had taught herself in her early work on cleft palates - it had become her lifelong hobby. She died in September, 1993, in Alnwick of bronchopneumonia aged 94, after a long and happy retirement.

It is impossible to do justice to a life so well lived and a career so creative and dynamic. I can do no better than quote Professor Donald Court, with whom she worked so closely for many years. He said of her, "How can we explain her energy, tenacity, vision, openness to new ideas and love of learning? The answer lay in her unwavering belief in the value of her subject and an unyielding commitment to its practice at the highest level. Like Cromwell's soldiers, she knew what she fought for and loved what she knew."

Professor Donald Court with Dr Muriel Morley in 1981.

Elizabeth Pease Nichol worked tirelessly for an end to oppression and inequality.

Elizabeth Pease Nichol (1807 - 1897)

Abolitionist, feminist and radical reformer

The life and achievements of Elizabeth Pease Nichol made such an impact in the 19th century that within two years of her death her biography had been published and to this day her portrait hangs in the National Portrait Gallery. She worked tirelessly for an end to oppression and inequality wherever she found it, whether in slavery, in the treatment of women or in animal rights. Her radical politics were rooted in her Quakerism and Christianity. Constrained as Victorian women were, she lived by the principle, "...however contracted your sphere, or however little you seem to have in your power, do that little, for individual efforts have been found to be eminently serviceable". (Pease to Weston 1841). Her life's work bears testimony to just how much one dedicated woman can achieve.

Elizabeth had the advantage of being born into a leading and politically active Quaker family in Darlington. Her father, Joseph, was a rich wool merchant, an entrepreneur and a philanthropist who served as Britain's first Quaker MP, elected to represent South Durham in 1834. Through extensive family and commercial connections, she was at the centre of a Quaker reformist network that included men and women across the British Isles and the US. She enjoyed a freedom of movement and social interaction which relatively few women of her day experienced, and she remained unmarried until she was 46 thus having more freedom to pursue her own interests. She was tall with intense blue eyes and a self-deprecating manner. Her dress was simple and she wore a Quaker bonnet. The ODB describes her as an,"earnest passionate and principled lady who only overcame her reluctance to speak in public at the end of her very long career".

Quaker doctrine insisted that all human souls, male and female, black and white, rich and poor, were equal before God, and that every Quaker should criticise and challenge all unjust forms of authority. As a Quaker she received an education equal to her brother's and was encouraged to develop personal administrative, organisational and communication skills.

The Pease home, Feethams in Darlington, developed into a centre of political activity in North East England, and while still young Elizabeth met many of the important reformers of her day, for example Daniel O'Connell, John Bright and Richard Cobden. After her mother's death in 1824, Elizabeth became her father's primary assistant in his reformist activities. She combined helping him with her own local work which centered around Darlington. She helped found a Mechanics' Institute, the local hospital, and Darlington chapters of the Temperance Society., the Bible and Religious Tract Society and the RSPCA. In 1832 she supported the Reform Act but felt it did not go far enough and after that supported universal suffrage.

In the 1830s, however, Elizabeth's major focus became the campaign to abolish slavery itself, and when British colonial slavery had been abolished, in 1833, she worked tirelessly for universal abolition, with a particular focus on United States of America.

Elizabeth Pease was determined that women's role in the process of abolition would be a powerful one, despite the fact that many men, even powerful reformists, were against female involvement in any political matters. William Wilberforce wrote, "For ladies to meet, to publish, to go from house to house stirring up petitions - these seem to me proceedings unsuited to the female character as delineated in the Bible." (letter to Thomas Babington 1826.) In the campaign to abolish the slave trade in 1807, women had not been allowed full membership of the men's societies, were not allowed to sign public petitions and were discouraged from appearing at public meetings, let alone speaking at them.

Denied participation in men's meetings, women formed their own independent organizations. By 1835 there were 73 such local societies including Darlington, where Elizabeth Pease was the driving force. As for not signing petitions women began to draw up their own. The Darlington Association gathered an impressive 5315 signatures for the Ladies' petition to the Queen in 1831. In 1833 the National Women's Petition against Slavery had 187,000 signatures. Overall in 1833, 800 women's petitions reached Parliament, signed by 300,000 women.

Women began to write powerful political tracts. In 1838 Elizabeth herself wrote an open anti-slavery letter for national distribution entitled *Address to the Women of Great Britain*." In it she urged women to speak out in public and form their own anti-slavery organizations as she said, "In the cause of God and of religion, of Justice and humanity, of injured women and helpless childhood, of severed ties and broken hearts".

Her campaigning led her to travel widely throughout England and Scotland to organise meetings and bazaars, she engaged speakers, kept minutes, and maintained an international correspondence. She also accompanied George Thompson, a national anti-slavery lecturer on a national tour to form new anti-slavery societies.

During the 1840s, Elizabeth Pease of Darlington, became the most influential anti-slavery woman activist in Britain and one of the key coordinators of support for the radical American abolitionists known as the Garrisonians, who described Elizabeth as, "one of the foremost women in the anti-slavery cause, in England, distinguished by her strength of intellect, generosity of spirit and nobleness of heart".

It is almost unbelievable, in the face of all she had done, that when in 1840, the first World Anti-Slavery Convention was held in London and despite her reputation, despite the dependence of both the British and the American Anti-Slavery Societies on the women's financial and moral support, and despite the fact that Elizabeth and other women delegates had travelled to London from all over the world to attend, they were not allowed to take part. Eventually a miserable compromise was reached, and Elizabeth Pease and seven other would-be women delegates, from America as well as Britain were allowed in but they had to sit in a segregated area, where they could barely see or hear and they were not allowed to speak.

Their marginalized position is clearly depicted in Benjamin Haydon's monumental painting of the Convention in the National Portrait Gallery. Elizabeth is one of eight women portrayed, sitting, as mere observers in the wings.

This awful experience, and the sheer powerlessness of the women outraged Elizabeth and strengthened her support not just for an equal role for women in the anti-slavery movement, but for full equality between men and women. From that date Elizabeth Pease became a leading figure in the women's movement.

In 1840 she wrote in a letter to John Collins, a friend, "I believe there are few persons whose natural feelings are so opposed to women appearing prominently before the public, as mine - but viewed in the light of principle, I see that prejudice, custom and other feelings will not stand the test of truth... and must be laid aside."

Her father's death in 1846 caused Elizabeth great sorrow but her work continued. In 1853, however she married, and for the next six years she lived in Glasgow as the busy wife of Dr John Pringle Nichol, Professor of Astronomy at Glasgow University and stepmother to two teenagers, her political activism on hold. The couple made their last visit to Darlington in 1854, when she opened the new Mechanics Institute Building at Skinnergate. She was the major donor, having founded the Mechanics Institute in Darlington in the first place, with a donation of £400 pounds, the equivalent of £50,000 in today's money.

After her husband's death in 1859, Elizabeth moved to Edinburgh, to Huntley Lodge, Merchiston, where she lived until her death 38 years later.

During the 1860s and 70s Elizabeth focused on women's rights. She

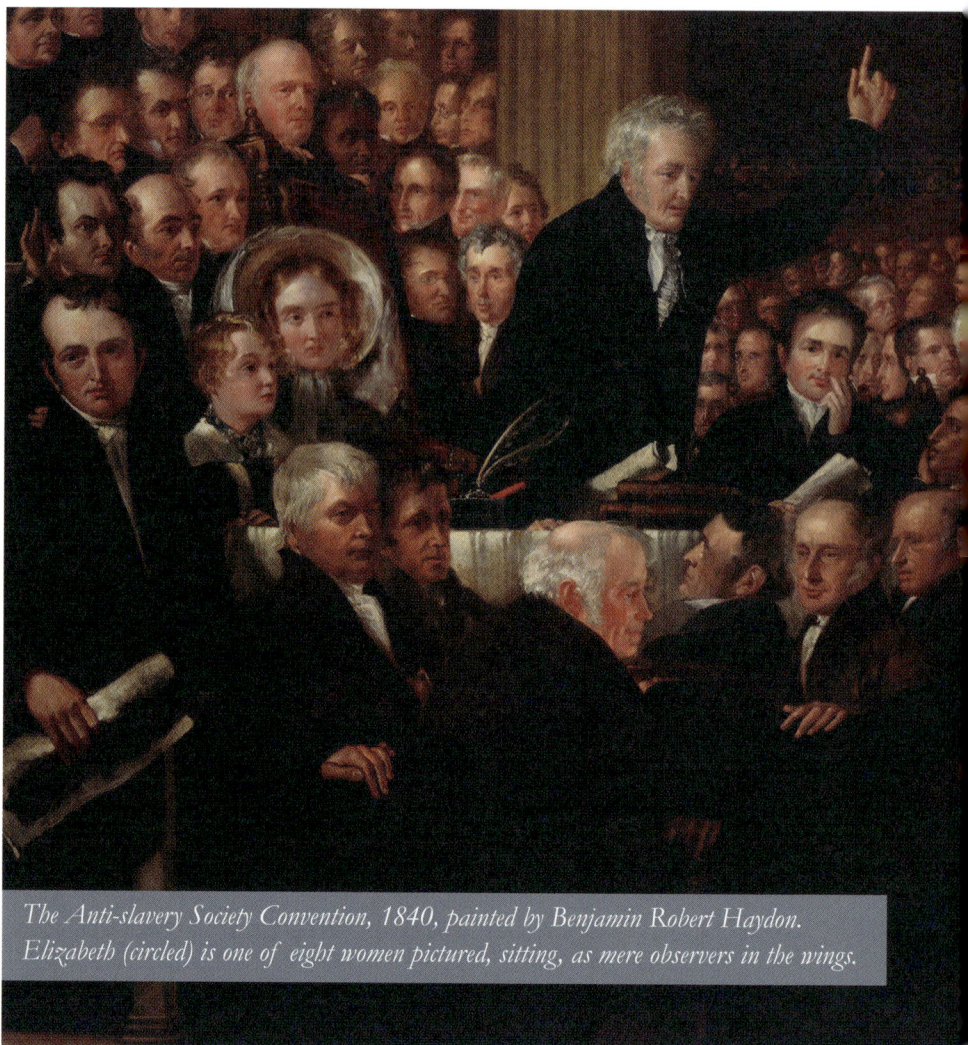

The Anti-slavery Society Convention, 1840, painted by Benjamin Robert Haydon. Elizabeth (circled) is one of eight women pictured, sitting, as mere observers in the wings.

became a member of the movement to admit women to Edinburgh University School of Medicine, reluctantly speaking on the matter at public meetings. She joined the Edinburgh Women's Suffrage Society becoming its President, and the Ladies Education Association. In 1880 Elizabeth Pease was among the 5,000 who took part in the Great Demonstration of Women in Manchester, and in 1884 was a signatory to the Letter from the Ladies asking for women householders to be given the vote. She became active in the movement to repeal the *Contagious Diseases Act* in 1870, to stop the unfair treatment of prostitutes and those suspected of being prostitutes. During this time, she worked closely with other leading activists such as Josephine Butler. Elizabeth brought to these feminist movements her reforming zeal and her exceptional training and extensive knowledge of procedure learned during her anti-slavery activities, as well as her national and international reputation.

Image © National Portrait Gallery, London

There is currently an Edinburgh-based project to honour Elizabeth Pease alongside her sister Quaker abolitionists, with a memorial to highlight their contribution to the great moral crusades of the 19th century.

Elizabeth Pease Nichol's political activism was curtailed in old age by her increasing blindness and, in 1888, her doctor forbade her to attend all meetings. She died peacefully shortly after her 90th birthday in February 1897.

Elizabeth Pease Nichol epitomizes the long tradition of political activism and support for progressive social movements in the North East. She used her life to shift public opinion on the great moral issues of the day, but never sought personal fame. She worked to encourage and inspire thousands on both sides of the Atlantic, to make vision a reality, not through words so much as by actions. Above all, she was effective despite the limitations imposed by gender and never did less than her conscience demanded.

Bella Reay, football star of Blyth Spartans.

Bella Reay (1900 - 1979)

Munitionette and football star

One of the great social changes arising from the First World War was the employment of women in the munitions industry, 950,000 of them. This in turn gave rise to another often forgotten phenomenon, the spectacular rise and fall of Women's Football. Bella Reay, born in Blyth, was both a munitionette and star of the unbeaten women's football team Blyth Spartans'.

Initially there was great reluctance to draft women in to the armaments industry but the shell crisis of 1915 made it inevitable and from 1916 the armaments industry became the biggest wartime employer of women. Armstong Whitworth & Co. alone employed 21,000 women to make guns and shells. The munitionettes, especially those filling the shells with explosives, worked with dangerous, volatile chemicals. During the course of the war, over 200 munitionettes lost their lives in accidents, explosions and poisoning from TNT. In the North East there were 27 munitions companies employing tens of thousands of women. Never before had such a large cohort of women found themselves thrown together so closely and naturally they enjoyed the camaraderie.

Having stepped beyond the bounds of normal social conventions in the workplace, women began to explore other avenues usually closed to them, football, until then a totally male preserve, was one of them.

They realized that women's football had entertainment value as well as great fundraising potential and was good exercise. Women's football teams sprang up in munitions factories all over the country, especially in the North East. Tyneside boasted 17 teams, Teesside 11, Sunderland at least three and Hartlepool four. The munitionette teams played matches against each other, charging spectators a fee to raise money for wartime charities. They generally played under the name of the companies they worked for, except the team that proved the most successful, Bella's team, Blyth Spartans.

Bella Reay was a miner's daughter, born in 1900, in Cowpen, Blyth. She was 17 years old when she started work as a munitionette in the South Docks area of Blyth. She worked in the munitions factory and loaded ships with ammunition for the Front, as well as unloading cargoes of used shell cases for recycling. In August 1917 the girls from South Dock decided they too would form a ladies football team, Blyth Spartans Ladies Team.

The women's teams wore mobcaps and normal football jerseys but their lower body clothing evolved from full-length trousers or knee-length skirts to knickers, as shorts were then called. The shorts did arouse cries of indecency and immodesty among the prudish and letters of complaint littered the columns of the local press as did the equally robust letters in defence of the girls and praise for their excellent work for charity. Blyth Spartans' strip was green and white stripes.

In 1917 a Munitions Girls Challenge Cup was announced. A solid silver trophy was donated for the winners of this knock out competition, the proceeds of all matches were to go to charities. 26 teams entered the competition including Blyth Spartans. Blyth reached the semi-final, having scored a total of 15 goals, Bella nine of them. The semi-final against Armstrong Whitworth's was played at St James' Park in front of a crowd of 10,000. Again, Blyth Spartans emerged victorious 2 goals to 1. The final against Bolckow-Vaughan's Munitionettes was fixed for 30th April, 1918, at St James Park, where a crowd of 15,000 spectators were disappointed by a goalless draw. The replay took place in May at Ayresome Park when, in front of a crowd of 22,000 spectators, Spartans won 5 -0, Wor Bella scoring four goals. They had won the Tyne Wear and Tees Munitionettes Cup, the first and only Ladies' football cup then in existence.

In that one season alone Blyth Spartans Ladies' Football team, despite working 12-hour shifts, had played 30 games, won 26, drawn 4 and lost none. The star of the team, the goal-getter, "Wor Bella," had scored 133 goals. The team had also travelled to play in the three adjoining counties and raised over £2,000 for charities. In today's money that would be an amazing £100,000.

From the viewpoint of its charitable objectives, Blyth Spartans, indeed the whole Football enterprise, was a huge success. Both local and national charities benefitted. Blyth supported the St. John Ambulance, the Joseph and Jane Cowen Home for the Retraining of Wounded Soldiers and the Sailors and Soldiers Orphan Fund and many others. It is hard to imagine the enthusiasm and passion of these young women for their football and for their fundraising. Bella's friend, Jennie Nutall, even played a match on her wedding day, for Blyth Spartans against Burradon Ladies!

When the Armistice was signed in November 1918 and the guns fell silent, the munitions industry began to lay off the women munition workers, and consequently their teams disbanded. Blyth Spartans Munitionettes ceased to exist after mid-September 1918. Nonetheless Bella did appear as a guest player in the second Munitionettes Challenge Cup in March 1919 at St James' Park in front of 10,000 spectators. She was centre forward for Palmers, Shipbuilding and Iron Co., against Christopher Brown Ltd. Snow covered the ground and the weather was atrocious, but Wor Bella scored the only goal of the match, winning her second winners' medal.

By the time the war was over, Bella Reay was known throughout and beyond the North East as a legendary centre forward and as the star player of an unbeaten ladies' football team. Her pioneering contribution to women's football over one hundred years ago has been commemorated by a blue plaque, which can be seen today in her home ground, Croft Park, Blyth. It reads: "Bella Reay born in Cowpen, Centre Forward for Blyth Spartan's Ladies (1917-1919) and England. Bella scored 133 goals in one season and was part of the team which went on to win the Munitionettes Cup in May 1918."

The rise of the Munitionettes Football teams from 1917 to 1919 was undoubtedly a force for good. It was a healthy outdoor activity for women and girls who worked 12-hour shifts indoors and with hazardous chemicals. The teams raised millions of pounds for the many war-related charities and gave huge pleasure to hundreds of thousands of spectators during the sufferings of the Great War.

After the war everything changed. Almost a million women who had enjoyed the freedom their wages gave them, the camaraderie of the workplace and the sense of achievement derived from their brave and unstinting work as munitionettes, lost their jobs and had to return home or seek work elsewhere. Bella married and became Mrs Henstock, and then a proud mother, and later a grandmother. But like all the other women footballers she had very little opportunity to play football, and that was not because of her domestic responsibilities.

What happened? Why did women's football just disappear?

In the early 1920s a few local teams were formed but generally the women's games went unreported or were mocked. There seems to have been a widespread desire to restore pre-war social norms and to stop women playing football. Then, outrageously, in 1921 The Football Association banned their members from hosting women's football matches. They asserted without any explanation, that, "Complaints have been made and the council feel impelled to express their strong opinion that the game of football is quite unsuitable for females and ought not to be encouraged". This was a death knell for women's football at that time. The 1921 ban on women's teams using F.A. affiliated grounds remained in force, until 1971, and to the F.A.'s eternal shame stopped the development of women's football for half a century.

Fortunately, gradual and hard-won changes in society's view of women meant that in 1969 women founded their own association, the Women'sFootball Association, the F.A. ban was lifted, and the Women's England National Football Team was founded. Recent years have seen an explosion of interest in women's football, so much so that the Football

Association has taken over the governance of the game, which ultimately should mean that more money is available to promote the game and make it available to more girls and women.

The "Lionesses", The Women's England Team, won the 2022 European Championship, beating Germany 2-1 in a sold-out Wembley stadium. This seems to me to have put the rather overpaid men's teams in the shade. The win will certainly generate further interest and produce a host of new women football stars. Lucy Bronze is one. A fellow Northumbrian she plays at National and International levels, she won the BBC Women's Footballer of the Year in 2018 and 2020 and was a member of the national team that won the European Cup. One hundred years after Bella, she too began her football career playing for a Blyth team, Blyth Town. She was inspired by the spirit of her heroine, the football legend, the high scoring centre forward to beat all, the shooting star that was Bella Reay.

The hugely successful Blyth Spartans team and, below, the blue plaque celebrating Bella's achievements

BELLA REAY BORN IN COWPEN
CENTRE FORWARD FOR BLYTH
SPARTANS LADIES (1917-1919)
AND ENGLAND

BELLA SCORED 133 GOALS IN ONE
SEASON AND WAS PART OF THE TEAM
WHICH WENT ON TO WIN
THE MUNITIONETTES' CUP
IN MAY 1918

Ellen Richardson (1808 - 1896)

Anti-slavery campaigner and promoter of education

Ellen Richardson was yet another of that extraordinary group of North East Quaker women in the late eighteenth and the nineteenth centuries who changed Britain, and even the world, for the better. She is best remembered today - understandably - for her key role, along with that of her sister-in-law Anna, in bringing about the liberation from slavery of two famous and celebrated African Americans - Frederick Douglass in 1846 and William Wells Brown in 1854. However, a cause equally dear to her heart was providing educational opportunity to the children of poor and working-class families who, until the educational reforms of the 1870s onwards and the introduction of compulsory education, were usually denied any schooling and were destined to grow up illiterate.

Ellen was born into a prominent Newcastle Quaker household. Her parents - George and Eleanor Richardson - had a house and business premises in the Old Flesh Market in the town. The site of their house was later occupied by the Old Town Hall, built in the 1850s, which was replaced by an office block in the 1970s. Her home is pictured in a booklet *In Memoriam* dedicated to Ellen's brother Henry and sister-in-law Anna and written by her nephew and niece Thomas and Emma Pumphrey in 1892, and they describe "the quaint bay window of their parlour."

Ellen was educated at Ackworth School in Yorkshire. She spoke of her life there as a boarder as "a time of Spartan discipline". Whether happy or unhappy her schooling certainly seems to have convinced her of the importance of education as, on returning home to Newcastle, aged 17, she quickly, and in various ways, demonstrated her keen interest in providing education for the poor and to those to whom it was denied. Her Quaker upbringing no doubt also influenced this interest and while, according to her own admission, it was a while before she wholeheartedly accepted the doctrine and practice of

Quakerism as an adult, the social causes espoused by the Quakers seem to have motivated her from the start.

Besides education, the abolition of slavery in the United States was a cause particularly dear to her heart. Ellen's commitment to the abolitionist movement was shared by other family members and manifested itself in various ways, including attending meetings, writing letters and articles and boycotting the produce of slavery. The Newcastle Quakers hosted visits by leading campaigners from America including slaves and freed slaves. In 1845 Frederick Douglass set sail for the British Isles not only to contribute to and support the campaign in Britain and Europe, but also, to evade possible capture in the United States and the fate of being returned to the slave owner in Baltimore whose property he legally was. During his stay in Britain he visited Newcastle and was a guest of the Richardson household.

History has credited both Ellen and Anna Richardson with the move to secure Douglass's freedom and it seems that both played a key role. Ellen is on record as saying that the original idea was hers and that she did not inform Douglass nor discuss her idea with him at any point as she wanted to prevent any disappointment if the efforts were unsuccessful. She was also aware that the move risked negative reactions from some prominent abolitionists who considered that paying money to secure freedom from slavery was somehow sanctioning slavery itself. She may also have had concerns that Douglass would have doubts about the idea and might not want it but she was convinced it was necessary if he was to be able to return to America and campaign effectively and openly as they all wanted.

The Richardson family had a cottage in Cullercoats where they frequently stayed in summertime and Ellen, in a much later letter to Douglass's second wife Helen Pitts Douglass, described how it was there where she first had the idea that "Frederick must be free"! She wrote, "Frederick, my sister and myself sat opposite Cullercoats sands with the sea rolling on the beach - that was one of the best day's work I ever did when I look at the result of F's freedom."

Anna Richardson was quick to help Ellen and was able to make contact with American lawyers, and to approach Douglass's owner Hugh Auld. Eventually the sum of £150 was agreed - Auld was brazenly keen to make a profit on his original investment in buying Douglass - and papers were signed in late 1846 with freedom being granted in December that year. While Frederick Douglass always attributed publicly the idea and its execution to Anna and Ellen alone, it seems that he did know something of what was afoot in a letter he wrote to Anna in August 1846, and he may have given her his assent to what was being planned at that time. What is crystal clear, however, is that he approved of the successful outcome and paid tribute to both women for their generosity for the rest of his life. He was certain that it was their efforts that allowed him to become America's leading spokesman in the crusade against slavery, his eloquence and effectiveness making him, in many ways, the Martin Luther King figure of the nineteenth century. Predictably, many white Abolitionists did indeed criticise the raising of money to buy Douglass's freedom but Douglass himself felt they did not fully appreciate or understand the terrible fear escaped slaves had of being recaptured, saying memorably that "it was not to confirm legitimacy on a remorseless plunderer" but "to release me from his power".

Frederick Douglass would remain close to Ellen, Anna and the Richardson family for the rest of his life. He visited Newcastle and Cullercoats as a free man, and as Ellen's guest, in 1859 and again in 1887. In 1860 he sent Ellen a copy of his second autobiography *My Bondage and My Freedom,* dedicating it to her "with the respect, esteem and most grateful regards of the author and as a token of the sentiments towards her, as the friend and benefactress, through whose active benevolence he was ransomed from American slavery."

Ellen and Douglass corresponded with each other for almost 50 years, right up to his death in 1895, just a year before Ellen's own passing. Ellen rejoiced in Douglass's successes and in his later prominence in American public life as a Marshal to the US Government. She told him "our interest in you never dies."

For most of Ellen's life, however, it was her work in promoting education that most occupied her. She was involved in the Jubilee School for girls in Newcastle from about 1825 onwards until its closure and absorption into the wider educational framework in the city almost 60 years later in 1884. For most of this time she was referred to as "Secretary to the Jubilee School", a position

Frederick Douglass, left, and William Wells Brown, whose liberation from slavery was helped by Ellen Richardson.

which involved much management and organisation. The school was founded in 1810 by philanthropists including Ellen's father and the jubilee it commemorated was the 50th anniversary of George III's accession to the throne. Its purpose was to educate children from impoverished backgrounds and became described later on as one of the "Ragged Schools" - that name being a graphic way of indicating the destitute children being taught. As well as her role as Secretary, Ellen also took on teaching duties, assisting in classes and specialising in scripture and in reading. She also took satisfaction in the school's work in training teachers and supervised that work which greatly increased the supply of teachers, not only in Newcastle but in many of the mining villages on Tyneside and in Northumberland. Until the end of her life she kept in touch with many of the teachers she had helped train and followed their later work with keen interest.

Her work impressed the Newcastle Corporation and in 1860, the Schools and Charities Committee of the Council asked her to organise and supervise their St. Mary's school for Girls in addition to her existing responsibilities at the Jubilee School. Undaunted she managed to run both schools for a number of years. An account of her supervising examinations at St. Mary's indicates that in 1865 the school had around 135 pupils.

Remarkably, she also founded a third school in Cullercoats along with her cousin Ann Richardson - later Ann Foster. This began as a "Creche-school" for those children - boys and girls - in the fishing community aged 18 months and older. This was a highly unusual initiative for the time but Ellen knew how difficult it was for the fishwives to look after babies and young children, when, at the same time, they were selling the fish their husbands caught around local neighbourhoods. Ellen was determined to support them and give their children a path to education. The school developed into an elementary school.

While steeped in these local initiatives, Ellen was also following the national debate about education and took a close interest in the various attempts to bring in legislation on educational reform. She corresponded with William E Forster, who through his Parliamentary Bill of 1870 set the framework for the schooling of all children between five and 12 years of age and thereby gave momentum to the move to provide free compulsory education for all. In 1874 Ellen published her own book outlining her education beliefs and approaches entitled *The Principles of Teaching in Elementary Schools*. This was described in one of her obituaries as urging "the importance of the culture of intellect, emotion and imagination". She saw education as mind expanding and enriching and as something that should be available to all.

Given the range of Ellen's educational responsibilities, it is obvious that, although her work was voluntary and unpaid it was also professional and full time. In addition, she undertook many other charitable activities, running stalls in bazaars or organising assistance for individual families as, in 1859, appealing energetically for help for a large Jewish family facing particular hardship. Cullercoats was a focus for many of her charitable activities. She valued her friendship with the fishing families and helped them in various ways enjoying their company and frequently inviting them to her cottage in Cullercoats or her Newcastle home in Rye Hill. There is an account of her in old age continuing to visit her fisher folk friends in her bath chair.

Ellen also pursued some other interests unrelated to her charitable work. She was a supporter of the "Peace Society" and attended some of their events. She also had some involvement with the Newcastle Society of Antiquaries and donated occasional items, including a book of Arabic prayers and, apparently, a document containing the seal of Elizabeth the First.

Over the years, Ellen had a number of family responsibilities to shoulder, which she seems to have managed to do willingly, despite her wider extensive responsibilities, and often in difficult and painful circumstances. In 1840 her brother Isaac's health deteriorated and she went with him to the Isle of Wight, which had been recommended as having a healthier climate. It was a long journey in those days and sadly he died not long afterwards in Ventnor.

Two years later, Ellen lost her only sister, Rachel, married to Thomas Pumphrey the superintendent of Ackworth School. From then on, Ellen devoted much attention to their four children and always remained close to them, taking care of them in subsequent years. Ellen also took responsibility when her mother died in 1846 - the year when she was busy organising Frederick Douglass's freedom - of looking after her father and becoming his housekeeper, a role she performed until he died in 1865 at the age of 89. Following his death, she moved house from the family home in Albion Street to Rye Hill to be nearer her cousins Robert and Ann Foster, and to be close to other members of the Richardson family circle.

Ellen's participation in the spiritual life of the Quaker community increased with age. She owned that it was a long time before she became fully integrated into Quakerism and adopted their beliefs wholeheartedly, but once this had happened, she felt both blessed and happy. She wrote a number of "Heart Communings and Prayers," giving proof of this spiritual journey. She also became an Elder of the Church, only relinquishing this role when her eyesight began to fail and she could no longer carry out the duties that this entailed.

Ellen died aged 87 in 1896 and was buried in Elswick Cemetery. The service at the grave was described as "Simple - in the manner of the Society of Friends." Her cousin, Mary Spence Watson, described her by saying "I believe she is the last proper Quakeress in Newcastle and the last who wore Quaker's dress ... and she was so splendid."

Anne Seymour in Biafra, Africa, in 1969.

Photo credit: Romano Cagnoni

Dr Anne Seymour FRCS, MBE (1935 - 2016)

Missionary doctor and charity worker

Anne Seymour was a real force of nature, a skilled trauma surgeon and committed Christian with a powerful social conscience, she dedicated her life to serving the poor and the needy. She worked in Africa as a missionary doctor for 16 years, and in South Shields for 33 years of her remarkable life.

Born in Bromley, Kent, Anne trained as a doctor at the Royal Free Hospital School of Medicine, University of London. She graduated in 1959, and worked in two pre-registration jobs, in orthopaedics and fevers before spending six months in general surgery at Leicester and another six months in casualty at Watford. However, as she herself wrote ... "from my school days, I had known I had a calling to work as a mission doctor and this would be in Africa". So, at the age of 26, in 1961, she travelled to a mission hospital in Biafra in south-east Nigeria where she worked as a general surgeon before, during and after the Nigerian Civil War.

From the outset, the mission hospital was very short of doctors and Anne found herself performing operations beyond her expertise and experience, and on occasion had to refer to a textbook for guidance while operating on a patient. But things got much worse. In 1966 there was a military coup followed by a full-blown civil war between the Nigerian Government and the state of Biafra, which wanted independence from Nigeria. The conflict, one of Africa's bloodiest civil wars, lasted for two and a half years and caused the mass starvation of over two million Biafran civilians and over 100,000 military casualties.

Throughout the war Anne worked in field hospitals where there were so many wounded that she barely had time to sleep. She was once forced to operate on a soldier at gunpoint.

Anne travelled to Britain in 1968 to raise awareness of the bloodshed and try to raise funds to alleviate some of the suffering. She petitioned MPs and gave television and radio interviews, before returning to Africa.

As the situation grew worse, Anne travelled around the country on a bicycle, a Honda motorcycle or a Volkswagen Beetle, providing urgent medical aid to local villagers. She worked during air raids and severe shelling. Throughout the crisis she had refugees living with her, sharing her food. She even cared for them in her home. Anne kept a diary during the 30 months of the war which gives a moving account of her experiences, of the dangers she faced and of the terrible things she saw, and the decisions she was forced to make.

"The last day at Isiukwator was a real nightmare. There were about 400 people at the clinic and we had to choose 40 to get midday meals at the "feeding centre"... being really firm we ended up with 96. Reasoning that 40 servings would cover 48 plates (they would spread the food a little thinner) we divided them up into two groups, one set to come on Mondays, Wednesdays and Fridays and the other set on the other days. Some of the mothers stood in the sun for four hours to try to get a child or children onto the list." (*Biafran Missionary Doctor* by Anne Seymour 1961-70 p58).

In 1969 the international photographer, Romano Cagnoni, spent a day photographing Anne's work at the Mission Hospital in Biafra. Cagnoni commented that Anne was one of the most beautiful people he had ever met.

By 1970 the war was over, the Biafrans were defeated and Biafra was incorporated once again into Nigeria, as the East Central State. Anne, who had worked with the Igbo in Biafra, began to be regarded as an anti-government influence and was in constant fear of being detained. She wrote: "While I still maintain that we were morally justified in going into Biafra against the wishes of the Nigerian Government, I never considered that entitled us to escape the legal consequences." As soon as she could and when the Nigerian Red Cross arrived to relieve her, she fled Nigeria and returned to England.

After nine years in Biafra, Anne took up a post in the Wirral before moving to South Shields in 1976. She was appointed consultant/surgeon in charge of A&E, at the Old Ingham Infirmary, which she ran effectively for the next 13 years. In this post she showed unerring professionalism and compassion for her patients, although having operated on people suffering terrible injuries during the Nigerian Civil War she would not suffer fools, particularly any drunken casualty cluttering up her A&E Department. One of her medical colleagues said, "In my experience the Mariner is only frightened of three things ... Cape Horn, Anaesthetics and Anne Seymour." A Staff Nurse said: "That may be true, she could be irritable, but Miss Ann Seymour is the only Consultant who ever made ME a cup of tea." Essentially, she was kind and compassionate and went out of her way to help those in need. She did many home visits out of hours or would drive people home if she felt they needed assistance. She often skipped a meal rather than interrupt a consultation. She ensured that no one had a pauper's funeral and would pay funeral costs out of her own pocket. She became a local legend during her own lifetime.

Anne was still drawn to Africa and in 1989, much to everyone's surprise, she took up the post of Medical Director/consultant in a rehabilitation centre for disabled children in Mabu, Bafut in the Central African country of Cameroon. It was the adopted mission of St Wilfred's Roman Catholic College in South Tyneside, and Anne would often write to them telling of her work. A parishioner from St Gregory's remembers receiving a letter from her written by the light of a hurricane lamp asking, "if the Parish might raise funds for a perimeter fence for her hospital ... to discourage wild animals." While in the Cameroon, she also helped out at two other hospitals, Shisong hospital in Kumbo and Martin de Porres Mission Hospital at Njinikom. In 1996, aged 61, and after seven years in the Cameroon, Anne decided to retire and return to her home in South Shields.

Her so-called retirement is an excellent example of how productive this phase can be in a person's life. Anne devoted her retirement to charity work. In 1987 she co-founded St Clare's Hospice in Jarrow, along with Lady Chapman and Dr. Alan Hill. Unfortunately it closed in 2018, but for 30 years it provided palliative care for adults in South Tyneside. Anne was also very involved with her parish church, St Gregory's in Harton, South Shields. For a time she ran the Girl Guides, English classes for refugees and Mother and Baby groups. She was an ever-present feature of the Annual Diocesan Pilgrimage to Lourdes, travelling with the sick and disabled year upon year, for which she received a Papal Medal. The parishioners of St Gregory's were among those who lobbied for the installation of a Blue Plaque to honour Anne's contribution to South Tyneside, which can be seen at the site of the old Ingham Infirmary, on Westoe Road in South Shields.

Anne's most outstanding "retirement", initiative though was that she founded STARCH (South Tyneside Asylum and Refugee Church Help) in 1999, a charity set up to support refugees in South Tyneside. The Charity organises drop-in sessions and access to a range of support services, as well as a safe haven for asylum seekers and refugees to meet and make friends. Having been a refugee herself in Nigeria, Anne was tireless in her support of asylum seekers and in 2016 the year of her death, she was honoured with an MBE "for her services to Asylum Seekers and refugees in South Tyneside."

Anne Seymour died peacefully in her sleep aged 80 and, subsequently, a beautiful headstone was placed in Harton Cemetery, South Shields to commemorate her.

When Anne died there was a huge outpouring locally of heartfelt grief and the local press was full of stories of her surgical skills and her many acts of kindness, from cooking Christmas dinner for anyone who had nowhere else to go, to giving away almost all she owned. Her personal disregard for fashion and her famous butterfly hats also received a mention.

The picture then is of a lady uninterested in material concerns, in no way egotistical, who applied her medical skills unsparingly and whose free time was spent helping those in need, old or young, either through personal intervention or through volunteer organisations. A woman of fierce intelligence, uncompromising, and no doubt challenging, but an inspirational woman of deep compassion.

Photo credit: Romano Cagnoni.

Environmental campaigner Jennie Shearan.

Jennie Shearan (1922 - 2005)

Fearless environmental campaigner and community activist

Jennie Shearan was born in Hebburn in South Tyneside and lived in that town for most of her life. It was there that she died in 2005, and it is there where today the lasting legacy of her campaigning and local activism is so clearly evident.

Jennie's early life, in a loving family environment but one in which money was very scarce, was largely shaped by the economic hardship in the North East of England caused by the Great Depression of the late 1920s and 1930s. During Jennie's youth Hebburn's neighbouring town, Jarrow, had 70 per cent male unemployment and Jarrow's economic plight gained national prominence with the Jarrow Crusade - that march of unemployed men from Jarrow to London, which eventually stirred the conscience of a nation and inspired a determination never again to allow hardship and poverty to exist in the country on such a scale.

The tenth child in a family of eleven, Jennie was only nine years old when her mother died, and she depended thereafter on the support of siblings and her father, a trade union official, to whom she was very close. This closeness and the nature of his work no doubt had the effect of making her aware from an early age of the economic and social ills affecting her neighbourhood and town. A belief in the importance of trade unionism and Labour politics were part of her upbringing.

By the mid-1930s, following the collapse of local industry including Palmer's shipyard, the biggest local employer, Jennie's father had left Hebburn to find work in Liverpool where some family members had already settled. Jennie, then a teenager went with him and remained there until almost the end of the Second World War. During her time there she worked in a munitions factory but was told that she was no longer needed after she had - successfully - argued for a pay rise on behalf of her fellow workers! It was in Liverpool during the war, aged 20, that she met a young Welsh sailor, David Shearan, whom she married in 1944. The war was still on when, as a wife and with a new baby, she decided to return to family in Hebburn to await the end of hostilities and prepare for the time when she and David could begin life together on a permanent basis.

David had begun his working life as a miner and, once his war duties were over, joined Jennie in Hebburn and gained employment at nearby Wardley colliery. After a period in one-bedroomed rented accommodation, in 1953 the couple were offered, and enthusiastically accepted, one of the new three-bedroomed council houses being built in the post-war period. It was in south Hebburn, on what would be known as the Monkton Lane Estate, close to the coke works that had been established in 1937 to provide local employment. However the estate was also on the edge of countryside and residents were told that the coke works only had a 20-year lifespan, due to expire in four years' time. The Shearans regarded their new house and garden as providing an ideal family home for the long term. The reality was to turn out to be very different.

Jennie relished her role as a wife and, over the next 18 years, as a mother of five children. She also played an active part in her local community and continued to take an interest in political and social issues. However her concern over the problems caused to her neighbourhood by the continued operation of the coke works became an increasing preoccupation. As early as the end of 1953 came the news that rather than ceasing operations as residents had been told, the coke works were going to be allowed to construct an additional battery of 33 ovens on land adjacent to those that would become defunct. Given the daily problems of black dust, fumes and noise from the plant, this expansion caused shock and dismay among those families, like Jennie's, living alongside it.

The use of coke, a smokeless fuel unlike coal, was expanding greatly in Britain in the late 1950s and 1960s, partly in response to the Great London Smog. Indeed, Hebburn was the first town in the country to be declared a smokeless zone, an extraordinary irony given the dark clouds of smoke and smog emanating continuously from the coke works and enveloping the houses in its vicinity.

By the beginning of the 1970s Jennie's children had mostly left home to start independent lives and she became freer to become more involved in local issues and politics. The local government reorganisation of the early 1970s had created new metropolitan counties and districts, and Hebburn found itself part of South Tyneside in the county of Tyne and Wear. As a Labour Party activist, Jennie expressed interest in becoming Hebburn's County Councillor and was duly selected - and then elected - in 1973. She took to her new role with enthusiasm, determined to represent effectively the people who had voted her in. She engaged with constituents, took up issues on their behalf and quickly made an impression through campaigning on issues as varied as providing ramps for disabled access, to being dubbed "Tyne and Wear Consumer Watchdog" through her work in monitoring prices in local stores and ensuring refunds for faulty products. She also embarked on a campaign to clean up her district, complaining not only of pollution from the coke works but demanding action to landscape areas of derelict land and calling for more funds to be directed to much needed environmental improvements as well as better facilities for the youth of the neighbourhood.

In 1980, in what amounted to a doubling of the coke works' capacity, National Smokeless Fuels gained permission to build an additional 33 ovens to replace the original defunct set. This new expansion would, in all likelihood, give the plant at least another 20 years of life, an appalling prospect for local residents. Jennie, who had begun to notice the high incidence of breathing problems and other health issues suffered by people in the area she represented, decided that tackling the pollution and harm caused by the plant must be her highest priority.

She began collecting soil samples and documenting the amount and frequency of black dust affecting local houses. She became an expert on what legal recourse against pollution was available to citizens, including European legislation which applied to Britain through its EEC, later EU, membership. By combing through records of County Council minutes she also found out that in 1963 experts had recommended that no more houses should be built near the coke works because of exposure to pollution. As a result of her work, in 1981 the council agreed to her demands to grant rent rebates to the affected tenants. This was important in itself but also meant that the scale of the problem had now been officially recognised.

Her efforts were not uncontroversial, however, because of the employment which the coke works provided. Given the history of unemployment in Jarrow and Hebburn, anything which seemed to threaten jobs was liable to cause concern. But Jennie was always clear in asserting that she was not trying to destroy jobs. Her primary aims were to ensure that Monkton should operate in such a way as not to cause pollution or damage the health of local residents. "The right to breathe clean air" - that was her mantra and it summed up the campaign perfectly.

In 1985 Jennie was chosen to be the Chair of Tyne and Wear County Council - a real tribute to her by her colleagues. She was the only woman ever to hold this position and, by force of circumstances, she turned out to be the last occupant of the role following the decision, a year later, by the Thatcher government to abolish metropolitan county councils.

In his excellent and moving biography of Jennie, her grandson Gianfranco Rosolia describes how the end of Jennie's council career coincided with "particularly bad incidents of pollution in Monkton Lane Estate with homes and cars coated in a yellow slime, and 80 mph winds scattering coal dust across the neighbourhood." Such incidents no doubt hardened Jennie's resolve to fight even harder for her area, whether an elected Councillor or not. And her resolve was immediately put to the test when, in 1987, National Smokeless Fuels put in a planning application to construct a power generation station at Monkton incorporating a chimney some 55 metres in height. In response Jennie and her supporters created a committee to oppose this further development and to highlight the extent of the environmental damage of the existing operation of the works. This committee became the Hebburn Residents' Action Group (HRAG).

In opposing the planning application Jennie and her group mobilised their supporters and presented a well-argued case that led to the application being unanimously opposed by the council. The group then began a series of protests and marches. They collected signatures to petition British Coal to clean up the coke works before any further expansion was considered. They organised charity and fundraising events and, using Jennie's already good press contacts, got good and widespread newspaper and television coverage. Indeed Jennie's TV performances were invariably excellent, showing her gift for plain yet authoritative speaking and allowing her undoubted sincerity and deep commitment to shine out.

Undaunted by local protests National Smokeless Fuels lodged a second application to expand the works and appealed to the Department of the Environment against the council's earlier decision. This led to a public inquiry at which Jennie and her group gave evidence and won again, convincing the Inspector of the inquiry that the application should be refused.

The campaign to clean up the works then gathered momentum, greatly helped by further TV coverage. Jennie had contacted the BBC programme *Watchdog* which took up the issue and portrayed how horrific the pollution was. This was later followed by an ITV-Tyne Tees documentary that was equally graphic. Jennie and her group - with generous support from local author Catherine Cookson - also lobbied the European Parliament in Strasbourg, meeting with Environment officials and MEPs on the Environment Committee.

British Coal and National Smokeless Fuels persisted in seeking to expand the plant and, on a technicality, were able to renew their application leading to a second public inquiry in 1990. They hired a top legal team to represent them, which posed a huge challenge to Jennie's group with their meagre financial resources and the limited time available in which to secure legal representation. However Jennie's campaigning had engaged the interest of Dr. Wendy Le-Las, an environmental campaigner and academic and she, via her own legal contacts, managed to get Charles Pugh, a barrister and expert on environmental legislation to act for the HRAG, pro bono. He would also be assisted by another environmental legal expert Philip Mead.

The outcome of this second inquiry gave outright victory to neither side. The Inspector was clear in his conclusions that the residents deserved a better quality of life but allowed the application to proceed with the important proviso that desulphurisation equipment be fitted regardless of cost.

At the same time some welcome news for the residents was that the council had decided to commission - and fund - a study by Newcastle University into the health effects of the plant, given the numbers of residents with respiratory problems, which Jennie and the HRAG had identified in their own prior community health study. However just as the official study was getting underway, British Coal announced suddenly and surprisingly that the plant was to be decommissioned. The public reason given was the decline in the demand for coke, although many suspected that the real reason was the cost of installing the anti-pollution equipment that the Inspector had insisted on at the conclusion of the public inquiry.

The relief that the plant's polluting activities were to stop was followed by dismay at British Coal's subsequent statement that the plant would be mothballed rather than demolished. This meant that it could start up again in the future and in the meantime the site could not be made available for any alternative form of employment. Then a further blow was dealt to the residents with the Secretary of State for the Environment, Michael Heseltine, overruling the need for desulphurisation equipment to be installed, thereby overturning the inquiry conclusions. In desperation, Jennie contacted a solicitor to see about serving papers on the Secretary of State and of appealing to the European Court of Justice. She was even prepared to sell her house to pay for this if necessary. She then waited months and heard nothing until January 1992, when another sudden announcement was made by British Coal that the coke works were going to be demolished. Hot on the heels of this announcement came the news that the Newcastle University study had concluded that residents near the plant were more likely than residents elsewhere on Tyneside to suffer from respiratory diseases and that health issues were linked to emissions from the works. Vindication of Jennie's long and tireless campaigning had at last been achieved.

Some eight years later in 2000, Jennie was present and spoke at the opening of the Monkton Community Woodland and Business Park on the coke works site. The area is now green and pleasant for the neighbouring residents to enjoy and the Business Park accounts for more jobs than the coke works when they were operating.

Jennie's non-stop campaigning and ultimate success shows clearly the virtues of persistence in pursuing a worthwhile cause. This persistence continued over the years despite her having to confront many personal and family challenges, including breast cancer, her husband's injury in a mining accident and his eventual illness and death.

Members of the Hebburn Residents' Action Group, such as sisters Jackie Grey and Jenny Lowry, have spoken of Jennie's inspirational leadership and the way that she motivated her supporters, convincing them that nothing would be too difficult for them to do in pursuing their goals. They admired how she was able to get influential people to help and speak up for them. Above all, they treasured the deep friendships and the many light-hearted moments they shared together and that enabled them to withstand setbacks and opposition cheerfully and purposefully.

Jennie's important campaign without doubt helped to ensure that never again would people be housed in such close proximity to industrial pollution. Her example has also inspired the work of the Environmental Law Foundation, which continues to help local communities the length and breadth of the country. It is heartening, particularly with the publication of her biography, that her work will now be permanently remembered in her home area of the country, the area which she loved so well.

Let us give the last word to Jennie herself. "If you can send a man to the moon, you can clean up Monkton Coke Works!"

Photos: Courtesy of Gianfranco Rosolia

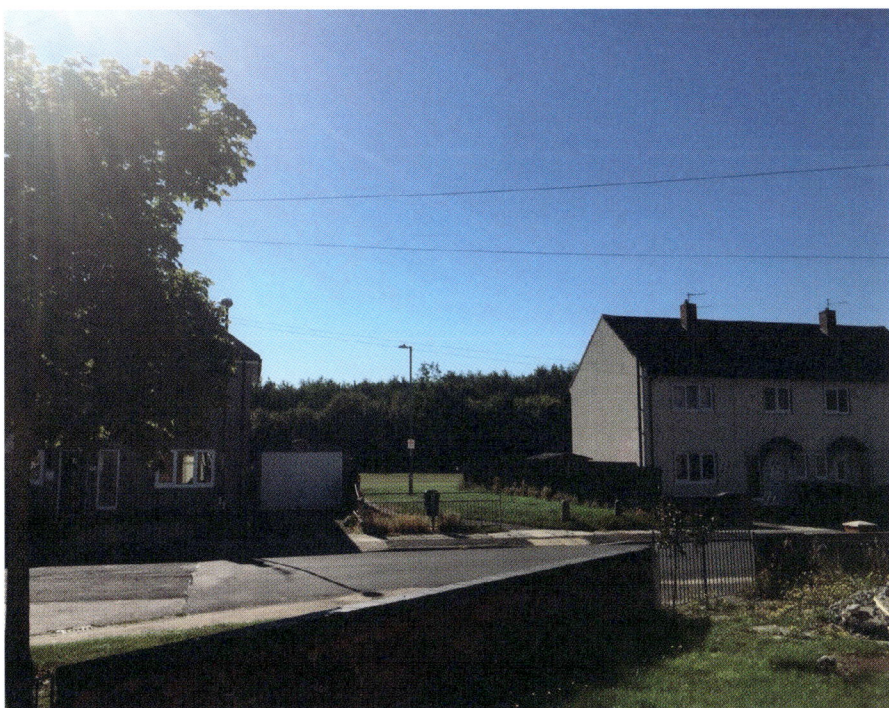

The difference in the local environment after Monkton Coke Works closed.

One of Elizabeth Shepherd's quilts on display at Beamish Museum.

Elizabeth Shepherd (Grey) (1875 - 1950)

Inspirational quilter

Quilts have been used as bed coverings since at least medieval times, and although the making of quilts, quilting, was a long-standing practice in the homes of many ordinary working people in different regions of the country, it has gone largely unrecorded until recently. This is the story of one archetypal quilter from the North East, Elizabeth Shepherd, of Coquet Island and Amble, a miner's wife, whose quilting skills enabled her to feed her family when her husband was too ill to work, and who produced beautiful artefacts that are today celebrated in print and have been exhibited at the Victoria and Albert Museum. The only known surviving specimen of her work is in the collection of Beamish Museum.

Before embarking on Elizabeth Shepherd's story, here is a brief outline of the processes involved in traditional quilting, the better to appreciate her work. The type of quilt produced in the North East is referred to as traditional or wadded quilting. These quilts consist of a sandwich of three fabric layers, two layers of cotton or cotton sateen with a layer of wadding in between. The wadding gave weight and warmth to the quilt, and by the 19th century cotton wool or cotton wadding was used as an alternative to wool. Quilting in the North of England became renowned for two types of quilt; "wholecloth" quilts which consisted of two pieces of fabric, often of different colours to give a reversible effect, with the wadding in between and "strippy," quilts which consisted of two contrasting materials split lengthwise and seamed together to make a top cover with between seven to 11 broad stripes. The different layers of material were held in place by a running stitch using linen or cotton threads, which also embellished the surface with decorative patterns. In the spaces between the lines of stitching the padding rises up so that the pattern is in relief.

The patterns were devised by the makers and were marked on the cloth in various ways, using tailor's chalk, blue pencil or they were simply needle-marked. The frames on which the quilts were made, were eight to nine feet long because the standard size for bed quilts was two and a half yards by two and a quarter yards. The frames did take up a lot of space but could be upended and stood against a wall when not in use.

These quilts were very labour intensive to make as all the stitching was done by hand. Having said that, several people, family members or friends, could and did work on quilts at the same time, and it was often a very sociable enjoyable process. Made in the home, quilts were often for use only in the home but sometimes they were made as a commercial venture, or to eke out low wages or in times of dire need, simply to put bread on the table.

Elizabeth or "Lizzie" Shepherd as she was known, was the sixth of seven children born to James and Elizabeth Grey. The family lived on Coquet Island, a small island that lies about a mile off the coast at Amble in Northumberland, and which today, although uninhabited by man, is a bird sanctuary, home to some 40,000 breeding seabirds. It was while living on Coquet Island that Lizzie, taught by her mother and stepmother, learned to make traditional quilts.

Lizzie's father was one of the island's three lighthouse keepers and the family home was one of two modest cottages there. Lizzie spent most of her early life on the island though she received some schooling on the mainland when the weather permitted safe crossing for the rowing boat. Lizzie's daughter, Belle, gives us a glimpse of Lizzie's early life when she says that, "her mother received very little education, that she sometimes stayed with her granny at Warkworth, and that she and her sister did all the sewing and knitting for the family - underclothing, shirts, dresses, mats, socks, fancy work and quilts. They also sewed for what was then called their bottom drawer which was their preparation for marriage." (Quilts 1700-2010)

Lizzie's mother died after her seventh child was born, sometime in the 1880s and although her father remarried, his second wife died too, and we find Lizzie still living on Coquet Island in 1901, aged 26 and housekeeper to her father.

However by November 1906, when Lizzie married, her address was given as 5 Panhaven Road, Amble, a two up two down terrace cottage, which can still be seen today, and which was to be her home for the rest of her life. She married a miner, John William Shepherd from Scott Street, Amble, who worked at the nearby Radcliffe Colliery. She was 31 years old and he 33. They had three children, two girls and a boy. However sometime after the end of the First World War, tragedy struck and John was seriously injured in a mining accident and would never work again.

Their daughter Belle Shepherd takes up the story:
"...my father was injured in the mines and he was denied compensation because the then doctors said his injury was due to natural disease. But he never worked again after the accident, the roof of the pit fell in on him and he was brought home battered and bruised from head to foot ... he lay untreated for at least a year ... and so my mother stuck in to quilting to help us out with the housekeeping. I had to go out and knock on people's doors and ask them if they wanted to join our club. And some refused, but many accepted until we

had a sufficient number to start off and we would stop collecting customers when we had reached twenty. And then we would start off and it took my mother a fortnight to make a quilt, she would sit down at about nine o'clock and carry on until dinner time without a break then rest for an hour or two and start work about three o'clock and with a break only for tea, would carry on at least until eight o'clock at night. And I helped with the housework and the quilt as soon as I was able to sit down.

"Well, my mother had many patterns, just at her fingertips. She was able to draw them quite easily, but when she was tired of the pattern she would look around and she would copy anything she could see, a curtain pattern or a chair seat pattern or anything she could copy and put on a quilt.

"The patterns were drawn on brown paper, then cut out for use. She drew the pattern onto the quilt in a day and a half, improving on them over the years. ... Well after taking a fortnight to make a quilt, my mother would have to bake on a Sunday it was the only time, then on Monday she would wash and she called that washing week, because she was always very tired and she would catch up on mending that week and extra housework ... She always got the material for the quilts from the Co-op and when I collected for the club I took all that money for the club up to the Co-op every week and the manager just let us have what material we needed as we needed it ... The customers chose their own colours. And this store, the Co-op manager, he gave us our own pattern book so that we always had it in the house so we could take it out to a customer and they would choose their pattern ... I collected the money every week, a shilling a week and took it straight up to the Co-op ... A full-sized quilt was three pounds ten (shillings) ... As far as I can remember the profit on a quilt was a pound to thirty shillings. I always thought it would have been more profitable to scrub floors, but my mother wasn't built that way! She had to stay in anyway to be with my father who was injured in the pit." *Traditional British Quilts*," Dorothy Osler (Batsford London 1987).

At least one quilt club, like Mrs Shepherds in Amble, was to be found in most mining villages in the North in the period up to the First World War and into the 1920s and 30s, because pit accidents, leading to injury or death meant that it was not uncommon for untrained married women to be forced to become the family breadwinner. What strikes you is how badly treated the miners and their families were, just left, bereft of any income, and mercifully, just how ingenious, persistent and stoical these women were in circumstances that would have overwhelmed many of us. The prices referred to above relate to the 1920s and 30s. The usual weekly sum was sixpence or a shilling collected until the full sum was paid off. Customers received their quilts in turn, often drawing lots to decide who received theirs first, second and so on. What is staggering is how little profit the quilters made given their skill and the time involved, to say nothing of their needs. Belle and Lizzie's sister, who lived a few doors away, helped with the quilt making especially in the evenings.

Dorothy Osler, author of *Traditional British Quilts*, interviewed Belle Shepherd in her mother's house in the course of her extensive research, and describes how Lizzie used her main living room for quilting. The standard traditional frame was set up in the 14 by 14 ft. room, which also accommodated a coal fired range and the stair alcove. The room must have been very cramped and, despite that, her poor husband had a bed in the alcove where he lay for most of the time.

As has been said, Lizzie bought all the fabrics for her quilts from the local Co-op, (today a Tesco Express shop and a Co-op Undertakers). Her receipt from the Amble Co-op for the purchase of Roman satin, wadding and thread, dated 1905, survives and is illustrated in the Bowes Museum exhibition book, *North Country Quilts*.

Despite accepting commissions for as many as 20 quilts at a time, Lizzie's work was of high quality and her design skills were better than the average club quilter. She was inspired by household objects such as the bentwood chair seat design used on the corner of the surviving quilt. She used the design on their family Bible for a quilt she made for her son and she copied designs from curtain fabrics. The surviving quilt made by Lizzie Shepherd is a lovely peach coloured wholecloth, and while the use of a shell design, is not particularly innovative, it is very beautifully executed, and so very appropriate for a quilt made in Amble, a fishing village as well as a mining village.

As Lizzie's reputation spread, by the 1930s she was receiving requests to make quilts from people further afield than Amble, from other places in Northumberland and from customers in Cromer (Norfolk) and Edinburgh for example. Lizzie also entered her quilts in the local shows, probably Warkworth, Alnwick and Glendale and she won many prizes. The prize money, usually about 10 shillings, would have made a welcome supplement to the family income. Lizzie went on quilting for many years though only one of her many quilts has been traced. She died in 1950 aged 75 years, by which time her daughter Belle, whom she had schooled so well, was making quilts on her own account.

Lizzie Shepherd was indeed a notable, inspirational lady. She was so strong and talented that, despite her lack of education, she was able to rise above a life of poverty, drudgery and hardship, and in cramped and difficult circumstances, was enterprising enough to create useful and beautiful artefacts, items which today we treasure as part of our national heritage.

Illustrator Amy Millicent Sowerby.

Amy Millicent Sowerby (1877 - 1967)

Illustrator of children's books and postcards

Amy Millicent Sowerby, who was born in Gateshead, was one of the most sought after and best-loved illustrators of children's books and postcards throughout the Edwardian period and beyond. Her utterly charming portrayal of happy, rosy cheeked, care-free children in idyllic settings, depicting fairy tales, nursery rhymes, and other traditional themes, endeared her to children and parents alike. Her imagination and the quality of her illustrations was such that even now her work continues to fetch high prices here and abroad.

Millicent was born in Low Fell, Gateshead, apparently with a silver spoon in her mouth. Her family were wealthy owners of the Sowerby Ellison Glassworks, which in the 1880s was the world's largest producer of pressed glass. However, their wealth was short lived.

Millicent's father, John George Sowerby, inherited this huge international glassworks business from his father in 1879. John George had six children. The eldest and only son was John Lawrence. The first daughter was Helen, then Githa, born in 1876. Only one year later came Millicent. The younger girls, Rachel and Ruth were born in 1880 and 1882. The family lived in a large Arts and Crafts' style house, "Ravenshill" in Low Fell, Gateshead, and kept seven servants and several gardeners.

As was typical in middle-class Victorian households, the five girls languished at home, educated by a series of governesses, isolated from local children and with only each other for company. Only Lawrence was formally educated, at Winchester College. The belief of middle-class society at the time was that women needed only minimal education as they were destined to marry or live a life of leisure. As events unfolded the girls' lack of either formal education or training, and their financial dependence on their father, would have proved disastrous had it not been for the talent and resilience of Millicent and her sister Githa.

Somewhat ironically, childhood for the Sowerby children was far from the happy ideal they later conjured up in their books. Their mother was rather stern and aloof and very content to hand the children over, first to a nanny and then to a stream of indifferent governesses. Their father ruled the household with a rod of iron, and their frequent house moves were very unsettling for the children.

Disastrously John George Sowerby's initial interest in the business quickly waned and while the glassworks flourished, John George's roles diminished. Instead of the glassworks, he spent his time on his two great passions, landscape painting and book illustration. He had artistic talent and enjoyed a modicum of success. He produced five children's books and exhibited some work at the Royal Academy, but he failed in his bid to make a living as an artist.

His financial mismanagement was such that in 1883, when Millicent was only six years old he was declared bankrupt and had to sell the family home to pay his debts. Gradually he severed all his links with the glassworks, moving the family every few years to ever-smaller houses to pay his debts, or sometimes just to give variety to the landscapes he could paint. In 1896 he foolishly sold his complete portfolio of shares in the company thus losing his main source of income. In 1903 he was again declared bankrupt. This time he moved the family from Reigate to Sutton Courteney in Oxfordshire, prime landscape painting country.

The impact of this second bankruptcy was devastating, it meant that John George Sowerby could no longer support his family. Although Helen and Lawrence were married by then, there were still four dependent, unmarried daughters at home.

However, from Millicent's point of view, disastrous though this bankruptcy was, it provided an escape route, an opportunity for personal independence and even for the artistic fulfilment she and her sister Githa craved. And so, in 1903, when Millicent was 26, driven by their father's improvidence and the need to support themselves, they set up home together in a small flat in London and planned a commercial venture, they would earn their own living and help to support their younger sisters by producing their own children's books in partnership. Githa would supply the poems and stories and Millie the illustrations.

Happily the sisters were both talented and determined. Millicent had shown an early aptitude for watercolours, which her father encouraged. She had attended some art classes in Newcastle when the family were living in Gateshead but was largely self-taught. Despite this lack of formal training, by the end of the century she had exhibited landscape paintings at the Bruton Gallery in Mayfair and the Royal Institute of Painters. She was very drawn to book illustrations for children and wrote, "It has always been the beautiful in childhood that has attracted me." She loved the work of the great illustrators of the day, Walter Crane and especially Kate Greenaway, and was inspired by the Arts and Crafts movement. Githa, on the other hand was interested in writing and already had some poems and articles published in magazines. She went on to become a well-known playwright.

The time was just right for their venture because at the end of the Victorian era rapid advances in printing techniques had made very good colour printing available to a mass market. This enabled artists like Kate Greenaway (1800-1901) and Walter Crane (1845-1915) and later Millicent Sowerby herself, to create beautifully coloured, high-quality illustrated children's books, and the market for children's books grew exponentially.

The partnership between the sisters was phenomenally successful. Financially they managed to earn the money they needed and artistically it led to the creation of 17 children's books over a 20-year period, with a later final publication, *The Glad Book*, in 1935. The fact that the sisters had complementary personalities helped enormously. Githa was forceful, dominant and assumed a leadership role. Physically she was the taller and more striking of the pair. Millicent had a reserved and quiet nature but was highly creative and equally confident in her abilities, determined to succeed and extremely hard working. She quietly did what she loved most, she imagined and painted pictures to delight.

Throughout the rest of their lives Millicent and Githa worked closely together and continued to live together until Githa's marriage in 1912. Thereafter Millicent either lived alone in her little flat and studio in Kensington or stayed with Githa and her family. Millicent herself never married but became doting "Aunt Mill", to Githa's only child Joan, and to her sister Helen's daughter Dorothy, with whom she was close.

The first book of their partnership was published in 1906 and was called *The Wise Book*. It was always only Millicent's name that appeared on the hard cover of their books presumably for marketing reasons, as initially, at least, she was better known than Githa. In 1907, came two more books, a fairy story called, *Bumbletoes*, and another poetry book, *Childhood*. These first three books made a very considerable impact, not least among publishers so that as early as 1907 Millicent Sowerby had become the "go to" children's illustrator and was invited by the publishers Chatto and Windus to illustrate, *Alice in Wonderland*. This was quite a scoop and Millicent was delighted to agree. "Alice" was the first children's book to have a strong-minded girl as its main character and Millicent was the first woman to illustrate Alice. The very next year she was asked to illustrate Robert Louis Stevenson's best-selling *A Children's Garden of Verses*. Reviewers described her illustrations as "characteristically excellent". Both books became children's classics.

Another milestone for Millicent was her association, in 1910, with the children's publishers Henry Frowde and Hodder and Stoughton. The first book with Henry Frowde was *Little Stories for Little People* for which Millie and Githa each received £35. (A one-off payment per book was normal.) Thereafter Millicent became Frowde's leading illustrator of books for the very young and unusually was paid a retainer by them. By 1915 she was earning £150 a year from Frowde's alone, and by 1921 double that amount. A review in 1911 of all the books she had illustrated proclaimed, "Millicent Sowerby is Kate Greenaway come to life again." This must have pleased Millicent enormously.

When, in 1922, Githa became a very rich woman from the unexpected bequest of a magnificent house in Kensington Square and a lump sum of £44,000 (equivalent to £5 million today), all their financial worries were over at a stroke. Imagine their relief. But it also meant that Githa could no longer commit to working on children's books, and at that point their children's book partnership of 17 years came to an end.

However, by that time Millicent was already successful in her own right. Her income did not derive from books alone, she had another important source of finance, picture postcards for children. Today hardly anyone sends postcards, but in 1871, 75 million were sent from the UK, and in 1910 the total had swollen to an incredible 800 million, many of which were picture postcards for children.

The first children's picture postcards appeared in Germany in 1898 and by 1902 they had become and remained an absolute craze in Britain for decades. They were a great novelty and children loved them. Their popularity was supported by a highly efficient, almost incredible postal service which guaranteed a 24-hour delivery from and to anywhere in the UK. The huge variety and high quality of these postcards meant that collecting them became as popular as sending them.

Millicent was quick off the blocks and as early as 1905, and for the next 20 years, she was commissioned by seven different publishing houses to produce whole series of children's postcards on themes such as fairy tales, the seasons or children's games. Her series for CW Faulkner, *Happy Childhood*, depicting Shakespearean scenes, was described as, "one of the daintiest sets ever produced." But by far the most successful was her series *Postcards for the Little Ones*. Commissioned by Hodder and Stoughton, these consistently sold in their thousands. The style of her illustrations, her images of blithe and beautiful children captured perfectly the atmosphere of the middle-class nursery and Millicent soon became one of the best-loved and most popular postcard artists.

Born in the reign of Queen Victoria, Millicent lived through two World Wars and the massive political and social changes that followed, however she lived quietly, unobtrusively dedicated to her work and her family. A keen seamstress she made clothes for herself, Githa and her nieces and cousins. Yet despite Millicent's dedication to the family, the family seem to have under-valued her. I am sure Millicent was unaware of this but it provides a useful reminder of how families can easily underrate each other. Githa's daughter

Joan had this to say: "I saw a lot of Aunt Mill of course because she was always visiting us and she worked very closely with Ma over the children's books. No one in the family realised that Aunt Mill was as talented as she was or that her illustrations and paintings would one day become so highly prized. Everyone underestimated her." (*Looking for Githa*. Patricia Riley. p102 recalled in an interview with Githa's biographer Patricia Riley in 2008).

Millicent Sowerby continued to paint delightful watercolours well into her 80s and died from a brain haemorrhage in her little flat in Bina Gardens, London, at the age of 89. Millicent's estate was worth £20,000 in today's money and was left to her niece Dorothy Green of Field Head, Broughton in North Lancashire. Sometime after her death, Dorothy, not realising how valuable they were, gave away a lot of her aunt Mill's paintings and made a bonfire of some of her drawings.

There can be no doubt that Millicent Sowerby's achievements were very considerable. She illustrated 18 books of verses and stories published under her own name. She was retained by Henry Frowde for decades and illustrated Rose Fyleman's *Sunny Book* published by Oxford University Press in 1918. And in parallel with this she was operating as an independent illustrator and producing postcards designed to transport children to beautiful worlds of adventure and fantasy, which sold in their thousands. She gave great happiness and enjoyment to countless children at home and abroad and, equally exceptional for a woman at that time, she achieved commercial success and managed to earn her own living.

Today Millicent Sowerby's illustrations sell for hundreds and sometimes several thousand pounds. Her postcards can be found on internet sites and are widely reproduced and framed with copies selling for around £50 each.

Millicent's Alice in Wonderland, 1907.

Children's picture postcards produced in 1915 by Millicent Sowerby including, above, Cinderella, and, opposite, Leap Frog and Cricket. Images: Mary Evans Picture Library

Elsie Tu (1913 - 2015)

Hong Kong people's champion

The indomitable and courageous Elsie Tu.

Lasting 102 years, Elsie Tu's life - both public and private - was an extraordinary one for its twists and turns. When she was a girl, her father - scarred by the suffering and pain he had witnessed in the First World War affecting both his fellow soldiers and in the communities near the Western Front where he was stationed - impressed upon her the need for education, and to use her education to work for the poor and for social justice. He would never have expected, that in taking this lesson to heart, his daughter would champion the cause of exploited and penniless people, not of her native Tyneside, but thousands of miles away in Hong Kong.

Elsie was born Elsie Hume, the second child of four, in Newcastle in 1913. Her childhood was not easy as the family had little money and Elsie's mother's behaviour was by all accounts controlling and unreasonable towards her husband and children. Elsie remembers, without fully understanding at the time, how her mother would accuse her father of having affairs during the long hours he worked as a tram conductor, when in reality the extra hours were simply an attempt to make ends meet. She also recalled how her mother's displays of favouritism towards one or other of her children at different times made all of them frightened and resentful. Later on, when Elsie was 16, a ghastly incident in the family home occurred when the husband of Elsie's elder sister Ethel, (who were both living with the family at the time) attacked his wife with a knife, injuring her and Elsie's father, who intervened to try to help avert the attack. Elsie ended up having to give evidence in court, although Ethel refused to incriminate her husband. As a result he got a year's prison sentence, to be spent in a psychiatric hospital depending on his state of mind.

Elsie's schooldays were also disrupted because of frequent family changes of address. She attended primary and junior schools in Heaton and Walker and for a while in West Jesmond, where she was looked down on because her family was badly off and lived in a poor neighbourhood. Her secondary education was at Benwell Secondary and then at Heaton Secondary Girls School where she was happier. She was an able pupil in every sense, performing very well academically but also showing prowess in sporting activities. At the time she left school her headmistress, Miss Cooper, wrote a glowing testimonial to her in the following words: "Elsie Hume was always an exceptionally high-principled and conscientious student and was also a very keen athlete. She was Captain of the First Lacrosse and First Rounders Teams and School Sports Captain in 1982. Elsie was always most public-spirited and energetic." Those last words, in particular, seem strikingly apt - and prophetic - in view of Elsie's later life and works. Elsie also received a Special History Prize at school from Florence Nightingale Harrison Bell, who had donated the prize in memory of her husband Joseph.

Elsie had at first envisaged getting some sort of job on leaving school in order to help family finances. However, given her academic record, the school persuaded her to apply to university, to Armstrong College, Newcastle (then a college of Durham University) to study education and get qualifications to teach - teaching often being the only viable career option for women in those days. She graduated in 1937.

During her teenage school years and at university Elsie's social conscience was stirred by the poverty she saw on Tyneside which was exacerbated by the difficulty of finding jobs after the First World War and deepened further in the aftermath of the 1929 Wall Street crash and the consequent great depression. She was particularly touched by the plight of middle-aged and older people and their feelings of despair and pessimism about their future. She began to articulate her views and although at first terrified of speaking in public, she discovered she could get people's attention and interest when doing so. She said in later life that "stage fright" had never been completely overcome, even after many years of living in the public eye.

At university, Elsie became a member of the Plymouth Brethren Christian sect. This followed previous experiences of evangelical Christianity but this time in a way which became all-embracing and exclusive. Her new beliefs were also strongly reinforced by her boyfriend at the time, with whom she was deeply in love and expected to marry. For a woman marriage within the sect meant domination by the husband whose responsibility was to abide by church teachings above all other commitments. Both she and her boyfriend aspired to become missionaries and to work abroad after finishing their studies and undergoing the necessary training and preparation.

At university Elsie suffered a painful illness that delayed her studies and her graduation day and that would eventually mean (although that wasn't quite understood at the time) that she would be unable to bear children.

Immediately after university Elsie sought full-time work and was offered a job in Halifax teaching English and history. She lodged with a Plymouth Brethren family, the Elliots, and divided her time between work and church, while keeping in touch with her boyfriend in Northumberland. He, however, began to write less frequently. When she returned to the North East their relationship ended, which caused her much pain and sadness.

Once more living at home, she first taught in Prudhoe for a while, commuting by train from Newcastle. After the Second World War broke out in 1939, she began teaching at Todd's Nook school in Newcastle. As the war progressed she saw for herself, in distressing circumstances, some of the wartime damage around the city, with one of her former homes being destroyed. On one occasion she encountered two brothers, both air raid wardens, who advised her to take refuge in an underground shelter and learned shortly afterwards that both of them had been tragically killed by a bomb that same evening.

At the beginning of the war Elsie also undertook some basic nursing and first aid training, something which was to prove unexpectedly useful in her later life.

She subsequently found herself evacuated with the children she had been teaching to Great Corby in Cumberland and, although obviously still very concerned about the war and its effects, she found life there peaceful, happy and satisfying. Throughout her life she retained the fondest memories of the natural beauty of that area.

Elsie had kept contact with the Elliott family in the Plymouth Brethren community in Halifax and received a marriage proposal from Bill Elliott, one of the sons of the family. He, like Elsie, aspired to missionary work. Elsie liked Bill but at first turned him down, not being in love with him and having already some doubts about the role of women in marriage as laid down by church doctrine. Eventually however, and after assurances from Bill that he would interpret church rules liberally and with understanding of her concerns, she accepted him and began to look forward to a missionary life overseas. After preparations, and family farewells, they set off with other missionaries at the end of 1947, arriving in China in 1948.

They first went to Nanchang in Jiangxi province and consolidated the mission there. Elsie was committed to the work and keen to educate children, spread the Christian message and seek converts. Not long after coping with the problems of finding accommodation, getting settled and beginning to engage with the local population, she found herself becoming uneasy with the attitude of some of her fellow missionaries towards the local Chinese population. She felt that they looked down on them, and in some ways they embodied some of the worst views and attitudes of colonial conquerors, seemingly unable to understand or appreciate local skills, culture and traditions. She applied herself to study Mandarin and was determined to succeed, particularly since she was told that married women usually did not manage to make much progress! Her knowledge of the language would prove useful in later years.

This was a turbulent period of Chinese history. The country was on the brink of civil war between the supporters of Chiang Kai Shek and those of the Communist party under Mao Tse Tung. Many people fled their homes, fearing reprisals from one side or another in the fighting. Missionaries were warned that their work would become impossible in the event of a Communist victory and, although Elsie felt that the scare stories about the Communist Party were not borne out by the orderly and disciplined nature of the take-over that she personally witnessed, she understood that religious proselytising and missionary activity by Christians from the countries that had previously colonised large areas of China would not be allowed in future.

Accordingly, and after only three years in China, she and her fellow missionaries and church members left the country and sought refuge in British-owned Hong Kong. Initially her church had expected Hong Kong to be simply a staging post on the way to Borneo, but in the end they stayed there and began missionary work in the poorer areas, particularly the squatter neighbourhoods where so many of the refugees had gathered.

It was difficult finding accommodation as money was tight and in the squatter neighbourhoods housing provision was of the most basic variety. Yet Elsie very quickly began to empathise with the plight of the local population and was struck by how much they were exploited. She particularly admired the exquisite needlework and embroidery of the Swatow women and was appalled that such beautiful and skilled work was rewarded with pittance wages that were not enough to live on. She was determined to combine her church work with her educational vocation, wanting to give the local children a better start in life that would equip them to begin the process of escaping poverty.

Through the church she met Andrew Tu, who had left his home in Inner Mongolia in China to try to make a better life for himself in Hong Kong. He too was a qualified teacher and he and Elsie both found that they wanted the children to read other books in addition to the Bible, which many of the church members felt was the only book they should read. Little did she realise at that stage how important Andrew would become to her but from the outset she felt he was an inspiring teacher. In her words "watching Andrew teach was a never-ending delight to me. I learned more from watching him than in all my years of training".

The cramped and insanitary conditions in which she and Bill were living occasionally caused dismay and amazement among other British residents that they sometimes came into contact with. At one point, a British resident they knew who was returning to the UK wanted them to look after their dog but on seeing their accommodation exclaimed that in no way would she let her dog live there. "We live in a house unfit for dogs," Elsie would joke thereafter. The housing in the neighbourhood was occasionally damaged or even destroyed by typhoons or other storms bringing torrential rain and wind.

Elsie and Bill kept open house for their Chinese neighbours, and with Elsie's nursing training frequently acted as a kind of unlicensed clinic, helping to treat a wide variety of ailments when people could not afford to access even the most basic of medical services.

Along with Andrew and some others Elsie started a school of her own given the lack of any state provision and it was particularly through this process that she became acutely aware of the corruption that characterized much of Hong Kong's economic life in those days. To get any jobs done very often involved bribes or paying protection money to the triad gangs that controlled many districts and who were often in collusion with corrupt police officers or government officials. Such personal experiences were to motivate her in her later work on highlighting corruption and campaigning to see it tackled at the highest levels of government and administration.

Elsie and Bill seem to have both tried to make their marriage work, but Bill's earlier promise to be a liberal-minded husband very much took second place to his desire to please his church and obey its every rule. This caused Elsie increased frustration and anger, boiling over into a public declaration in the church that she could not accept its decrees. While some members - usually secretly - sympathised and agreed with her, others did not and even spread rumours about her, accusing her of affairs or other improper behaviour.

During this difficult time, Bill developed a tubercular infection which, it was felt, should be treated back in England and, reluctantly, Elsie felt she must accompany him while regretting deeply not being able to continue the hard and difficult work that she had become so committed to. Once back home, Elsie renewed contacts with her own and Bill's family and records how astonished they were at her gaunt appearance and her thinness, the result of overwork, poverty and poor diet. The unpleasantness on the part of some of the members of the church in Hong Kong also made itself felt in England because of letters that some of them sent to the church authorities in the UK, again accusing Elsie of unwifely and improper behaviour. Elsie was dismayed that Bill, although certain that she was completely innocent of the charges, refused to criticise or contradict the church and would not defend her publicly.

Bill decided that he did not want to go back to Hong Kong, which caused Elsie to confront her own wishes both with regard to her marriage and her teaching vocation. After much heart-searching and confiding in her oldest and best friend from her schooldays in Newcastle, she made the decision to return to Hong Kong alone and do her utmost to make her school a success. Nervous that the church would try to stop her, she made her travel arrangements in secret and successfully returned to Hong Kong after an arduous sea journey, during which she experienced mental turmoil about what had happened and what the future would hold. Bill did not want a divorce, which his church opposed, but, although that troubled her, it did not stop Elsie in her determination to live her own life and to pursue what she felt would be a much more purposeful existence in Hong Kong.

Her return to Hong Kong was far from straightforward but, after many trials and difficulties, Elsie and Andrew managed to get a new school up and running and had the satisfaction of seeing it grow and expand. Finances remained a challenge and, in order to balance the books, Elsie also took on a job working in a college. She became active in campaigns and organisations to improve the lot of the countless poor of Hong Kong whose voices had gone unheard for so long. Her matter-of-fact account of her workload and schedule at the time, as described in her autobiography, leaves the reader astounded at the sheer stamina she must have possessed as well as her strength of character in not getting overwhelmed by pressure.

In the 1960s she began to lobby not only the Hong Kong authorities but also the British Parliament, alerting MPs to the lack of democracy and the poor living and working conditions of the people in what was still a British colony. The 1960s was the decade of widespread decolonisation in Asia and Africa, but in contrast to this changing landscape Hong Kong seemed to be in a time warp and embody many of the problems of the past. Elsie joined the Reform Club - a quasi-political party, loosely allied to the Liberals in Britain and got elected to the Urban Council in 1964 aged 51. For the rest of her long life she was a well-known public figure. She wrote letters to British newspapers calling for educational and social reforms in Hong Kong and within the Urban Council, she spoke up for higher wages, better housing, better public transport, free primary and secondary education for all and proper access to healthcare. She was particularly known for calling out corruption whenever she came across it and for defending victims of corruption and whistle-blowers who sought to expose it, often at great risk to themselves.

Elsie was to serve on the Urban Council for 32 years. Apart from her first election as a Reform Club candidate, she always stood as an Independent. She continued with Andrew to run her school and by the time they retired from teaching in 2000 they had managed to increase their pupil numbers from only 30 at the very beginning to 3,000, spread over three different sites!

In the early years of her service on the Urban Council she had to face some difficult and dangerous situations. The most dramatic example occurred at the time of the Star Ferry protests in 1965 when fares were increased to a level which many people dependent on the service could not afford. Elsie had voted against the increase but the protests against the plans turned violent and Elsie was blamed for this, the riots being dubbed the "Elsie riots". She was the subject of abuse and media smears and it took a long time for her to clear her name.

With much courage she held her nerve and continued to expose corruption such as the protection rackets whereby traders had to pay money to triads, some of which was then siphoned off to elements of the police service who were condoning such behaviour. She was often told she was a fantasist about corruption (although she had numerous documented examples). Her opponents sought to discredit her, saying she needed psychiatric help or alleging that she was naïve and believed everything that anyone would tell her. She would reply indignantly that nothing could be further from the truth and that she always investigated claims thoroughly before taking up cases. She set up a fund of justice to allow people some legal aid, especially those exposing the triads and corrupt officials.

Things began to improve markedly in the 1970s when Elsie established an excellent relationship with the new governor of Hong Kong, appointed in 1971, Sir Murray MacLehose. He was to be the longest serving governor with four successive terms in office. It was during his tenure that conditions for the people of Hong Kong improved dramatically. He brought in free compulsory education for all up to the age of 14, he launched an extensive housing programme, he established systems of social welfare and legal aid. He prepared the way for a comprehensive public transport system, promoted public parks and green spaces for people to enjoy, and importantly recognised Chinese as an official language. Above all he set up the Independent Commission Against Corruption (IAC) in 1974 under encouragement from Elsie herself.

Her personal situation improved too, as around that time she moved to Kowloon and got a room with a bathroom attached, which she described as "sheer luxury". She gradually became able to afford a better diet and more comfortable living conditions and thus started to benefit from the increasing prosperity and the economic boom in the colony, which took place from the 1970s onwards.

Her tireless efforts were also rewarded with a number of honours. Sir Murray MacLehose recommended her for a CBE, awarded in 1977. She recalled that in pinning on the medal, Sir Murray told her that this was for "great courage and achievement". He also publicly acknowledged her role in motivating him to introduce his widespread reforms and to tackle corruption. That same year she received the Queen's Silver Jubilee Medal. In 1976 she had been awarded the Ramon Magsaysay award. This is a highly prized award given to individuals and organisations working in Asia who "address issues of human development in Asia, with courage and creativity, and in doing so have made contributions which have transformed their societies for the better."

In 1988, she received an Honorary Doctorate from the University of Hong Kong and in 1997 she was presented with Hong Kong's highest honour, the Grand Bauhinia medal, in the first year in which it was awarded. She was the only woman among 12 recipients. It is given to recognise those who have made a significant and lifelong contribution to the wellbeing of Hong Kong.

Throughout these years of achievement, Andrew was a constant presence and she said that "without Andrew's support I could not have gone through all the difficulties of those years." They remained close friends, but at first neither of them could contemplate anything more than that while Elsie remained married to Bill. However eventually, much to Elsie's relief and surprise, Bill did agree to a divorce, having found someone else he wanted to marry. Elsie and Andrew visited the UK on a few occasions and sometimes had time to visit some of Elsie's favourite places of the past, including Whitley

Bay, Hexham, the Roman Wall and Cragside. These were happy times with Andrew falling in love with Northumberland and Elsie's family taking to Andrew and, apparently, expressing their hopes that he and Elsie would eventually marry!

A long and deep friendship such as they had enjoyed did indeed prove to be a good basis for a future life together and Andrew and Elsie married in 1985. The book they began jointly, which Elsie completed and published in 2003, *Shouting at the Mountain: a Hong Kong story of Love and Commitment* chronicles their friendship and enduring love, which continued until Andrew's death in 2001. Besides Andrew's abilities as a teacher and his association with Elsie's cherished causes he was a committed environmentalist, before environmental concerns gained their current prominence and urgency. He was also a longstanding campaigner for compensation and reparations to be given to victims of the Japanese in the Second Sino-Japanese War, calling for an official apology to be given by the Japanese Government.

Elsie was not convinced by Governor Chris Patten's reform programme when he became governor in 1992. She felt that he was needlessly antagonising China when everyone knew that the handover of Hong Kong to China had been concluded and that his actions were in conflict with the agreement that the UK had entered into, showing bad faith. However, when accused of being pro-China she responded fiercely "I'm not for China, I'm not for Britain. I've always been for the people of Hong Kong and for justice. I will do the work I've always done and stand for the people who get a raw deal."

However, being seen as pro-Beijing did lead to her losing her seat on the Urban Council in the election of March 1995, thus bringing her 32-year stint to an end, even though she retained much personal popularity. Indeed, one commentator described her as "the pro-Beijing camp's only worthy, authentic, popular hero," a description undoubtedly meant to be complimentary although Elsie would likely have bridled at the label.

Elsie largely retired from political life once she had turned 80 but nonetheless occasionally showed her independence of mind when speaking or writing in protest against government policies in post-1997 Hong Kong which she felt were unjust or insufficient.

Indeed, even at age 100 in 2013, she was still prepared to speak out, criticising the growing income disparity within Hong Kong, complaining about the selfish behaviour of some "rich men without conscience" and expressing sympathy with striking dock workers.

On the occasion of her 100th birthday a banquet was held and the Elsie Tu Education Fund was set up in her honour. When she died aged 102 on 2nd June 2015, her funeral was practically a state occasion with Hong Kong's three most senior political figures acting as pallbearers. Elsie's ashes were then buried with the remains of her beloved husband Andrew.

It is something of a paradox that Elsie, who was a household name in Hong Kong, is virtually unknown in her home area of Tyneside where she lived all her early life. However, her alma mater, Newcastle University, did honour her in 1996 when she was awarded an Honorary Doctorate in Civil Law.

The citation, recognising her as one of the most distinguished graduates of the University described her as "for over forty years the voice of Hong Kong's social conscience, fiercely dedicated to the protection and the welfare of the poor and disenfranchised" and her life as having been "so fruitfully dedicated to the civil and political rights of those whose voices would otherwise never have been heard."

A heartfelt tribute indeed to an indomitable, courageous and compassionate woman.

Elsie and Andrew Tu in 1995.

Elizabeth Spence Watson (1839 - 1919)

Campaigner for women's suffrage and for better economic and social conditions

Spence Watson/Weiss Archive

Photograph of Elizabeth, her husband Robert and their six children: Mabel, Ruth, Evelyn, Mary, Bertha and Arnold, c.1890

In his book about Robert Spence Watson, published in 1914, Percy Corder describes Robert's marriage to Elizabeth as "the beginning of an ideally true comradeship in the joint enterprises of life both small and great." He continues, "to her he owed the constant stimulus and encouragement of a high-souled nature". He describes Elizabeth as "a keen lover of justice and gifted with an untiring zeal in the furtherance of all good causes."

Elizabeth Spence Watson, so often referred to as Robert Spence Watson's wife, deserves to be remembered in her own right. Researching her life and reading her journals reveals just how many significant activities and causes she pursued with determination and flair over many years.

Elizabeth was born in Newcastle in 1839, the third daughter of Edward and Jane Richardson of Summerhill Grove. Her family were well known Quakers and the household was one where women were rated intellectually equal with men and where education for both sexes was felt to be very important. The family also had a long and distinguished history of involvement with the campaigns against slavery and the slave trade, and boycotted the produce of slavery such as sugar.

Elizabeth was educated at Lewes School and then studied in the School of Art in Newcastle, where one of her teachers was the famous pre-Raphaelite artist William Bell Scott. It was when she was a student that she became engaged to Robert Spence Watson, whom she married in 1863 at the Friends Meeting House in Newcastle. She was aged 24 and he was 26. Setting up home together, they eventually, after Robert's father's death in 1875 moved into Robert's family home - Bensham Grove, Gateshead - where they lived and brought up six children, five daughters and one son. The house, a vibrant Community Centre today, was set in five acres and is frequently referred to by Robert and Elizabeth in family papers as "our beloved home" where "we have spent so many happy years." It would become, over time, not only a treasured family house but a place that welcomed many illustrious Victorians as visitors - including people from the world of politics, industry and the arts. It also hosted many local activities.

Elizabeth was devoted to her home and family and was keen to support her husband in his national and local roles. Her support was far from passive - she saw her role as actively promoting causes that she and Robert jointly held dear and this involved campaigning, organising and attending meetings in her own right. On occasions Elizabeth and Robert would share platforms and both of them would be asked to speak. Robert, from all the evidence, thoroughly approved of this and rejoiced in Elizabeth's work. He had a long record as a strong advocate of women's rights, declaring that there would be "no remedy for the ills of the world until women get political power."

Describing Elizabeth's wide range of activities is a daunting task but they can roughly be listed under the following headings: women's suffrage; women's rights; Liberal party politics; anti-slavery; education; measures to tackle poverty; and last, but not least, peace and international relations.

The struggle for women to obtain the vote was a long one and Elizabeth was involved in suffragism from mid-Victorian times, in the 1860s and 1870s long before the later and better-known suffragette campaigns that gained momentum after the formation of the Womens Political and Social Union at the beginning of the twentieth century. She supported the efforts of various MPs to promote legislation to give women the vote which began with John Stuart Mill in 1866 and which were followed by debates on the subject in almost every year in the 1870s and 1880s. She was involved in the Women's Franchise League, set up in 1889, and in 1897 she co-authored a public letter, alongside Elizabeth Garrett Anderson and others, commending those MPs who had voted in favour of women being given the vote that year. She co-founded the North East and District Women's Suffrage Society in 1900 and was a Council member of the North of England Society for Women's Suffrage.

Along with many suffragists and in line with Quaker pacifism, Elizabeth did not support suffragette campaigns where violence was involved, such as stone throwing or attacks on property. However, she frequently expressed understanding at the frustration that had led to such demonstrations, conceding - in a statement to the *National Graphic* newspaper - that "it must be remembered that quieter methods have been pursued during a long course of years with apparent want of success." It is notable that in the North East, which was a hive of suffragette activity, there were many good relationships and friendships between suffragists and suffragettes and whatever differences about tactics existed there was overwhelming recognition of that common goal which they both wanted to achieve. Fittingly, Elizabeth was to chair - in April 1918 - the year before she died, a rally in Newcastle to celebrate the passing of the Women's Franchise Bill in Parliament.

While seeking to separate the various campaigns and causes Elizabeth was promoting it is clear that there was overlap between them. Elizabeth was active in Liberal Party politics - hardly surprising given that Robert was President of the National Liberal Foundation. When she set up the Newcastle Central Women's Liberal Association in 1886 (and became its first President) she opened its inaugural meeting by saying that the members "did not wish it to be a mere party movement or additional machinery available for electioneering purposes" ... but that "the principle of the Association was to educate both men and women that women were capable of being full citizens and should be given the franchise".

She was to head the Newcastle Liberal Association for over 25 years, standing down from the role a year after Robert died in 1911. Throughout her Presidency of the Association, she was also active in setting up new branches, particularly in other parts of the North East, and she acquired a reputation as an excellent organiser, activist and public speaker. Meetings of the Association were devoted to a huge variety of political issues. While women's suffrage and "a woman's place in modern politics" were always recurring topics, other matters of regular interest were municipal reform and local government, Ireland (including Home Rule) and international affairs. There were also discussions about how the Liberal Party should engage with the new, emerging Labour Party and Labour candidates, and how both parties could encourage working men's representation in Parliament. There are many tributes to Elizabeth's public speaking skills, with the well-known Liberal MP John Morley being moved by "the beautiful speech" of his friend Elizabeth at the time of his retirement from politics.

Belonging to a family with a longstanding and ardent commitment to the anti-slavery movement, it is not surprising that Elizabeth strongly shared her husband's outrage at the order given to British ships by Prime Minister Disraeli in 1875 that they should return any stowaway slaves to their owners. Robert, Elizabeth and others threatened to indict Disraeli as a result, should he persist with this policy. Robert and Elizabeth were proud of their continuing links with anti-slavery campaigners and indeed their home, Bensham Grove, had welcomed many of the key people involved in the fight against slavery including the celebrated former slaves Frederick Douglass and William Wells Brown.

Within Gateshead, in particular, Elizabeth was active in promoting educational opportunities for all, but always focusing especially on the needs of those from disadvantaged backgrounds where money was tight. She served for a number of years as Secretary to the Committee of the Ragged and Industrial School for Girls and later, with Robert, was "a prime mover in the founding of the High School for Girls in Gateshead." For 18 years she was also a Guardian of Poor Law at Gateshead's workhouses. She was concerned about good nutrition and health, promoting cookery classes for women of differing backgrounds and needs. She was a member of the Gateshead Nurses Association, of the Girls Friendly Society, the Newcastle and Gateshead Vigilance Association, the Band of Hope and the British Women's Temperance Association.

Even women's fashions concerned her as can be seen in a letter she wrote to the *Daily News* in London in 1907 complaining that the paper had given coverage to "a London modiste" urging women to lace tightly to get the tiny waists beloved of high Edwardian fashion. She remonstrated "In these days when the evils of tight lacing have been so often and so continually shown, when hygiene and the rules of health are taught in our schools, when we had begun to think that tight lacing had gone out of vogue, it is truly deplorable to read of such teaching, made all the worse by insidiously beginning with the mothers of the young girls whom it is sought to influence ..."

Her major interest, outside women's suffrage, was undoubtedly the great issues of war and peace. In 1888, in the Women's Liberal Association, she was already talking about how to prevent "useless and wrong" wars, supporting John Morley MP and others in their views. She was active in opposition to the Boer War where she felt Britain was acting like a bullying imperialist and around this time she became President of the Tyneside Branch of the Arbitration and Peace Association (Labour arbitration being something that had been pioneered by her husband, Robert).

Elizabeth also supported conscientious objectors in the First World War and was horrified at the treatment meted out to long-standing German residents in Britain. Even when well over 70, she intervened physically to try to prevent a local German shopkeeper being assaulted by an angry crowd. She also continued to write to newspapers in protest at the arms escalation by both Britain and Germany and at the increased bombings by both sides. In 1916, in the middle of the war, she attended a Peace Conference in Leeds and supported other peace initiatives.

Elizabeth acknowledged that amongst the many causes she espoused, her principal goals were those of securing the suffrage for women and advancing the cause of world peace. In 1911 she reflected, in the Annual Report for the Newcastle Women's Liberal Association, that "women are now admitted to town councils, education is free ... and the Parliamentary franchise is almost in sight". However, "as for peace ... over the restless waves of what inland seas or mighty oceans does peace securely spread her wings?"

While Robert and Elizabeth were devoted to public life over many years, they did also treasure their family and their home life with their children. The family papers make this very clear, and reveal how much they enjoyed travelling, both within Britain and abroad. Elizabeth, a gifted water colourist, made many sketches of the places and different countries they visited. However, they also had a very sad bereavement to overcome with the death of their only son at age 18 from pneumonia. A contemporary newspaper account of his death describes him as a young man whose studies and way of life had shown him to be "full of promise."

In the last few years of her life after being widowed in 1911, she continued to be engaged politically and socially. Her appetite for travel and new experiences was equally undimmed and at the age of 75 she climbed Mount Wellingon (4,170ft) in Tasmania while visiting her daughter, who had married the Headmaster of the Friends school in Hobart.

Elizabeth died in 1919 aged 80. She bequeathed her home in Bensham Grove for public use and it initially became an "Educational Settlement". Today Bensham Grove still serves the people of Gateshead as a Community Centre.

The Dean of Worcester spoke of her after receiving news of her death, saying: "we are now accustomed to women in public life such that we hardly realise how much Elizabeth Spence Watson was a pioneer". Let us hope that well into the 21st century her pioneering record will continue to be honoured.

Bensham Grove, the home of Elizabeth Spence Watson.

Select Bibliography

Dame Allan *(Moira Kilkenny)*
Report on the Statue of Dame Eleanor Allan on College House, City Campus
By Simon Buck and Drs J Aston and C van Hensbergen, Pub Northumbria University
Philanthropy North East, Allan, Dame Eleanor, Online source
An Impartial History of the Town and County of Newcastle, by John Baillie 1801
History of the Parish of Wallsend, by William Richardson, 1923

Susan Auld *(Joyce Quin)*
Oxford Dictionary of National Biography
Wikipedia entry
The British Newspaper Archive
Oral information from the Northumbrian Pipers Society
Obituary in *The Times, (14/3/2002)*
Information from Martin and Charles Auld, sons of Susan Auld

Florence Nightingale Harrison Bell *(Joyce Quin)*
Article by Michael Proctor for the Heaton History Group; *The Redoubtable Mrs Harrison Bell: campaigner and social reformer*
Researching the Origins of Florence Nightingale Harrison Bell, Newcastle Suffragist and Social Reformer by Professor John Heckels, *NDFHS Journal,* Spring 2019
The British Newspaper Archive
Labour Woman and other periodicals and records in the Archive and Study Centre, The People's History Museum, Manchester
Wikipedia

Norah Balls *(Moira Kilkenny)*
Deeds Not Words by Nina Brown, Old Low Light 2022
To Make Their Mark by David Neville, Centre for Northern Studies 1997
Magnificent women and Their Revolutionary Machines by Henrietta Heald 2019, CPI Group Croydon

Matilda Burgh and Margaret Usher *(Moira Kilkenny)*
John Sykes. Local Records. vol. 1, 1866 Patrick & Shotton
To Make Their Mark by David Neville, 1997

Dame Annie Maud Burnett *(Moira Kilkenny)*
ODNB Burnett. Dame (Annie) Maud by C M Fraser
Ladies Elect Women in English Local Government 1865- 1914 by Patricia Hollis, Clarendon Press Oxford 1987
The Shields Daily News of 17th Feb. 1931, records that Dame Annie Maud Burnett was honoured for her services to Tynemouth and North shields by the presentation to the Borough of a life-sized and beautiful portrait which is currently housed in the Quadrant, North Tyneside Council (the Silverlink N.Cobalt Business Park N.Tyneside) and can be seen by the public

Christine Elizabeth Cooper *(Moira Kilkenny)*
Oxford Dictionary of National Biography, Susan L Cohen
Munks Roll. Entry for Christine Elizabeth Cooper, 1986, Vol V111. J.M.Parkin
The Care of children in Hospitals 1947, J.C.Spence
Sir James Spence 1975, Archives of Disease in Childhood. Donald Court
Discussions and primary source materials kindly supplied by Professor Sir Alan Craft MD, FRCPCH, F.Med.Sci., and Dr Nigel Speight. These included the following;
Obituary notice for Dr Elizabeth Cooper by I Kolvin
In her own hand, lecture on Centenary Meeting Medical school. *Overseas Connections of the Dept. of Child Health*
Dr Cooper's own copy of her CV, dated 1977
Lecture notes for Liverpool University (Feb 1962) describing her visit to Ghana, Sierra Leone and Gambia, and similar lecture entitled Visit to West Africa

Dame Rosemary Cramp *(Joyce Quin)*
A century of Anglo-Saxon sculpture, Cramp, R. 1977 Frank Graham
Recollections of Rosemary Cramp from Durham University Archaeological Department 2023
Material and information provided by Beth Rainey, University of Durham
Material provided by Professor Adrian Simpson, Principal of St. Mary's College, University of Durham
Evensong: people, discoveries and reflections on the church in England, Richard Morris, London 2021
Material provided by Helen Milner, niece of Rosemary Cramp

Margaret Rebecca Dickinson *(Moira Kilkenny)*
Margaret Rebecca Dickinson: A Botanical Artist of the Border Counties, Dr. Elizabeth Towner, 2021, by Berwickshire Naturalist's Club
Women Naturalists of North East England, Claire Jones and Sarah Seeley, Natural History Soc. of Northumbria
Wikipedia
Online Gallery, The Watercolour Drawings of British Wild Flowers by Margaret Rebecca Dickinson, (Natural Hist. Soc. site,)

Pauline Dower *(Moira Kilkenny)*
Living at Wallington, Pauline Dower, 1984, Mid Northumberland Arts Group
The Fight for Beauty, Fiona Reynolds, 2016, One World
The Women who Saved the English Countryside, Mathew Kelly, 2022, Yale

Mary Baxter Ellis *(Joyce Quin)*
Oxford Dictionary of National Biography
British Newspaper Archive
Wikipedia
FANY Invicta. Ward, I, 1955
Obituary, *The Times* (29/4/1948)
FANY website.
Popham, H. FANY, 1984
FANY Gazette (various editions)
Artists of Northumbria, Marshall Hall
Blog by Beth Brook for LGBT History project 18/2/2014 on FANY - The women of the First Aid Nursing Yeomanry

Anne Fisher *(Moira Kilkenny)*
A new Grammar with Exercises in Bad English, Anne Fisher 1754 edition. Held in Newcastle City Library
Local Records; or Historical Register of Remarkable Events Vol. 1, Newcastle upon Tyne John Sykes
Thomas Slack of Newcastle, printer, 1723- 1784, Archaelogia Aeliana 3rd series vol. XV111 James Hodgson.1920
Anne Fisher: first female grammarian, 2002 Maria Rodriguez Gil
Eighteenth Century Newcastle upon Tyne P.M.Horsley, Oriel Press 1971
Myer's Literary Guide to the North East, Alan C. Myer 1997
Newcastle Printers in the Eighteenth Century, Richard Welford 1896
The Feminist Companion to Literature in English, B.T. Batsford 1990. Blain, Clements and Grundy

Dorothy Forster *(Moira Kilkenny)*
Men of Mark Twixt Tyne and Tweed. Vol 2 Richard Welford, Walter Scott Ltd, 1895
Dorothy and the Forsters of Bamburgh, John Bird, Printspot

Jane Gomeldon *(Joyce Quin)*
The Medley, Gomeldon J. 1766
The Feminist Companion to Literature in English. Blain, Cléments, Grundy. Batsford,
London, 1990
The Oxford Dictionary of National Biography
Wikipedia
Sykes, John. Local records, 1833

Mary Elsworth Greaves *(Joyce Quin)*
Mary Elsworth Greaves by Professor John Heckels. *Journal of Northumberland and Durham Family History*
Work and Disability: Some Aspects of the Employment of Disabled Persons in Great Britain,
Greaves, Mary, 1969
Defeating the Pied Piper, unpublished memoir from the Disability Income Group, Greaves,
Mary
No Feet to Drag – Report on the Disabled, Arthur Butler and Alfred Morris, Sidgwick and
Jackson 1972
Disability Legislation and Practice, Duncan Guthrie, 1981
Alf Morris – People's Parliamentarian, Derek Kinrade, 2007, National Information Forum
"No Limits" – The Disabled Peoples Movement, Hunt, Judy, 2019.
Hansard Parliamentary Record, 5th June 2008
Obituary of Mary Greaves, *The Times* (17/01/1983)

Jane Grigson *(Joyce Quin)*
Jane Grigson: her life and legacy, The Guardian, 15/3/2015
Jane Grigson, by Geraldene Holt, *Food and Drink, the Cultural Context,* edited by Don Sloan,
2013
Desert Island Discs. BBC Radio 4 (8/9/1978)
The Food Programme (A Tribute to Jane Grigson, Part 1 and 2) BBC Radio 4, (10-11/5/2015)
Food with the Famous, Grigson, Jane, London 1979
Wikipedia.

Mary Jane Hancock *(Joyce Quin)*
Women Naturalists of North East England, Natural History Society of Northumbria
Obituary of the Natural History Society of Northumbria 1896
Watercolours and oil paintings of Mary Jane Hancock, the Library, the Great North Museum
Men of Mark Twixt Tyne and Tweed, Richard Welford, 1895
Thomas Bewick, His Life and Times, Robert Robinson, 1887, reprinted 1972
Nature's Engraver: A life of Thomas Bewick, Jenny Uglow, 1988
Artists of Northumbria, Marshall Hall
A fine and Private Place - Jesmond Old Cemetery, Alan Morgan, Tyne Bridge Publishing 2000

Hannah Hauxwell (Joyce Quin)
TV Documentaries by Barry Cockcroft. "Too long a Winter", 1972. "A Winter too Many" 1989 "Innocent Abroad" 1992
Hauxwell, Hannah and Cockcroft, Barry.
"Seasons of my Life" 1989, "Daughter of the Dales" 1991

Grace Hickling *(Moira Kilkenny)*
International women in science:a biographical dictionary to 1950. Stevens, Catherine and M.C.Haines. (2001)
Transactions of Nat.Hist. Soc. of Northumbria. Vol. 55 5-11 1988.
Women Naturalists of North East England, NHSN 2018

Dr. Marie V Lebour *(Joyce Quin)*
Women Naturalists of North East England, the Natural History Society of Northumbria
"Dr. Marie V Lebour" Obituary by Sir F. S. Russell. *Journal of the Marine Biological Association of Great Britain.* August 1972
"Pioneers of Plankton Research: Marie Lebour." By J. R. Dolan. *Journal of Plankton Research,* August 2021
British Newspaper Archive.
Wikipedia.

Constance Leathart *(Joyce Quin)*
Small Enough to Conquer the Sky (Jim Denyer *Mr Newcastle Airport*) John Sleight, Newcastle Libraries 1993
Wish me luck as you wave me goodbye, Jane Torder
Mount up with Wings, Mary de Bunsen
The Female Few: Spitfire Heroines, Hyams and Poad
A-Z of Gateshead, Brack, Hall and Lang
The Picture and the Pilot, Marshall Hall, *The Northumbrian,* 2000
Northumberland County Archives, Woodhorn,
Various Press Clippings
Interviews with Mary Gray, (friend of Con Leathart) Hexham and with Eileen Burn, (cousin of Con Leathart) Carrycoats, Northumberland

Sarah Losh *(Moira Kilkenny)*
The Worthies of Cumberland, Henry Lonsdale, 1873
The Pinecone. The Story of Sarah Losh, Romantic Heroine, Architect and Visionary, Jenny Uglow. 2012.
The Architectural Review, 142, July 1967, P65-67
England's Thousand Best Churches, Simon Jenkins, 1999
The Buildings of England Cumberland and Westmorland, Nikolaus Pevsner, 1967
Pugin, Rosemary Hill 2009

Mary Ann Macham *(Moira Kilkenny)*
Martin Luther King in Newcastle upon Tyne, by Brian Ward, 2017, Tyne Bridge Publishing
Black People and the North East in *North East History,* by Sean Creighton
Hidden Chains, the Slavery Business and North East England, 1600-1865, John Charlton. Tyne Bridge Publishing 2008
Exhibition at Low lights Heritage Centre, Breaking Chains 2020

Teresa Merz *(Joyce Quin)*
Northern Pageant, Spencer, James R, 1937
The Life and work of Teresa Merz of Newcastle-upon-Tyne, Elizabeth O'Donnell
Womens History Journal, Spring 2017
Merz and Spence Watson family papers in Tyne and Wear Archives
Quakerstrongrooms website
Connected Voices website
Philanthropy North East website

Mary Midgley *(Joyce Quin)*
Beast and Man, M. Midgley, Routledge 1978
Wickedness, M. Midgley, Routledge 1984
The Owl of Minerva - a Memoir, M. Midgley, Routledge 2005
The Essential Mary Midgley, D. Midgley (ed), Routledge 2005
Are you an Illusion, M. Midgley, Routledge 2014
Professor Jane Heal. Obituary of Mary Midgley. *The Guardian* 12/10/2018
Interviews and conversations with Professor Jane Heal and Marion Anderson

Muriel Morley *(Moira Kilkenny)*
Bibliography; Craniofacial Society of Great Britain and Ireland; Honorary Member
Biographies Dr. Muriel Morley. 1899-1993
Commemoration of the Twenty Fifth Anniversary of the The Founding of Britain's First University
Department of Speech. 1959-84., With an appreciation of Dr. Muriel Morley, Newcastle 1984
Profile of Dr Muriel Morley by Society of Speech Therapists. Date unknown

Elizabeth Pease Nichol *(Moira Kilkenny)*
Elizabeth Pease Nichol by Anna M Stoddart 1899, London: J M Dent
Nichol, Elizabeth Pease ODN, by Clare Midgeley.
Women Anti-Slavery Campaigners, with Special ref. to the North East, by Clare Midgeley, *North*
East Labour History, Bulletin 28, 1995
Elizabeth Pease; One Woman's Vision of Peace ,Justice, and Human Rights in 19th Century Britain.
by Karen I Halbersleben
Martin Luther King in Newcasle on Tyne ,the African Freedom Struggle and Race Relations in the
North of England, by Brian Ward, Tyne Bridge Publishing, 2017

Bella Reay *(Moira Kilkenny)*
The Munitionettes; A History of women's football in North East England during the Great War, by
Patrck Brennan, 2007 Donmouth Publishing.

Ellen Richardson *(Joyce Quin)*
Richardson family material on the website of Benjamin S. Beck "ben@benbeck.co.uk
The Birthplace of your Liberty – Purchasing Frederick Douglass's freedom in 1846, Hannah Rose
Murray, University of Edinburgh, New North Star 2020
Women in the Quaker Community: The Richardson family of Newcastle, c1815-60, Mood, Jonathan
Quaker Studies 2005
Frederick Douglass in Newcastle-upon-Tyne, England, Cools, Amy, Sept 2018, blog for
Ordinary Philosophy, September 2018
Thomas and Emma Pumphrey. "In Memoriam" 1892
Quaker Library, London.
Tyne and Wear Archives.

Anne Seymour *(Moira Kilkenny)*
Exhibition arranged by Dominique Bell, entitled *Anne Seymour: Doctor, Missionary, Refugee,* at
South Shields Museum and Art Gallery, July 2018

Jennie Shearan *(Joyce Quin)*
CLEAN AIR by Gianfranco Rosolia, TJ books, (27/08/22)
British Newspaper Archive
Author's political papers

Elizabeth Shepherd *(Moira Kilkenny)*
Traditional British Quilts by Dorothy Osler, Batsford, London 1987.
Quilts 1700-2010 ed. Sue Pritchard,V&A Publishing
North Country Quilts: Legend and Living Tradition, Dorothy Osler, Bowes Museum, 2000
Selection of Dorothy Osler's research papers, unpublished, 2020

Amy Millicent Sowerby *(Moira Kilkenny)*
Bibliography; Postcards from the Nursery Peter & Dawn Cope, Pub Cavendish, 2002
The Dictionary of British Women Artists. Sara Gray, Casemate 2009
Looking for Githa, Patricia Riley, *New writing North*, 2009
The Discovery Museum in Newcastle holds copies of all 18 children's books produced by
Millicent and Githa Sowerby.

Elsie Tu *(Joyce Quin)*
Elliott Elsie. Crusade for Justice – an autobiography, Elsie Elliott, 1981, Kings Time Printing
Colonial Hong Kong in the eyes of Elsie Tu, Tu Elsie, Hong Kong University Press 2003
Shouting at the Mountain: A Hong Kong story of Love and Commitment, Tu, Andrew and Elsie,
Chameleon Press, 2004
Heaton History Society (Peter Sagar, Arthur Andrews and Chris Jackson) *Elsie Tu –
Champion of the Poor.* 18/10/2021
Citation for the award of Honorary Doctor of Civil Law to Elsie Tu. Newcastle
University 1996.

Elizabeth Spence Watson *(Joyce Quin)*
A short life of Elizabeth Spence Watson, Corder, Herbert, 1919
Life of Robert Spence Watson, Corder, Percy 1914
The Genteel Militant: Elizabeth Spence Watson's Work for Women's Suffrage and Peace, Craven, Ann,
Journal of the North East Labour History Society. Vol 47, 2016
Dingybutterflies.org
Material in the Quaker Library, Euston Road, London
Family papers in Tyne and Wear Archives.

Acknowledgements

In addition to the sources and bibliography at the end of each chapter we would like to thank the following organisations for their invaluable help: The Literary and Philosophical Library, Newcastle upon Tyne; the Quaker Library in Euston Road, London; Tyne and Wear Archives and Museums (particularly Rachel Gill and Lizzy Baker); Rebecca Knight and staff of the Library of the Great North Museum; the Northumberland County Archive service at Woodhorn; the Heaton History Society; Newcastle University; the People's History Museum, Manchester, the Libraries of the House of Lords and the House of Commons, Barter Books, Alnwick, the South Shields Museum and Art Gallery, the Old Low Lights Heritage Museum in North Shields, the Newcastle Association of City Guides and the Northumbrian Pipers' Society.

Many individuals have supplied information to us including valuable and hitherto unpublished material and we would like to thank all of the following, indicating in brackets the name(s) of the women concerned. Nicola Alexander Dent, Jackie Grey, Jenny Lowry, Susan Pinchen, Gianfranco Rosolia, (Jenny Shearan); Marion Anderson and Professor Jane Heal (Mary Midgley); Charles and Martin Auld, Andy May (Susan Auld); Alan Bell (Dr. Anne Seymour); Nina Brown (Norah Balls); Eileen Burns, Lucy Gordon, Mary Gray, Julian Leathart, Becky Milligan, Kate Milligan and Anthea Lang (Connie Leathart); Paul and Di Copeland (information on nineteenth century women naturalists); Sir Alan Craft (Dr C E Cooper and Dr Muriel Morley); Dr Janet Webster, Head of Speech and Language Sciences at Newcastle University (Dr Muriel Morley); Professor John Heckels (Mary Greaves); Chris Kilkenny (Margaret Usher and Matilda Burgh); Mary Manley (Elizabeth Shepherd); Helen Milner, Beth Rainey and Professor Adrian Simpson, Durham University (Rosemary Cramp); Dorothy Osler (Elizabeth Shepherd). We would also like to thank Rachel Kilkenny and Guy MacMullen for their valuable help with proof reading. Finally, and loudly, we would like to thank our publisher Derek Tree of Tyne Bridge Publishing for his constant help and advice throughout in preparing our work for publication in a form which we believe does justice to our inspirational subjects.

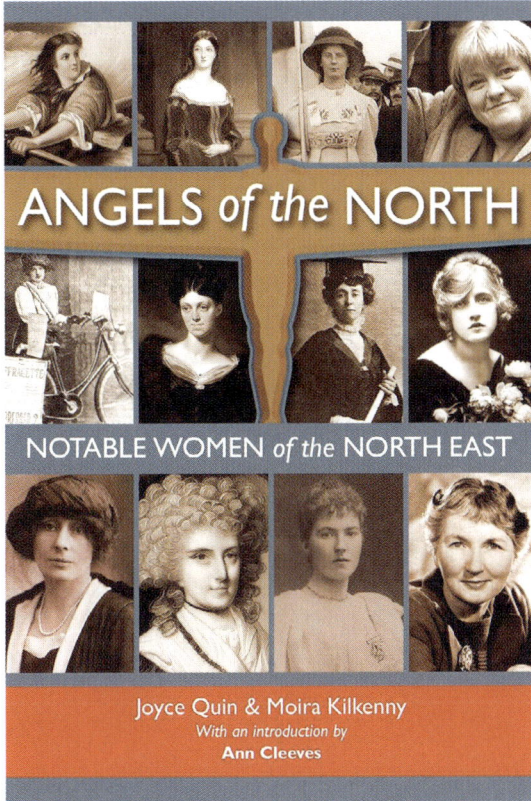

ANGELS of the NORTH

NOTABLE WOMEN of the NORTH EAST

Joyce Quin & Moira Kilkenny
With an introduction by
Ann Cleeves

Volume One of Angels of the North is available in all good bookshops, Newcastle City Library Gift Shop and online from Tyne Bridge Publishing